I0114740

WAR FOUGHT
AND FELT

CONFLICTING WORLDS

NEW DIMENSIONS OF THE AMERICAN CIVIL WAR

T. Michael Parrish,
Series Editor

WAR FOUGHT AND FELT

THE EMOTIONAL MOTIVATIONS OF CONFEDERATE SOLDIERS

JOSHUA R. SHIVER

LOUISIANA STATE UNIVERSITY PRESS

Baton Rouge

Published by Louisiana State University Press
lsupress.org

Copyright © 2025 by Louisiana State University Press
All rights reserved. Except in the case of brief quotations used in articles or reviews,
no part of this publication may be reproduced or transmitted in any format or by
any means without written permission of Louisiana State University Press.

Designer: Kaelin Chappell Broaddus
Typefaces: Garamond Premier Pro, text; Ultra Regular, Kensington Compressed
Black, FM Bolyar Pro Bold, and Ephemera Kingsford Regular, display

Cover photograph: Detail of an ambrotype featuring First Lieutenant James N. Bell
and his wife Emmeline with their daughter Nannie Claudia Bell. Liljenquist Family
Collection, Prints and Photographs Division of the Library of Congress.

Cataloging-in-Publication Data are available from the Library of Congress.
ISBN 978-0-8071-8505-6 (cloth) | ISBN 978-0-8071-8581-0 (epub) |
ISBN 978-0-8071-8582-7 (pdf)

TO RICHARD SHIVER

The man who taught me to
love history, value relationships, and
put others before yourself.
I miss you, Pops.

CONTENTS

Contents

ACKNOWLEDGMENTS

No man is an island. Much like those of the subjects of this book, my efforts would have been in vain were it not for the support of those around me. I would like to thank my best friend and wife, Morgan, and my parents, Rick and Sharon, all of whom stood by me and encouraged me through the preparation, writing, and completion of this book. Likewise, I would like to thank the many friends and colleagues who have patiently encouraged me through writing and editing of this manuscript. In particular, I would like to thank Dr. Brett Derbes, whose encouragement and friendship helped me through some of the most difficult moments of grad school. I would also like to thank Dr. Michael Megelsh and Dr. Daniel Cone, whose listening ears kept me going when I wanted to give up. Gentlemen, ours too was a shared burden of suffering. Additionally, I want to thank the many amazing mentors and professors who have guided me and shaped me throughout my academic career. All of them have taught me the importance of academic rigor, unwavering perseverance, and unceasing kindness. Thank you, Dr. Kenneth Noe, Dr. Chris E. Fonvielle Jr., and Dr. Peter Carmichael. I would also like to thank Mr. Rand Dotson, Editor-in-Chief at LSU Press, for his patience and guidance in preparing and revising this manuscript. Finally, I would like to thank God. Without Him, none of this would be possible.

In researching and writing this project, I benefited greatly from the generous support of various organizations that deserve more recognition than I could offer. Their financial support and belief in this manuscript were instrumental to its completion. These organizations and the awards that they offered include the Clinton

Jackson and Evelyn Coley Award from the Alabama Historical Association, the Wayne Flynt Endowed Graduate Research Award in Alabama History and Culture from the Caroline Marshall Draughon Center for the Arts and Humanities, the Student Research Fellowship from the Friends of the Alabama Archives, the Archie K. Davis Fellowship from the North Caroliniana Society, and the Milo B. Howard, Malcolm C. McMillan, and Edna Floyd Booth Awards from the Auburn University Department of History. Thank you to everyone who kindly donated to these awards and who made this book possible. All mistakes and errors herein are the fault of the author solely.

WAR FOUGHT
AND FELT

HISTORICAL HETERODOXY
A NEW VIEW OF EMOTIONAL EXPERIENCE

On August 7, 1864, Lieutenant L. White Duggar of the Gid Nelson Alabama Light Artillery was hunched over a small scrap of paper as the city near him—the all-important rail center of Atlanta, Georgia—was aflame. As part of General Joseph E. Johnston's Army of Tennessee, Duggar and his comrades found themselves partially surrounded and under siege by Union forces under the command of General William Tecumseh Sherman. Gazing into this small scrap of paper, Duggar wrote in almost perfect cursive a poignant letter to his "beloved mother." Rather than wax eloquently about the Confederate cause or the state of the war, Duggar wrote blithely about life in camp and his desire to come home before recounting the recent loss of his friend, Freddie.

"There were two Yankee batteries in our front playing on us," he wrote, and while his fellow artillerist and friend Fred finished loading his cannon to respond, "a shell from the enemy's gun struck him as he turned to the right—just back of the right ear cutting off half of his head leaving his two ears and the lower part of his nose." A nearby soldier felt the smack of Fred's skull against his body, knocking him to the ground. "I could not turn from the horrible sight," Duggar noted, "his brains lying scattered two feet or more on the ground." Worse yet, in the heat of battle, Duggar could not retrieve Fred's body and it instead fell on one of his messmates to drag his corpse to the rear. As the battle drew to a close, Duggar quickly made his way to the rear with a fellow comrade and both men carried what remained of Fred to the closest ambulance—a mile behind the front lines. In the rear, Fred's remains were "tied up and put in a cut pine coffin made for him. He was buried the next day by ten oclock in the cemetery. . . . His coffin has a brass belt plate marked C.S. on it (and inside the box) and is in a large pine box." Unlike thousands of unidentified soldiers who were buried in mass graves, Fred was carefully buried in his own marked grave. The devotion Duggar felt toward his friend—a devotion so deep that he personally carried Fred's bloody pieces over a mile to their final resting place—is representative of the love felt by thousands of other soldiers for their comrades who shared the burden of war's suffering.

On paper, Freddie's death is just one more number added to the growing body count of the war. Historians often portray the war's brutality in terms of sheer numbers and the American Civil War was one of the bloodiest wars in the Western Hemisphere. Yet to Duggar, Freddie was not a number, but instead a boon companion whose loss was deeply felt. "Dear Mother, since I wrote the above I have been out to Freddie's grave and put the shed over it and fixed it," he wrote to her, "planted a nice piece of arbor vitae at his head. The shed is well white washed and looks [smart?]." Duggar could not leave the shattered remains of his friend to the anonymity of the Georgia wilderness and his marker ensured that Freddie would not be forgotten. The more that the young lieutenant wrote about his friend, the more his heart swelled with emotion until he exclaimed, "Poor dear Fred! Little did we think that so soon we would miss his good voice and merry whistle among us."[1]

In an age in which southern men were expected to stifle emotion and display individualistic self-confidence, Duggar's letter is reflective of a tectonic shift that occurred among thousands of Confederate soldiers during the war.[2] Dripping with vulnerability and loss, his words run contrary to the prevailing cultural expectations of southern masculinity marked by self-mastery. For nineteenth-century southern elites, this idea refers to the belief that a man should be individualistic, uncontrolled by anyone but himself, and in some cases willing to moderate his behavior.[3] Particularly in public, southern men were expected to control their emotions.[4] Yet Duggar seemingly felt secure sharing his feelings with his mother and contrary to advice manuals, newspaper columns, and diaries written during this period, Duggar was not reticent about sharing feelings. The horror of his own personal loss melded with years of suffering in service of the Confederate Army, leaving Duggar without the need to carefully craft or control his image. Instead of falling back on social conventions, he fell back on primal emotions shaped by his experiences. Like thousands of others, he took part in a war that was both *fought and felt.*

❧

Historians' recent reconstruction of the emotional inner worlds of southern men has led to groundbreaking work that has further illuminated our understanding of the individual soldier's experience of war. Much of this research frames nineteenth-century male emotions within the larger context of social expectations and the masculine pursuit of fulfilling them. Yet the concentrated suffering endemic to war deconstructed and reshaped many of these social expectations and soldiers often took it upon themselves to weave new gendered constructions of emotional norms. The American Civil War represented a period of remarkable change among southern men in which societal expectations of emotional restraint gave way to growing acceptance of previously taboo outward expressions of fear, sadness, love, loneliness, and powerlessness.

Historians have long recognized the importance of fear in understanding southern men in the nineteenth century. At their root, southern men are often seen as products of fear—fear of losing power, fear of losing the institution of slavery that undergirded their entire economic and social system, and fear of their loss of autonomy and independence—and it is in this fear that many historians find the roots of the social and political turmoil of the sectional crisis in the decades leading up to the American Civil War.[5] It is helpful to understand this fear through the lens of what psychologist and neuroscientist Ralph Adolphs calls a "functional concept of fear," in which fear is "caused by particular patterns of threat-related stimuli," which are "in turn causing particular patterns of adaptive behaviors to avoid or cope with that threat." Thus, the threatening stimulus is directly linked to patterns of behavior.[6] Southern men who were exposed to the same set of stimuli often reacted with patterns of behavior that were shaped by cultural norms of race, economics, and religion. Yet the American Civil War represented a watershed moment in which the collective aspiration of appropriate emotional expression gave way to the individual's need to express love, affection, and sorrow within the confines of

{3}

interpersonal relationships. Understanding these relationships, and the emotions that they generated, is paramount to understanding the motivations of Confederate soldiers during the American Civil War.

Until recently, historians have been slow to grasp the importance of human emotion in understanding human motivations and historical change. This is particularly true among Civil War historians who have greatly expanded our understanding of what motivated soldiers to fight over the past few decades. Their explanations have included ideology, politics, masculinity, religion, cultural expectations, and even boredom, among others. Yet the potency of human emotions has evinced little historical research and the result is that we are left with a limited understanding of the influence of emotions on soldiers' motivations and psyches. While this research is invaluable, it unfortunately ignores the more primal aspects of human existence and more recent research in the fields of neuroscience and psychobiology have provided historians with an additional avenue for understanding historical figures. The goal of this book is to provide greater nuance in our understanding of the interrelationship between masculinity and male emotions in shaping Confederate soldiers' motivations for fighting. Rather than painting southern males as automatons who were primarily shaped by and motivated by hegemony, patriarchy, white supremacy, or insecurity, this book builds upon these concepts by rooting them in their emotional origins.[7] While influenced by external sociocultural factors, these emotions also had intrinsic biological origins that influenced individuals to act outside of prevailing cultural norms. It is important to understand the biological root of these emotions, how soldiers were motivated by them, and how their resultant actions represented a marked departure from normative social patterns.

Until recently, much of the historical literature's conception of the experience of southern males was rooted in cultural expectations of the present day.[8] The cultural frameworks surrounding masculinity today have been applied to those of the past and the result has been an imbalance in our collective understanding. Whereas social constructivism has yielded some valuable insights into the past, historians have too often wielded its hammer, seeing many of history's difficult questions as their proverbial nails. This book represents an attempt to add more nuance to the discussion around social constructivism by providing a concrete link between certain socially constructed gender norms and the unassailable reality of human biology and emotions. In this way, I hope to provide a fuller picture of the Confederate soldier and his experience of war as a man who, though expected to restrain his emotions, found himself pulled taut between the cultural expectations of the world around him and the overwhelming feelings that he could neither shake nor repress.

⁓⁕⁓

In 1996, sociologist Michael Kimmel wrote that centuries of male-centric historical analysis did not "explore how the experience of being a man, of *manhood,* structured the lives of the men who are their subjects, the organizations and institutions they created and staffed, the events in which they participated." This discrepancy, Kimmel maintains, is because historians of gender often see American masculinity through the lens of idealistic advice books as well as because of the limited writing of women from the periods being studied. As such, "masculinity" is often understood as a cultural force in which men are expected to vie for domination, control, and power, as this was considered the ideal display of one's manhood.[9]

Whatever the ideal may have been, historians have often been quick to apply a historical period's cultural prescriptions (or even those of their own age) to explain why human beings act in certain ways. Yet men like Lieutenant Duggar were not only products of cultural norms but also reactionaries to those norms. They were not automatons who were inseparably chained to the masculine expectations of their world. In order to understand why historians have taken this approach, it is first necessary to understand the relationship between masculinity and cultural norms through the lens of structuralist and poststructuralist approaches. "Structuralism" refers to "a method of analysis in which individual elements are considered not in terms of any intrinsic identity but in terms of their relationship within the system in which they function." Structuralists thus approach these systems from a scientific and naturalistic perspective and in terms of southern masculinity, they would often argue that men were products of the social, religious, political, and economic systems in which they were immersed. On the other hand, "poststructuralism" promotes the "decentering" of a historical subject, arguing against the "very possibility of the closed system of which structuralism is predicated."[10] Thus, "poststructuralists" eschew the deterministic importance of social systems in shaping masculinity

{5}

and emotional expression and, unlike structuralists, who argue that agency is determined by systems, poststructuralists argue for individual agency, which is not strictly tethered to structural systems. Poststructuralism challenged the idea of objectivity inherent in the social sciences and by extension, the belief that empirical historical research could somehow objectively uncover the truth of the past.[11]

The research for this book indicates that understanding the influence of male emotions requires us to go beyond the structuralist approach. While structuralism helps the historian neatly categorize individual and collective actions, thousands of Confederate soldiers acted outside of cultural norms. Though historians have previously focused on the potency of southern social expectations of masculine emotionality, they have not examined their durability. While prewar social dictates prescribed the goodness or rightness of the expression of men's emotions, the war and the struggle for survival meant that they found themselves adapting to the situations that they faced by redefining acceptable masculine norms of emotional expression. Many were forced to navigate an emotionally ambivalent state of existence in which the cultural and ideological pressures which had defined the prewar years could no longer be adhered to. This redefinition of emotional norms was demonstrative of the pragmatic nature of Confederate soldiers. Though they had inherited these cultural norms through their parents, siblings, friends, and social institutions, they also stretched and/or redefined them through their own personal actions or, more often, through their relationships with others. It was these "others" who often gave them the permission needed to express their feelings in new ways. Historian Nicole Eustace noted that in the century before the outbreak of the American Civil War, "eighteenth-century actors could not conceive of a self entirely separate from the social order, and so their expressions of emotion could never be entirely personal. Rather, they were inherently relational."[12] Yet the American Civil War represented a marked change in the relationships between men and the outward expression of their feelings. Moreover, what drove much of this change was the homosocial relationships built throughout the war as well as the permissive nature of their familial relationships, which gave them leeway to not only feel, but to let others know how they felt.

In this book, I examine the positive nature of these relationships by looking at the emotional push-and-pull that they exerted on Confederate soldiers. It seeks to understand how southern men *saw themselves* and how the war fundamentally changed their self-perception and their relationships to others. I argue that the emotional "push-and-pull" of interpersonal relationships between Confederate soldiers and their parents, sweethearts, friends, and children is foundational to understanding why they fought and why the Confederate cause lasted so long. It builds upon previous works that argue for the primacy of ideology, religion, politics, masculinity, knightliness, and more, to include the most potent factor tethered to all of these categories—primal human emotion. Without the emotions engendered by these relationships, the war itself may have never begun and Confederate soldiers may not have fought for so long. Moreover, it argues that the period of the American Civil War represented an important period in our understanding of southern masculinity as white southern males abandoned socially acceptable norms of emotional reticence in favor of emotional effusiveness on a vast scale hitherto unseen in the short history of America. While lasting only a short time, this restructuring of emotional norms is best seen in the letters of the soldiers themselves. While advice manuals continued to enforce pre-existing cultural and emotional norms, soldiers who bore the painful burden of the experience of war redefined those norms for themselves and their comrades.

The prewar ideals of southern manhood and self-mastery were tailor made for times of peace. Southern men lived within a matrix of sentimentality, Christian morality, masculinity, self-sacrifice, and an expectation that they would be more nurturing to their families than their colonial forebears had been. These social expectations shaped the contours of romantic and familial relationships during the American Civil War. Scholars have often argued that southern males were hegemonic lords of their familial manors. While this may have been true in many cases, it is also true that this was often honored more in the breach than the observance. Whether or not white southern males attempted to exert control, they were also expected paradoxically to be stoic leaders within their communities while also being emotionally available to their families.[13] Likewise, though expected to be paragons of Christian morality, many also promoted the institution of chattel slavery and sexual access to these slaves. During the war, they were also expected to carry on their masculine duties to their families even when they were physically absent. Thus, Confederate soldiers were pulled taut between competing social expectations, which, though marginally bearable in times of peace, meant that they were stretched beyond their limits during the crisis of the American Civil War. To survive, many would have to choose to either redefine these social expectations, ignore them, or allow themselves to be crushed by them.

In *War Fought and Felt,* I attempt to present a nuanced picture of emotional expression rooted less in social expectations of masculinity and more in the realities of the soldier's need for expediency and survival. Evidence for this project indicates that white southern men were less concerned with nationalism, politics, and individual rights during the war. This is not surprising, considering that soldiers, who most bore the costs of the war, increasingly found themselves disenchanted by its continuous demands of personal sacrifice. The relative peace of the prewar period meant that southern newspapers, politicians, and religious figures could wax poetically about individual rights, the importance of "the Cause," and the expectation of self-mastery. But actual war forced men to become more instinctual, stripping them of the veneer of masculine control, which among other things, argued for mastery of one's emotions.

The statistical source base for this book rests on the careful reading of 1,790 letters exchanged between 200 soldiers from one lower South state (Alabama) and one upper South state (North Carolina) and 366 family members and fifteen friends. The use of two states allows for more statistically relevant examples of broad social trends, which would not be the case if these letters were drawn from all over the Confederacy. In other words, picking a handful of soldiers from each Confederate state would not provide the same statistical accuracy as examining two hundred soldiers from two states. This greater breadth and shallower depth would be statistically problematic. Additionally, using one upper South state and one lower South state allows for sociocultural differences between the two regions to be apparent. Each of these letters was analyzed, counted, and grouped with others to provide a quantitative statistical analysis from each state. Though some letters have been incorporated from soldiers outside of Alabama and North Carolina to provide context, none were included in the 1,790 cited above nor were any included in the statistical analysis.

Of the one hundred soldiers from North Carolina, seventy were privates (70 percent), five were corporals (5 percent), seven were sergeants (7 percent), thirteen were officers (13 percent), and five were of unknown rank (5 percent). From the letters themselves, forty-one out of one hundred were married (41 percent) and twenty-eight out of one hundred (28 percent) had children. None of the soldiers from North Carolina could be identified as courting sweethearts back home. Additionally, soldiers from North Carolina accounted for 759 of the 1,790 letters (42.4 percent), which were sent to 188 identified family members including wives, parents, and children, as well as ten identified friends. Fifteen of these one hundred North Carolina soldiers (15 percent) were noted from the letters as being prisoners of war at sometime during their service. Of the one hundred soldiers from Alabama, fifty-nine were privates (59 percent), three were corporals (3 percent), eleven were sergeants (11 percent), twenty-four were officers (24 percent), and three were of unknown rank (3 percent). From the reading of the letters, seven soldiers were identified as courting (7 percent) while forty-one were married (41 percent) and thirty-seven had children (37 percent). The 1,031 letters written by these soldiers were sent to 178 family members including wives, parents, and children as well as five friends. Ten out of one hundred Alabama soldiers (10 percent) in the sample were noted as being prisoners of war at sometime during their service.

Beyond the demographic makeup of this sample of soldiers, I have provided a statistical analysis of the number of letters that express emotion or affection, provide descriptions of battle, formulate religious declarations, make inquiries about or references to children, or express declarations of ideology or duty. "Emotional expressions" include demonstratable declarations of love, anguish, "thoughts of another," or affectionate language. For this project, letters were privileged over diaries for several reasons. First, letters are more plentiful as soldiers generally did not keep personal diaries. Letters were also typically written closer in time to the period in which the events being described occurred—sometimes even during battle. Unlike today, rather than describing one's feelings, diaries of the period typically recorded the "comings and goings" of camp life. Finally, because these letters were written to trusted loved ones, they represented private avenues for men to express their genuine feelings without fear of others' prying eyes. As Private James R. McCutchan of the 14th Regiment Virginia Cavalry charged his wife: "Don't let any body see my letters, if [they] want to know what is in them read it to them, the part you want them to hear."[14]

To understand how this adds to the existing literature, it is important to understand the historiographical milieu in which it was born. The field of Civil War "soldier studies" can be divided into three distinctive epochs. The first consisted of histories and remembrances written by soldiers either during or shortly after the war. These primary source materials became the bedrock upon which all future research depended, and since they were generally written by those who participated in the war, they focused primarily on the heroics, daring, and sacrifice of those who fought. The second epoch began during World War II with the publication of historian Bell Irvin Wiley's 1943 book, *The Life of Johnny Reb: The Common Soldier of the Confederacy*.[15] Unlike soldiers' memoirs, Wiley pieced together a pastiche of hundreds of disparate primary source materials to form an interlocking web of competing motivations. Soldiers' motivations (that is, why they fought), he argued, included hatred of their opponents, a desire for adventure, and social pressure stemming from the masculine and cultural norms surrounding enlistment.[16] Ideology was not a factor in enlistments, he believed, and men's reliance upon each other—called "primary-group cohesion"—was what helped them endure their time of service. This approach shaped historians' perspective for the next seventy years, and Wiley's methodology (and many of his conclusions) became the status quo for understanding soldiers' motivations.[17]

The third epoch of Civil War soldier studies emerged in the 1960s and 1970s during the Vietnam War and stretches into the present day. This epoch was marked by a new understanding of Civil War soldiers as victims manipulated by insidious political or social forces that forced them into war.[18] Increasingly, historians looked at structural forces that shaped and manipulated the ideology and cultural forces of southern society. Some saw sociocultural forces as primary motivators while others saw ideology as the driving force behind soldiers' willingness to enlist and fight. Sociocultural explanations were rooted in distinctly southern notions of gender, hierarchy, masculinity, religion, race, family, camaraderie, and community. Likewise, ideological explanations were rooted in distinctly southern notions of political rights, rhetoric, political structures, nobility, nationalism, patriotism, slavery, honor, and manhood. Some works even combined both approaches.[19]

Within the past few years, it could be argued that we have entered a fourth epoch in the field of soldier studies, in which historians continue in the vein of trying to understand the soldier's personal experience of war. Rather than focusing exclusively on sociocultural factors or ideology, however, they now seek to illuminate soldiers' visceral and emotional experiences of war. This emphasis, which is rooted in sociocultural and ideological frameworks of the past, has become firmly entrenched in the historiography. The first book to take this approach was Stephen W. Berry's book *All That Makes a Man: Love and Ambition in the Civil War South,* published in 2003. It was later followed by Diane Miller Sommerville's *Aberration of Mind: Suicide and Suffering in the Civil War-Era South* (2018), James J. Broomall's *Private Confederacies: The Emotional Worlds of Southern Men as Citizens and Soldiers* (2019), and Dillon J. Carroll's *Invisible Wounds: Mental Illness and Civil War Soldiers* (2021), among others. This new understanding of the emotional "inner world" of Civil War soldiers has not only provided new avenues for understanding the soldiers' experience, but has also provided far more nuance to previously uncovered sociocultural and ideological explanations. However, the Achilles' heel of some of these works is that they rely on only a handful of historical actors who act as microcosms for larger trends—largely because these individuals had extensive primary source materials attached to them. While this provides an excellent source base for understanding change over time, it does not provide a large enough statistical example for larger extrapolations.

This new approach to understanding the Civil War soldiers' inner world runs contrary to the strict adherence of many historians to a purely "scientific" or "reason-based" approach to the past in which history is rooted in direct statements made in primary source materials. Emotions cannot always be interpreted from direct statements and instead must be inferred. "Despite a generation's worth of social and cultural history, the discipline has never quite lost its attraction to hard, rational things," writes historian Barbara H. Rosenwein. "Emotions have seemed tangential (if not fundamentally opposed) to the historical enterprise."[20] The more recent turn toward "emotional history" was originally born in Europe in response to the long-held belief in the "myth of modernity, the myth of the more rational, more scientific European individual, whose internalized regulation of emotion makes 'him' superior to others."[21] Historians of emotion argue that the expression of emotion is socially constructed and historically contingent. One of the downfalls of this new approach to history is that the primary source base underlying our understanding of the historicity of these emotions rests on those created by social elites—those who were the most literate and well-educated. This detracts from our understanding of the emotional norms of those of lower social or economic classes and thus, those who were probably less educated or literate due to the expense of private education.[22]

War Fought and Felt fits firmly within the fourth epoch of the field of "Soldier Studies" and represents a much broader approach to the study of the emotional inner world of Confederate soldiers. Rather than focusing on a few individuals, it instead analyzes two hundred white Confederate soldiers of varying educational and socio-economic backgrounds. The goal of such a broad sample is to understand the wider emotional norms exhibited by these men within the larger sociocultural and ideological milieu in which they lived. In analyzing their writings, I utilize information from other academic fields including soldier psychology, attachment theory, sociology, neurobiology, and philosophy to understand the broader panoply of exhibited emotions. By "reading against the sources"—that is, interpreting the emotions as well as the words connected to those emotions—this approach is admittedly more subjective than most historians would be comfortable with. But the use of modern psychological and sociological approaches is designed to mitigate some of this subjectivity.

Historian Nicole Eustace notes that "cutting-edge neuroscientists are discovering what linguistic theorists have been arguing all along: that language fundamentally shapes both the expression and the experience of emotion" and that "conceptual processing and the cognitive categorization of affect fundamentally shape the perception of emotion."[23] Because emotions are difficult to capture, I have largely depended upon words that represent feelings, which may include statements such as "I miss you" or "I wish that I could see you," which represents a feeling of longing and painful separation; "I love you," which represents feelings of love and affection; and more. Thus, I do not take a completely subjective approach to understanding soldiers' emotions as there must be verbal or written evidence of emotions.

As such, this book is about the *expression of emotions*. I cannot objectively uncover the totality of a historical individual's emotions without resorting to almost total subjectivity. As historian Barbara H. Rosenwein noted, for the historian "the ways in which emotions are expressed are, in fact, our only pathway to them."[24] What individuals *say* offers an important window into how they *felt,* but historians must look at the totality of an individual's extant letters to actually understand their feelings. As is the case today, many people either parrot or try to embody cultural norms that they may not truly believe in. Thus, though many Confederate soldiers repeated the public discourse surrounding southern masculinity, their letters also offer paradoxical or contradictory implicit and explicit examples of their disagreement with these standards.

The world in which white southern males grew up to "become men" was one in which social norms and politics were welded into one overarching system of self-protection rooted in defending their race, their power, and their system of economic advancement (that is, slavery).[25] This need for control did not necessarily define every aspect of the generation that fought in the American Civil War. These men were individuals who made their own decisions to either adhere to or redefine these social expectations and how and why they did so was often rooted in their emotional responses to external stimuli.

War Fought and Felt represents an attempt at understanding these felt responses. Though structural and behavioral norms *are* imperative to understanding of why soldiers fought, research for this book indicates that soldiers often mimicked the verbiage of social norms while also redefining them as the situation required. This mental flexibility is reflective of human beings who in the midst of overwhelming crisis found that their ability to adapt often meant the difference between life or death, sanity or insanity. Thus, their lived experience was not always reflective of wider communal norms and the research undergirding this study indicates that this was more prevalent than previously supposed. In pursuit of this, I acknowledge historian Diane Sommerville's assertion that "southern men and women bore a greater emotional cost than their counterparts in the North," due to the larger percentage of adult males serving in the Confederate Army, the larger size of southern families compared with their northern counterparts (that is, more members of each family served), most battles being fought on Confederate soil and thus posing greater immediate threat, and the fact that southerners alone lost the war and thus were forced to accept the bitter reality of their defeat. Since they faced a different set of external stimuli than that of their enemies, it is reasonable to assume that some Confederate soldiers' emotional reactions contained in this book may have been markedly different in either their totality or scale from those of Union soldiers.

The research contained in this book pushes back on the growing "dark turn" of recent Civil War historiography. Using many of the motifs endemic to studies of the Vietnam War, this recent approach paints the war's participants as unwitting and psychologically broken victims whose suffering was the result of unchecked ideologues bent on gaining or exerting power. However, my research indicates that, even if they were in some ways unwitting victims, Confederate soldiers often truly believed that what they were fighting for was the preservation of their homes, their families, and their "way of life." The politics that they imbibed were simply constructions that fed into their belief that this war would be a tectonic struggle for the safety and betterment of those they loved. In their eyes, civilians depended upon their soldier-husbands and soldier-fathers for their physical survival while these same soldiers depended upon families and friends for their emotional survival. While many were struck down by bullets or disease, previous research indicates that most Confederate soldiers were not psychologically broken by the war and of those who survived it, most neither committed suicide nor were institutionalized. Many successfully reintegrated back into society at war's end.[26] It is my contention that the relationship between soldiers and their families and friends provided an emotional buffer that prevented a great collective psychological collapse among Confederate soldiers. Indeed, relationships—and the positive emotions engendered by these relationships—are fundamental to understanding how Confederate soldiers made it through the war with remarkably less emotional degradation than could be reasonably assumed.

War Fought and Felt examines three sets of overarching relational categories: romantic, friendship, and parental relationships. These relationships represented external stimuli that shaped the emotional expression of the soldiers being studied in the prewar, wartime, and postwar periods. Within each of the broad categories studied, some soldiers felt an emotional "push" that impelled them to enlist, endure, fight, and sometimes die in the military, while others endured a "pull" that either kept them from enlisting or drew them away from their military service through desertion. Emotions were the tethers by which families and soldiers experienced this push and pull and my research indicates that soldiers often felt a symbiotic "push" and "pull" that led to truly unsettling emotional oscillations.

Because of its emphasis on the individual, I do not attempt to address every aspect of the Confederate soldier's relational world, including an in-depth primary-source-based analysis of the relationship between white southerners and African Americans. The complexity of this subject would require an additional, monograph-length work, and I instead only begin to touch on the thorny issue of race relations during the war. The dearth of contemporaneous written records left by enslaved or free African Americans makes providing a statistically significant insight into their feelings toward white southerners exceedingly difficult. Thus, the chapter of this book that touches on race relations does not include the quantitative approach taken elsewhere. Additionally, though I address how soldiers' wartime emotional constructions played into their postwar lives, I do not go into great depth on this subject, as there are other books which have already dealt with this subject in far more thorough and authoritative ways.

Chapter 1 examines the growth and acceptance of emotional expression by American males from the country's nascent beginnings into the antebellum period. In it, I consider attachment theory and how society, parents, and other intrinsic motivators influenced the development of ideals of manhood. Specifically, I seek to understand how those ideals of American manhood changed over time, how those ideals were reconstructed in the South, and how attachments between men, parents and children, and husbands and wives shifted over time in the colonial and antebellum periods. By examining this evolution, I am attempting to establish a baseline with which to measure the changing nature of attachments during the war and thereafter establish how those attachments emotionally sustained Confederate soldiers when nationalism and societally induced ideals of honor and courage eroded in the caustic cauldron of war.

Chapter 2 examines the importance of romantic relationships in sustaining soldier motivations during the war. In it, I look at how romantic love undergirded a soldier's willingness to enlist and continue to fight even as war psychologically and emotionally eroded male self-confidence so highly emphasized in prewar masculine ideals. Fewer than half of the two hundred soldiers sampled for this project were either married or courting, yet they represented the majority of soldiers who expressed emotion in letters during the war. The argument that white southern males were emotionally reticent is refuted and the evidence demonstrates that men often turned to their wives and sweethearts for emotional and physical succor. Through an emotional pragmatism along the lines of what historian Peter Carmichael describes, they eschewed traditional notions of masculinity when war threatened to become their masculine, psychological, emotional, and physical undoing. Simply put, white southern males could not have endured the war apart from the support of their loved ones back home.

Chapter 3 examines the emotional push and pull of interpersonal relationships between soldiers during the war. In it, I argue that camaraderie and emotional tethers between men, which had their origins in the prewar period, provided an emotional bulwark against the personally deleterious effects of war. These ties became more immediate and tangible than those provided by family members back home. Furthermore, I examine how the changing nature of prewar ideals of masculinity and homosocial relationships reached a dramatic climax during the war years, allowing for greater public displays of emotional intensity than those seen before or after the war. Comrades became a sort of chosen kin that, in the physical absence of blood family, protected the individual from the destruction of their individual identity and humanity. Rather than becoming more "standoffish" or emotionally distant during the war, white southern men instead became more emotionally pointed and expressive as the war eroded traditional masculine and emotional norms.

Chapter 4 looks at the emotional intimacy between Confederate soldier-fathers and their children. In it, I argue that white southern males were not emotionally distant from their children, nor did they grow hardened by the war to the point that they were emotionally reticent with their children. To the contrary, the emotional tethers that connected soldier-fathers to their children prevented the psychological collapse of many soldiers. Soldiers' love for their children motivated them to fight even when the bloodletting became overwhelming. As a result, Confederate soldier-fathers came to define the war less in terms of ideology or duty and more in terms of protecting their children's futures. Family members for whom separate spheres marked so much of their prewar lives were now bound tightly together in a bid to survive. At least for the duration of the war, the rigid boundaries of prewar masculine, feminine, and juvenile spheres became far more permeable.

Chapter 5 examines the complex emotions felt by southerners toward African Americans before, during, and after the war. Whereas the relationships between Confederate soldiers and their loved ones were often symbiotic in nature, the relationship between Confederate soldiers and African Americans was generally one-sided. The emotions felt by Confederate soldiers toward African Americans often were far more complex than those directed toward their white compatriots and they were rooted in an individual and collective cognitive dissonance based on racist beliefs designed to justify slavery. Whereas relationships between white southerners were often marked by tender affection, the relationships between Confederate soldiers and African Americans were more often tinged with bitterness, anger, and fear. As a whole, African Americans represented a mudsill class that undergirded a system of white hegemony. Because white southerners embraced the lies of paternalism, many seemingly felt a strange affection toward their slaves, so long as they were obedient and danced to the tune of racial stereotypes. Those who refused often left their "masters" to navigate their feelings of bewilderment, betrayal, and seething rage. In this way, African Americans exerted a lot of control over the emotions of those who were supposed to be controlling them. These emotions are fundamental to understanding the unrelenting outpouring of white rage during Reconstruction.

Finally, in the Conclusion, I synthetically address the postwar period and specifically examine how the new relational dynamics constructed during the war evolved during Reconstruction. Pulling from more recent works on demobilization and Reconstruction, I argue that this period represented a return to the prewar masculine ideals of mastery that helped plunge the nation into war in the first place while also altering the trajectory of American life into the twentieth and twenty-first centuries. At the heart of postwar white rage were feelings of embarrassment, betrayal, and insecurity from the upending of a racial order that, at least for whites, was supposed to provide a sense of superiority and security during the tumultuous postwar period.

This is the story of real people within the context of their own time and place. It is my attempt to recover more of the soldier's agency while also holding the explanatory power of larger social pressures in tension. However, my research counters the overwrought idea that white southern men were primarily obsessed with self-sufficiency and self-mastery. As a result of their suffering during the war, the prewar social expectations of self-reliance gave way to mutual interdependence and emotional effusion. In order to understand this change, it is important to understand the evolution of masculine emotional expression in the decades leading up to the outbreak of the American Civil War. This prewar period provides a baseline for understanding how dramatically male emotional expressive norms shifted during the war.

CHAPTER 1

MASTERS
OF
MANHOOD
THE SHAPING OF THE SOUTH'S MASCULINE ETHOS

With the outbreak of the American Revolution, the world convulsed with immense cultural, economic, and political changes. The old monarchical order faded as this revolution, ignited by the Enlightenment, overturned centuries of hierarchy. Ideas that were once primarily the purview of philosophers and critics, only a century before, had now filtered down to the masses, altering one's relationships with government, family, and self. These alterations, and their differing interpretations amongst men from northern and southern states, are fundamental to understanding how southern men came to view themselves as distinct from their northern counterparts. Moreover, they are central to how southern men defined "manhood" and how they saw themselves as the true guardians of the ideals of the Revolutionary generation. The widespread emotional paroxysms of southerners in response to what they perceived as threats to the Revolution's cherished ideals led to widespread unrest before the outbreak of the American Civil War. Undergirding this feeling of being threatened were deeply entrenched ideals of manliness, honor, community, and family.

The locus of southern life in the prewar period was family and community. The ideal of the "traditional patriarch" in which a man led his family while also representing it within the broader community through acts of service was what all men aspired to attain. Within the familial hierarchy, wives and children were expected to submit to the headship of their husbands and fathers, while these were expected to submit only to the symbolic heads of their communities such as church and civic leaders. As heads of their respective families and leaders in their communities, men were expected to control themselves and their families by cultivating their own virtue and restraining their own emotions, guiding their sons toward virtuous citizenship, and restraining the conduct of their wives.[1] This model of manhood originated in Britain and traveled with settlers to the New World. In the heady years of early British settlements in North America, the need for control seemed to be of paramount importance. Having sailed across the ocean for the wildwoods of North America, British settlers were repeatedly faced with their own powerlessness at the hands of nature and, as they believed, nature's God. Facing pressures from within due to starvation and disease and pressures from without due to increasingly hostile Native Americans, early English settlers found that hierarchy and rigid leadership was the only way to pull communities together in order to survive. This approach was embodied by John Smith at Jamestown—an approach that was credited by many with saving the burgeoning settlement. Over time, as tobacco became an important cash crop and the threat from hostile Native tribes abated, probusiness British mercantile policies pushed many families into higher socio-economic classes, many of whom no longer struggled simply to survive. This growing freedom allowed families to pivot primarily from providing mutual physical support to also cultivating familial affection and indulgence.

Historians James and Dorothy Volo divide colonial families into four main categories: nuclear families, extended families, stem-nuclear families, and clan-like families. The "nuclear family" consisted of a married couple with children living under one roof that was set apart from all other relatives. An "extended family" was a kinship network involving blood relatives who lived in separate households within the same community. "Stem-nuclear families" consisted of married children who lived within their parents' home and who had their own children. Finally, "clan-like families" were essentially nuclear, but each member of a clan "claimed a common ancestry, usually carried a common name, and most importantly, recognized a common identity beyond the bounds of the nuclear family that was largely unaffected by any daily living arrangement." They could reside in different households in the same village or even in different colonies, yet still claim a common identity. The kinship ties between these four categories of families provided economic and social support for each member.[2]

The idea of family was central to southern society—even in the colonial period. A man's life was not considered complete unless he had a wife and child who were considered central to his own vitality and happiness. In colonial North Carolina, James Iredell noted that "a young Man without the joys of a private Family leads a very dull, and I may add, a less improving Life."[3] The ideal of a companionate marriage marked by emotional connection was a central pursuit of young men and women in the American colonies. A companionate marriage did not translate into legal equality between men and women, however. As the American colonies evolved from frontier outposts to become more civilized and economically stable, elements of English common law were adopted in which a woman's legal status was subsumed by that of her husband. The transition from singleness to marriage was marked by a loss of legal opportunities for women. At the same time, though a single woman was expected to contribute to her community, a married woman was expected to turn inward and the bulk of her contributions were to extend to her family.[4] Famed Spanish explorer Francisco de Miranda, who toured America in 1783, wryly noted that "the married women maintain a monastic seclusion and a submission to their husbands such as I have never seen. . . . Once married, they separate themselves from all intimate friendships and devote themselves completely to the care of home and family." He went on to note that "during the first year of marriage they play the role of lovers, the second year of breeders, and thereafter of housekeepers. On the other hand, the unmarried women enjoy complete freedom and take walks alone wherever they want to, without their steps being observed."[5]

While a woman's influence was most seen in the home, men were expected to exert influence over the community. White males were expected to be leaders and contributors to the wider community and they were increasingly expected to do so through the cultivation of their own virtue. This individualism was wrought in part by the Enlightenment. German philosopher Immanuel Kant defined "enlightenment" as "*man's emergence from his self-incurred immaturity. Immaturity* is the inability to use one's own understanding without the guidance of another."[6] The revolutionary ideas of the Enlightenment—including rational challenges to authority, detachment from organized religion, an emphasis on empiricism and skeptical inquiry, the glorification of humanity in the arts, and the attempt to understand the world through scientific inquiry rather than religion—created an environment in which it was believed that man could improve himself to heights of perfection through the rational workings of his own mind.[7]

Not only did the Enlightenment encourage individualism among American males, but it also reshaped familial structures. English philosopher John Locke argued that as a temporary stage of development, children's reliance on parental authority rested on the unequal power structure arising from the child's temporary incapacity and weakness and resulting dependence on parents. Whereas previous generations believed in a natural hierarchical order within the family wherein children were often seen as weaker but necessary vessels for survival, Enlightenment thinkers argued for the importance of nurturing children and preparing them to become self-governing adults through the maturation of their minds and reason.[8] Reflecting this impulse, Scottish philosopher Francis Hutcheson argued that "the child is a rational agent, with rights valid against the parents; tho' they are the natural tutors or curators, and have a right to direct the actions, and manage the goods of the child, for its benefit, during its want of proper knowledge."[9]

This growing emphasis on self-cultivation and individualism permeated the masculine ethos of North American society. Men increasingly saw themselves as the embodiment of a new rugged masculinity that was marked by a growing distaste for dependence. Particularly with the outbreak of the American Revolution, *independence* was the clarion call of North American men even as the Revolution also unleashed a torrent of egalitarianism and expectations of greater emotional affection, particularly toward one's children. The ideal of the emotionally stoic "traditional patriarch" had begun its slow erosion.[10]

Historians are often quick to emphasize both emotional stoicism and patriarchy as the linchpins for understanding colonial men; they have been slow to recognize that these ideals of stoicism and unalloyed patriarchal authority were typically more honored in the breach than in the observance. Historian Kenneth Lockridge noted that the Revolutionary period was one where men were "caught between the exaggerated imperatives of domestic patriarchy as they constructed it—that they must control sexuality and indeed all things in their households—and the fact that both in and out of households women had substantial power."[11] After the "Edenton Tea Party" of 1774, in which fifty-one women in Edenton, North Carolina, organized a boycott of tea and other British products in response to the passage of the Tea Act in 1773, British men ridiculed the audacious act—a clear violation of standard patriarchal norms.[12] In a letter to his brother who lived in

North Carolina, one British citizen asked, "Is there a female congress at Edenton too? I hope not, for we Englishmen are afraid of the male congress, but if the ladies, who have ever since the Amazonian era been esteemed the most formidable enemies; if they, I say, should attack us, the most fatal consequence is to be dreaded."[13] While the women of the Edenton Tea Party were mocked back in Britain, they were generally praised by both men and women throughout the colonies.[14] "The battle of the sexes was fought on uneven terms, but women made it perhaps more of a contest than we have realized," Lockridge notes and then continues, "it was often real *economic* power in the hands of women that excited a not-always-successful misogyny in men."[15]

Even the language used to describe the family was imprinted with the rhetoric of equality. Though the laws of coverture gave husbands full control over their wives' property still governed marital relationships, Revolutionary ideology nonetheless imbued women with a sense of their own independence, and family increasingly became a republican institution—that is, an institution of emerging equality.[16] Eschewing the almost parent-child relationship that marked previous generations of husbands' relationships to their wives, marriage became an increasingly coequal institution built on mutual love and admiration. In a 1784 edition of the *Gentleman and Lady's Town and Country Magazine,* one author asked, "Wherein does the happiness of the married state consists?" to which this reply was given, "In a mutual affection, a similarity of tempers, a reciprocal endeavor to please, and an invariable aim to each other's comfort."[17] Likewise, in 1789, essayist Judith Sargent Murray wrote that "mutual esteem, mutual friendship, mutual confidence, *begirt about by mutual forbearance*—these are the necessary requisites of the matrimonial career."[18] Historian Steven Mintz noted that this era "popularized an antiauthoritarian ideology highly critical of patriarchal authority, social hierarchy, and defense."[19] To avoid overstating the case, it must be noted that this marital egalitarianism was not evenly applied across the whole of North America. Some areas and families eschewed egalitarianism while others heartily embraced it. At the same time, the *emotional egalitarianism* of marriage did not necessarily translate into legal or political egalitarianism. Nonetheless, this impulse picked up steam throughout much of the post-Revolutionary period and into the mid-nineteenth century.

If the relationship between husbands and wives increasingly centered on emotional connection and companionship, the relationship between parents and their children increasingly emphasized personal development and mutual love. To this end, mothers were expected to instill civic virtue and self-discipline in their children.[20] Embracing John Locke's philosophy of the *tabula rosa,* or the idea that the human mind at birth is a "blank slate" shaped through sensation and reflection, mothers were expected to inscribe upon their children the ideals of personal virtue and mutual service.[21] American lexicographer Noah Webster, considered the "Father of American Scholarship and Education," reflected this idea, stating: "Youth is the time to form both the head and the heart . . . the seeds of knowledge should be planted in the mind while it is young and susceptible and if the mind is not kept untainted in youth, there is little probability that the moral character of the *man* will be unblemished."[22] At the same time, influenced by Protestant evangelicalism, mothers of the Early Republic sought to prepare their children for the afterlife through self-cultivation while also emphasizing the brotherhood and sisterhood of all believers. Mothers were impelled by secular philosophers and religious thinkers alike to take an active part in the personal physical, emotional, and spiritual development of their children.[23] They were thus seen as the inheritors and disseminators of revolutionary, religious, and social expectations that shaped the sociocultural and ideological expectations and beliefs of the following generations.

Though the colonial period was marked by the near-absolute power of the male over his wife and children, the period of the Early Republic concurrently witnessed the growing social and ideological influence of women. Before the American Revolution, the idea of "virtue" referred to the masculine sacrifice of self. After the war, as women's influence grew, traditionally "feminine qualities" such as love and benevolence became increasingly melded into the collective ideal of virtue. Moreover, the perceived ability of women to stimulate feelings of sympathy and morality while encouraging the development of affectionate relationships were qualities that could bind the fragile new republic together. Preparing children and future husbands and fathers to assume the mantle of republican citizenship became the first and most important obligation of American women in the post-Revolutionary period.[24] In 1796, American journalist and newspaper publisher Samuel Harrison Smith noted that "virtue or the vice of an individual, the happiness or the misery of a family, the glory or the infamy of a nation, have had their sources in the cradle, over which the prejudices of a nurse or a mother have presided."[25]

The growing influence of mothers on the family and, by extension, on society was reflective of an increasing social egalitarianism within the family. While in the public sphere, the old social hierarchy of patriarchy and male dominance seemed firmly entrenched, within the private sphere these stratigraphic lines between family members were increasingly blurred. An elderly U.S. congressman, Paine Wingate, lamented in 1788 that "fathers, mothers, sons & daughters, young & old, all mix together & talk & joke alike, so that you cannot discover any distinction made or any respect shewn to one more than to another. I am not for keeping up a great distance between Parents & Children, but there is a difference between staring and stark mad."[26] Exactly how men felt about this is not readily apparent. Though men were certainly at the top of the social hierarchy in the United States, historians examining period diaries note that relatively few recorded their personal motivations or feelings. Diaries from this period were not necessarily tools for self-reflection or processing one's feelings. Rather, they were typically used for recording economic transactions or daily comings and goings. Some, like historian Jan Lewis in her study of pre-Revolutionary Virginians, took this as a sign that colonial men "did not live in a psychological realm. They did not examine motivation, nor did they muse about the complexities of human behavior. They neither had the taste nor the skill for self-examination. They did not probe the depths of the human heart."[27] However, if the pre- and post-Revolutionary periods were marked by a masculinity that emphasized emotional stoicism, it should not be surprising that men were largely unwilling to pen their emotions. Certainly, they felt them. Regardless of what men were willing to express, historians have noted that in the post-Revolutionary period, the American family increasingly became the locus for emotional expression and exploration. Indeed, as religious awakenings swept through the colonies, evangelicals saw emotional expression as evidence of real internal change. At the same time, the influence of Romanticism sparked an age of sentimentalism that redrew the relational boundaries of the seventeenth and eighteenth centuries. But it had not always been this way.

American males' distrust of emotion may have been rooted in the Scientific Revolution and the Enlightenment. The Scientific Revolution's focus on a mechanistic and deterministic universe and the Enlightenment's emphasis on reason and logic represented a new approach to understanding the world and man's place within it. As the Scientific Revolution and the Enlightenment deemphasized the spiritual and emotional in favor of the rational, masculinity now emphasized the external physical and social display of strength. By the early nineteenth century, however, the limitations of this approach were increasingly becoming apparent.

The emergence of the Romantic movement toward the end of the eighteenth century shifted the gaze of many toward the emotional inner world that so many were unable to deny. Emotions are potent and central to human decision making. Deemphasizing their importance was increasingly problematic and, in the eyes of many, reduced human beings to machines. "It was into this transcendental vacuum," historian Tim Blanning wrote, "that the romantics moved. In doing so, they were initiating a new phase in long-running dialectic between a culture of feeling and a culture of reason." This emergence of Romanticism represented a time of intense inner focus, which German philosopher of history Georg Wilhelm Friedrich Hegel described as a period of "absolute inwardness."[28] While Enlightenment philosophers emphasized reason, balance, order, harmony, rationality, and intellect, the Romantics emphasized the individual, emotions, imagination and subjectivity. Moreover, they argued that emotions were more important than reason and that the world is better understood through the senses.[29]

It is within this dialectic of emotion and reason that many white southerners found themselves in the middle half of the nineteenth century. Scanning the letters and diaries of Confederate soldiers, one finds, though the soldiers may not have always known it, cultural beliefs emanating from the Romantic movement and the Enlightenment bled through these pages—particularly those of the wealthy and well-educated. At least in the South, Romanticism may have held greater sway over the populace as they increasingly celebrated emotional exuberance in their religion, romance, family, and politics. As the United States careened toward war, it should be no surprise that when, in 1856, Republican U.S. senator Charles Sumner attacked South Carolina representative Preston Brooks's cousin, South Carolina senator Andrew Butler, he argued that slavery was both a harlot and his mistress. Sumner's goal was to be inflammatory and to elicit an emotional reaction. In response, Brooks evinced great emotion as he viciously caned Senator Sumner in the Senate chamber, severely injuring him. Southerners celebrated Brooks's outburst, as he stood up for his cousin's "honor," celebrating his emotional reaction. Rather than denigrating Brooks for his unrestrained rage, southerners went so far as to send him new canes.

⎯⎯❧⎯⎯

While southerners embraced the works of the Romantics, religion held greater sway over the populace. The emphasis on emotional expression among evangelicals was an important catalyst leading to a noticeable shift in emotional norms among white males. While evangelicalism was imported to the United States from Europe in the eighteenth century, it became tightly woven into the fabric of America with the outbreak of the First Great Awakening in 1730. Unlike mainline denominations, evangelicals emphasized an individual's personal and intimate relationship with God. Beyond assenting intellectually to God's invitation of salvation, evangelicals also believed that people must emotionally assent to God's offer of salvation. So fervently did they believe this that many preachers judged the success of their sermons on the emotional response of their congregants. Indeed, as famous evangelical preachers such as George Whitefield and Jonathan Edwards spoke of heaven, hell, and salvation, audiences responded with emotional anguish or exuberance. Evangelical preachers wrote blithely of the throngs of congregants who responded to their preaching with outpourings of tears, anguish, delight, and joy. This, they believed, was evidence that God had wrought a spiritual change in their congregants' hearts. For some evangelicals, the seemingly overwrought emphasis on one's emotional response to preaching meant that individuals may have been responding to God's offer of salvation out of fleeting emotions rather than careful intellectual assent.

During the First Great Awakening, the dialectic between the heart and mind became the central debate among pro- and antirevivalists. Some famous pastors and preachers argued that the passions, which were prone to situational turbulence, should be reined in by one's intellect. Reason, they believed, could buffer the undulating waves of human affections and this approach favored a commitment to truth over feeling. Others, however, argued that intellectual assent was much easier than allowing oneself to be vulnerable enough to bear the emotional weight of one's own sinfulness and God's goodness. Finally, others such as the famous Congregationalist pastor and theologian Jonathan Edwards, found a middle ground in which the outward affection and the inward intellectual assent were indicative of salvation. At the time, most religious Americans eschewed Edwards's middle ground and instead fell into one of two major camps. The "Old Lights" were antirevivalists who argued that salvation should be devoid of emotional influence while "New Lights" celebrated the emotional enthusiasm of revival meetings.[30]

Nonetheless, the First Great Awakening was distinguished from earlier strains of Protestantism by "dramatically increased emphases on *seasons of revival,* on *outpourings of the Holy Spirit,* and on *converted sinners experiencing God's love personally.*"[31] New Light evangelicalism may have been heavily influenced by the Romantic movement as well as by the egalitarian impulses of liberalism emanating from the Enlightenment. Compared with the rigid and hierarchical Calvinist churches that dotted early British North America, evangelical churches increasingly allowed for women and nonwhites to take positions in church administration such as deacons and elders. The poor, rich, parents, children, whites, and nonwhites commingled freely in many evangelical churches and, as Historian Thomas S. Kidd noted, "in the revivals, the world seemed to turn upside down as those with the very least agency in eighteenth-century America felt the power of God surge in their bodies."[32] The fact that rich and poor, Black and white all felt this power "surge in their bodies" echoes the Apostle Paul's startling assertion in the Book of Galatians that "in Christ Jesus you are all children of God through faith, for all of you who were baptized into Christ have clothed yourselves in Christ. There is neither Jew nor Gentile, neither slave nor free, nor is there male and female, for you are all one in Christ Jesus."[33]

That anyone of any gender, race, or class could have a personal relationship with Christ was problematic in the American South. The leveling effect of Christianity ran contrary to the rigid social and racial hierarchy endemic to the South. Southerners looked with great suspicion on northern evangelicalism during the First Great Awakening. However, in the eighteenth century, the American South seemed like a backwoods mission field in great need of the civilizing power of northern Protestantism. Increasingly, New Light evangelicalism swept through the South and, after the American Revolution, the arrival of Methodist missionaries led to a radical shift in southern society. According to Kidd, "what once had been viewed by northerners as a godless mission field was now beginning to turn into an evangelical stronghold." Yet in a classic case of religion being reshaped by social norms, southern evangelicalism increasingly reflected elements of the surrounding hierarchical, proslavery society.[34] Still, the emotional expressionism of Protestant evangelicalism did not wane.

The Second Great Awakening from 1790 to the late 1840s witnessed an even more intense focus on emotional expressionism. Revivalist preachers such as Charles Finney sought to stir the emotional embers of the First Great Awakening by focusing their preaching on the potency of God's love for people and their need for an emotional response. In this way, the Second Great Awakening represented a more positive approach to salvation and emotion compared with the First Great Awakening's emphasis on an emotional response to preaching about hellfire and damnation. Both methods were designed to elicit the same result: a profound emotional response to God's offer of salvation.[35] Likewise, the egalitarianism that marked the First Great Awakening became even more prominent during the Second Great Awakening. The naturalistic and mechanistic understanding of the world among intellectual elites and the merely intellectual approach to faith common in many religious circles were now seen as elitest, undemocratic, and contrary to genuine religious feeling. Revivalists of the Second Great Awakening often downplayed the necessity of rigorous intellectualism in favor of heartfelt emotionally laden devotion to God. One day, revivalist Charles Finney took the stage to preach the Gospel in a small town of mainly Dutch Reformed Christians. As he preached the Gospel with a torrent of emotion, he soon noticed among the crowd that "a deep and universal feeling seemed to pervade the whole assembly. Those that were truly pious among them, poured forth their tears of mingled joy, gratitude, and deep solicitude for their anxious and distressed neighbors."[36] For Finney, emotional outbursts were evidence of God's power and love poured out among His people.

The emphasis on emotion over intellect was particularly appealing to middle- and lower-class Americans, who often could not afford formal education. Intellectual development required expensive books, tutors, and schools. Emotion was natural and above all, free. Noted revivalists such as Francis Asbury and Lorenzo Dow even went so far as to excise theology from their sermons, relying instead upon the universal, innate, and cross-cultural medium of emotion to make their message more accessible to those who they believed lacked the education to understand more complex theology. Grief, joy, ecstasy, fear, delight, sorrow, and rejoicing all demarcated the experience of the Christian convert now. Finney, Asbury, Dow, and other revivalists believed, in the words of historian Claudia Stokes, that "mere words or verbal professions of faith can be easily counterfeited," and that "tears, as outward excretions of the unseen workings of the heart, metonymically affirmed the sincerity of these private convictions." Mere intellectual assent to the Christian faith was no longer enough.[37]

The influence of Romanticism and the First and Second Great Awakenings on emotional norms represented a growing trend toward sentimentalism in the nineteenth century. For southern men, taut between the old-world ideal of the emotionally stolid male and the developing ideal of emotional expressiveness, new ideas emerged about the role of men and their families. Increasingly, families were seen as less of an economic unit of survival and more as a safe space where one's emotional needs could be met. This approach had long been the purview of American women, who were expected to take care of their families while men worked outside of the home. Increasingly, men turned inward toward their families in order to meet their emotional needs.

It was within the safe confines of the family that men privately released their pent-up emotions, which preserved their public persona and thus maintained their honor. This idea of "honor" was one that held an almost sacred significance to southern men. Historian Bertram Wyatt-Brown argued that "honor" was a pre-Christian system of behavior that consisted of a "cluster of ethical rules, most readily found in societies of small communities, by which judgments of behavior are ratified by community consensus."[38] To be honorable was to be accepted by the wider community and, as Wyatt-Brown noted, "honor resides in the individual as his understanding of who he is and where he belongs in the ordered ranks of society." Honor is primarily concerned with social reputation.[39] On the horizontal axis of existence, honor was dependent upon one's reputation, while on a vertical axis, it was dependent upon patriarchy. By extension, the place of one's family in society was marked primarily by the reputation (or lack thereof) of the husband and father. To maintain one's public honor, white southern males were expected to master their own emotions. Yet those emotions needed somewhere to go, and it was within the household that they were generally unleashed. Love, joy, sadness, fear, and anxiety were emotions that were considered taboo in public and acceptable—and even expected—in private.

White southern males often found themselves hamstrung by ideals of manhood and masculinity that they were frequently unable to fulfill. Sociologists have long argued that individuals traditionally measure themselves and their self-worth in direct proportion to their reputation among members of their community. White southern men lived in a bifurcated world split between the "private" and the "public" self. The former represented the aspects of one's personality, being, thoughts, dreams, hopes, and faults, all of which were largely hidden away from the public and displayed only to one's most intimate of companions. The latter was constructed to align oneself with broader social and communal standards. Both were shaped by emotionally laden relationships.

Within the family, white southern men were considered masters of their own homes. The family unit became a reflection of the larger social hierarchy of society wherein wealthy slaveowners and planters ruled over the yeoman middle class and the poor. In a society in which the rights of women and children were on the ascendency and yet still lagged significantly behind those of men, this is not surprising. South Carolina politician and future Confederate States secretary of the treasury Christopher Memminger noted in 1851:

> The Slave Institution at the South increases the tendency to dignify the family. Each planter is in fact a Patriarch—his position compels him to be a ruler in his household. . . . Domestic relations become those which are most prized—each family recognizes its duty, and its members feel a responsibility for its discharge. The fifth commandment becomes the foundation of Society. The State is looked to only as the ultimate head in external relations, while all internal duties, such as support, education, and the relative duties of individuals, are left to domestic regulation.[40]

In her study of white yeoman farmers in South Carolina, historian Stephanie McCurry noted that both yeoman *and* planters shared "a definition of manhood rooted in the inviolability of the household, the command of dependents, and the public prerogatives manhood conferred. When they struck for independence in the fall of 1860 . . . lowcountry yeomen acted in defense of their own identity, as masters of small worlds."[41]

And yet, more recent scholarship indicates that our understanding of southern patriarchy requires more nuance. Historian Michael P. Johnson noted that patriarchy "placed various kinds and degrees of coercion and inequality in the context of family relationships," and yet the more coercive nature of patriarchy often caused more tension in southern families than has previously been understood. Whereas historians have couched "patriarchy" in stark and unblinking terms of coercion and power, male headship was, in the words of Johnson, "tempered by affection, between the patriarch and his dependents." Among planter elites, the typical southern family represented an emotionally nuanced web of entanglement. The rigid top-down approach of leading planter patriarchs was often tempered by concurrent feelings of compassion and tenderness. "Planter families were not cold and emotionless like the 'restricted patriarchal nuclear family' that prevailed in England between 1550 and 1770," Johnson notes. "Instead, the planters combined patriarchal ideas about authority with deep personal and emotional ties to their wives and children."[42]

Over the past four decades, historians have been focused upon the influence of patriarchy and power within southern families—often to the detriment of other external factors. The emotional ties between family members became more acceptable in the decades leading up to the American Civil War, and they are of far greater importance than many historians realize. It was these emotional tethers between parents and their children, as well as between husbands and wives, that opened the door to interpersonal influence. Though the familial power structure in the South is most often presented in terms of power flowing from the top (the male) down to the bottom (the wife and children), the truth is that influence could also flow from the bottom up. Though they generally did not exert social or political power on their husbands and fathers, wives and children did exert immense emotional influence on them. Love was one of the few avenues down which those on the bottom of the family hierarchy could influence those at the top. By opening themselves to feel love for others, white southern males were in some ways diminishing their patriarchal powers. It was through these relationships that men learned to examine themselves, define their feelings, and reshape masculine ideals. As historian James Broomall noted, "Self-examination, emotional release and control, and demonstrations of manliness became processes by which Southerners learned the contours of manhood and explored themselves and their place in society."[43]

The private act of self-examination and emotional release stood in stark contrast to normative constructs of male patriarchy that emphasized emotional staidness and interpersonal control. This bifurcation between the "private" and "public" self has proven problematic for historians as antebellum men did not always record their feelings or beliefs for posterity. In her study of colonial and early antebellum Virginia, historian Jan Lewis noted that men in the first half of the nineteenth century continued to use diaries as account books for their economic transactions, much like their colonial forebears. However, "they also began gradually to write diaries to explore and to soothe their feelings. Sentimental religion, by holding that purity of heart was more important than correctness of action, encouraged Virginians to record and examine the emotions of their hearts."[44] As Broomall noted about diaries, "in writing and within the domestic sphere, feelings ran more freely, and private exposure was more expressive."[45] The outbreak of the American Civil War represented an important sea change as men were torn from their families and forced to *share* their private and innermost feelings with others. The act of writing allowed men to interact with the parts of themselves over which they often felt little sense of power or mastery—their emotions.[46] Of course, diaries were most often kept by the wealthy and this does not give us a clear perspective on those of the lower classes and often less educated. Nonetheless, social mores and expectations do tend to trickle down from the top rungs of the social ladder toward the bottom. Moreover, it can be argued that during the American Civil War, when men faced the sobering prospect of their imminent demise, this same level of introspection and the exposition of the private self was translated into letters back home. Indeed, the letters read for this book indicate that, at least during the war, the expression of emotion through the written word was both well accepted and highly sought after.

The fact that men often wrote with an intense depth of feeling was surprising when one considers that antebellum men often lived in an emotional chasm in which many felt deep, nagging doubts about their ability to fulfill the masculine mandates of the broader community. At the same time, striving to achieve the highest levels of a society's socially enacted ideals of excellence, southern men faced immense feelings of insecurity and uncertainty, often leading to competition with their fellow men. Moreover, this competition and insecurity bred an obsessive individualism that hampered their ability to relate to others. Historian Stephen Berry notes that while white southern men grew up together and often developed deep friendships, their relationships were often marred by constant self-assessments of their standing among their peers as well as an overwrought alertness to perceived slights to their honor. "Even in friendship," he notes, "there was a standoffishness, an unwillingness to appear weak, vulnerable, or emotionally needy."[47] This predilection toward defining one's masculinity in relationship to other males is what sociologist Michael Kimmel calls the "homosocial enactment of masculinity."[48] The relationships between men in the prewar period defined masculinity's boundaries while also providing the rubric by which men could grade their attempts at fulfilling communal expectations.

If it is true that southern men were often overwhelmed with feelings of uncertainty and self-doubt in relationship to each other, it is no wonder that many sought solace or self-worth in members of the opposite sex. The pursuit (and winning) of a woman's heart was seen by men as evidence of their own goodness and worth. At the same time, southern women often served as de facto enforcers of masculine norms as well as cheerleaders for male visions of grand accomplishment.[49] The archetypal southern white female of the first half of the nineteenth century supported a man's economic, social, or political endeavors while also imbuing him with greater self-importance and social standing through her own purity, piety, domesticity, supportiveness, and submissiveness. The stature of a husband and wife in a community had as much to do with their fulfillment of social expectations as with economic gain. Historian Stephen Berry noted this pattern, writing that women "were supposed to bear witness to male becoming, to cheer men to greatness, and to comfort them along the way. Every free white man had a personal empire to build. . . . And each man had another empire to build in a woman, through whose eyes he could see himself succeed." Male aspirations—including accomplishments in business, in life, or in fulfilling cultural mandates—were achieved through the support and reassurance of women.[50] During his grand tour of America, famed French traveler Alexis de Tocqueville noted that "it is not uncommon for the same man, in the course of his life, to rise and sink again through all the grades which lead from opulence to poverty. American women support these vicissitudes with calm and unquenchable energy: it would seem that their desires contract, as easily as they expand, with their fortunes."[51]

Men and women thus took important and somewhat equal roles in the pursuit of the fulfillment of masculine ideals. The socially constructed symbiosis was woven deeply into the fabric of Victorian romance. Courtship in the antebellum period was markedly different than that of the colonial period. During the colonial period, marriage was often extolled due to the social, economic, or political gain for either one or both individuals involved. Yet it was also a transition period in which romantic love became the melting pot of the Enlightenment's individualism, the egalitarianism of the American Revolution, and the celebration of emotional expression by the Romantics and revivalists. By the antebellum period, individualistic romantic love based on sentimentality outweighed the importance of the economic or social benefits of marriage in many social circles. Women now held even greater power over these decisions as male suitors were forced to win them over and the woman's decision to either accept or reject marriage largely lay with her own conscience and desires. Romantic relationships increasingly centered on the "felt" need of connection, love, and interpersonal suitability fueled by physical attraction and emotional appeal.[52]

Companionate marriage was now designed to safely contain the entire spectrum of human emotions. Even before marriage, courting couples probed one another's psyches to determine their romantic compatibility. The rural nature of the South meant that courting couples, hampered by the limitations of technology and travel, often conversed in the form of written letters. Writing was an intentional act which generally required planning and forethought, allowing individuals to think about what they wanted to say and how they wanted to say it—a benefit largely missing from verbal communication. It thus represented an important medium for understanding how people truly felt as they worked through their feelings internally. This was even more true in an age in which men and women grew up in separate spheres in which separation between the sexes often led to a sense of insecurity when one sex had to interact with another.[53] And yet, even though letter writing carried such significance during the decades leading up to the war, its usefulness as a tool could be limited by one's lack of education, which inevitably led to a reduced vocabulary by which one could translate emotions into words. Between 1799 and 1809, the illiteracy rate (the inability to sign one's name) among American army enlistees (with an average age of 25.1) was 42 percent—a number which dropped to 25 percent by 1850.[54] Most southerners were nonelites who were either middle-class or poor and in an age in which public education was virtually nonexistent in many areas, lower-class white southerners either had to teach themselves or be satisfied with receiving comparatively little formal education.

While diaries allowed men to reflect on their inward feelings, letters were part of a larger process of pushing these feelings outward toward others. Concurrently, letters helped men draw others into their emotional worlds. Letters, coupled with verbal communication, were part of a larger process of emotional enmeshment between men and their romantic pursuits. This enmeshment was marked by private expressions of vulnerability and self-surrender that were balanced with public acclamations of emotional reservation and self-mastery. To southern white males, surrender to one's superior was acceptable and this was part and parcel of southern identity. Southerners expected to surrender themselves collectively to God while southern men could also, to a lesser extent, surrender themselves to women, who were seen as the moral exemplars of southern society. In a society marked by the ideal of republican motherhood and the celebration of women's familial and communal contributions through piety, servitude, and quiet strength, southern men virtually worshipped the ideal woman. Though romance in no way replaced organized religion, the language surrounding southern womanhood had an almost ethereal quality that was marked by sincere reverence. The ideal southern woman was everything that the average southern man was often lacking.

The collective exaltation of southern women theoretically enabled them to wield greater power over their husbands and children. While historians often focus on the narrow political and social constraints faced by southern women, in terms of *emotional power,* women often held immense sway over their husbands and children. This power existed in symbiosis, however. While women could wield immense power over their husbands, at times they were also expected to reorient their lives to support their husbands' social ambitions and economic conquests. Southern women often restrained their own ambitions in favor of their husbands' and this, coupled with the fact that many women lived in rural areas with little contact with others, meant that they typically lived very circumscribed lives. Unless she lived in a city, a woman's social circle rarely extended outside of her family. Family, then, became their focus both by social fiat as well as sheer circumstance.[55] For many southern women, this narrow but potent place in the social order was not unexpected. After his grand tour of America in the 1830s, famed chronicler Alexis de Tocqueville wrote that "no American woman falls into the toils of matrimony as into a snare held out to her simplicity and ignorance. She has been taught beforehand what is expected of her, and voluntarily and freely does she enter upon this engagement. She supports her new condition with courage, because she chose it."[56] Even though they may have "chosen it," they had little choice otherwise.

Although wives and mothers represented the familial and societal locus of moral and spiritual goodness, fathers embodied the family's ambitions and aspirations and by extension, white southern men *collectively* embodied the South's economic and social ambitions. Family provided men with physical, emotional, and spiritual support for the fulfillment of their grand visions and ambitions. At the same time, a woman's influence could temper the ambition of the family patriarch when it threatened to harm the family—particularly if he violated socially prescribed moral boundaries. With this influence, wives were not only protecting their husbands but, more importantly, they were protecting their families and their honor. This mutual reciprocity, emphasis on romantic feeling, and sentimentality led to greater emotional development between husband and wife. These prewar relational bonds became powerful sources of support when war finally erupted.

Concurrent with the emotional reshaping of marital and romantic relationships in the lead-up to the American Civil War, the emotional relationship between parents and children also witnessed a fundamental shift. Parent-child relationships in the colonial period were marked by a strict authoritarianism that, in the wake of the Romantic movement, Great Awakenings, and American Revolution, moved more and more toward sentimentality and egalitarianism. "I think that, in proportion as manners and laws become more democratic," Alexis de Tocqueville wrote, "the relation of father and son becomes more intimate and more affectionate; rules and authority are less talked of; confidence and tenderness are oftentimes increased, and it would seem that the natural bond is drawn closer in proportion as the social bond is loosened."[57]

Awareness of this propensity toward tenderness and intimacy between parents and their children is vital to our understanding of the depth of emotion expressed by Confederate soldiers during the war. Recent work in the field of attachment theory is demonstrative of how vital relationships are in shaping how children develop and see the world around them. "Attachment" refers to the emotional tethers between human beings that both guide and shape their feelings and behaviors. These include "attachment thoughts"—that is, how one thinks about one's relationship to others—as well as "attachment emotions"—that is, interpersonal feelings such as love, jealousy, anxiety, and devotion. Both, according to psychologist Jean Mercer, "combine to form an *internal working model* of emotional and social relationships, a set of feelings, memories, ideas, and expectations about people's interpersonal attitudes and actions."[58]

According to attachment theory, in the first year of life, an individual develops deep emotional ties to their primary caregiver. It is during this period that a parent's response to an infant's needs (especially when they feel stressed or threatened) is thought to define how that infant will respond to similar stressful or threatening situations in the future. Consistent emotional responsiveness to an infant's needs on the part of a parent creates "secure attachments," which will eventually lead to the development of healthy relationships while unemotional or inappropriate responses create "insecure attachments," which will eventually lead to unhealthy relationships later in life.[59] Through healthy attachments, children develop a sense of their own identity while forging new internal working models that unconsciously guide how they process information and approach novel situations. In essence, by modeling healthy attachments, parents not only meet the innate emotional needs of their children, but they also help them feel more secure, and by extension, more confident. Confidence is inherently rooted in a feeling of security with oneself and others. At the same time, this modeling of healthy attachments encourages children to seek out and develop healthy relationships. These internal working models are resistant to alteration but major life events such as divorce, the loss of one's parents, or serious physical impairment can alter their construction or utilization.[60] The depth of emotion exhibited in the letters of Confederate soldiers in this book indicates that many soldier-fathers held secure emotional attachments with their children.

In the private sphere, southern families felt and expressed emotion with regularity. At the same time, the power of these emotions coupled with the influence of concurrent intellectual and religious movements meant that the public-facing image of antebellum southern families as a rigidly hierarchical unit wherein the father served as the patriarchal master of his family may not have told the entire story. Within the private sphere, the emotional power of relationships marked by mutual sentimentality and love meant that wives and children could exert more influence over their husbands and fathers than historians are prone to admit. In effect, the lines drawn by society between family members which seemed so crystal clear from afar are in fact much blurrier under the microscope of historical examination.

This "blurring of the lines" was remarkable when one considers the separate spheres in which men and women developed. In the prewar period, adolescent males and females generally operated within separate spheres defined by different culturally appropriate activities. The sharp delineation between these separate spheres shielded young men from exposure to feminine characteristics while also repeatedly affirming masculine characteristics. Young boys were expected to pursue traditionally masculine activities that emphasized individualism, competition, and community responsibility through pastimes such as hunting, fishing, debate, and even participation in literary societies. In the same way, this separation shielded young women from exposure to masculine characteristics while also simultaneously reaffirming feminine and domestic characteristics. Young women were expected to spend their time sewing, corresponding, and reading. When men and women came together in matrimony, these separate spheres were designed to coalesce into a cohesive and complementary whole. They were trained for this marital dance their whole lives.

Though the separate spheres of cultural expectations between men and women were supposedly impermeable, young boys and girls learned to relate to the opposite sex through play, social engagements, and regular communication with their siblings. Even as they grew older and went their own separate ways, brothers and sisters corresponded regularly through letters that now provide valuable insight into the patriarchal impulses of young men. Even at a young age, boys often offered advice and direction to their sisters with a fatherly tone.[61] Whatever the ideal, families were not always dictatorships in which men asserted their patriarchal powers over their loved ones like masters over slaves. The letters read for this book rarely indicate this sort of performative power. It would seem as if rigid patriarchy was often more honored in the breach than the observance.

Though historians have long accepted a social constructivist view of human society and relationships, relatively few have examined the southern family on a granular level. Even fewer, if any, have sought to understand the role that emotions played in whether or not these norms were actually fulfilled. According to psychologist Klaus R. Scherer, "emotion" is best understood as a spectrum that includes "feelings" (which are a subjective interior reaction) but also as a process of appraising situations or events that can evoke physiological responses, such as tears, a racing heart rate, sweating, or heavy breathing. Reactions can also include facial or verbal expressions. These emotions and feelings are elicited by "stimulus events" in which "something happens to the organism that stimulates or triggers a response after having been evaluated for its significance." These stimulus events can either be internal—such as memories or thoughts—or external—such as witnessing or participating in an activity. Such internal and external events are appraised by an individual as being of importance, thus eliciting emotion.[62]

Though *expressions* of emotion can be socially constructed, it is now believed that human emotion is rooted in human biology. As such, the First and Second Great Awakenings, the Romantic movement, and the egalitarian impulses of the American Revolution did not in any way *create* emotional intimacy per se, but rather they made the *expression* of emotion more socially acceptable. This was particularly true if these emotions were expressed within the private confines of one's home and between the members of one's family.

In the South, manhood was intertwined with conceptions of honor, self-sufficiency, the ability to provide for loved ones, service to the community, self-mastery, and control of others. These ideals and social constructs were tailor made for times of peace. Yet in war, these ideals withered. Though they never fully disappeared, their influence is largely lacking in the sample of letters for this book. In the vast majority of them, Confederate soldiers wrote relatively little about manhood, honor, duty, or political ideology, focusing instead on whether or not their families were safe, news from home, explaining the humdrum nature of camp life, and sharing their feelings for their loved ones—often in case of their own demise. Indeed, though many spoke broadly of politics and rights before the war, letters written during the war (particularly as it progressed) were mostly about the minutiae of daily life, the grinding nature of camp and drill, and the fear of imminent death and separation from loved ones. It is possible that this last concern often narrowed the vision of many soldiers to their families and loved ones. As the war ground on, Confederate soldiers increasingly relied on each other and their families to endure a conflict that was so brutal that political ideology and social expectations were not enough to sustain their willingness to fight. To survive, many soldiers understood that their motivations would have to be far more personal. It was, they came to believe, a war fought to protect those they loved. And it was a war, they soon discovered, that they could not endure without the emotional succor of those for whom they were fighting and dying.

CHAPTER 2

EROS
AND
IMPETUS
HOW ROMANCE AND PASSION
ENCOURAGED DEVOTION TO THE CAUSE

On the evening of September 18, 1862, Private William R. Stilwell of the 53rd Georgia found himself close to the blood-stained battlefield of Antietam in Maryland. Only weeks before, marching north with General Robert E. Lee's 55,000-strong Army of Northern Virginia, Stilwell and his fellow Confederates saw themselves as liberators of the crucial border state from Yankee domination. Private James B. Painter of the 28th Virginia Infantry Regiment—a member of Lee's invading army—believed that he could see the end of the war in sight, writing that "the Maryland Boys is Joining us verry Fast we have seen verry hard times but I trust this war wont last long."[1]

In reality, Maryland was a state of deeply divided loyalties and the reception for Lee's army was relatively subdued in many areas. As Private Stilwell penned a letter to his wife Molly on the evening of September 18, little thought was given to the state's political fate. Less than thirty-six hours before, he had endured the trial of battle and watched the deaths of many of his dearest friends and comrades along the rushing waters of Antietam Creek. The bumblebee-like buzzing and whirring of hundreds of Minié balls cutting through the air, coupled with the occasional smack of lead against flesh or bone, still reverberated in his ears. His eyes welling up with tears, the young private's emotions flowed through his pen: "Molly, I think of you while the cannon roars and the muskets flash," he declared. "I have often thought of having to die on the battlefield, if some kind friend would just lay my bible under my head and your likeness on my breast with the golden curls of hair in it that it would be enough." Men like Stilwell faced the war with one eye to the enemy and the other toward their homes. Women like Molly served as a source of comfort in a world marked by barbarity that stretched the bounds of human imagination. Men found themselves without the immediate succor of a wife or mother with whom they had learned to regulate their emotions before the war. Indeed, Stillwell's emotions swelled from a faint trickle into a roaring torrent before he finally declared, "Molly, I shall have to close for my eyes are bathed in tears till I can't write."[2]

Stilwell was not alone in seeking comfort and strength from his wife. Over two years later, on November 2, 1864, as the fortunes of war turned against the Confederacy, Sergeant Jobe R. Redmon of the 5th Battalion North Carolina Cavalry scrawled a lengthy four-page letter to his wife and three children back home in Kinston. Sometime in October, Redmon and his friend Obediah B. Jarret had deserted from their unit before they were quickly captured and court-martialed. Had they been captured earlier in the war when volunteers were plentiful, they may have faced flogging or another form of corporal punishment. Instead, having deserted in 1864 when General Robert E. Lee struggled to stem the flow of deserters, both men were sentenced to death. "I am sory to inform you that I have but 7 dayes to live," Redmon wrote to his wife, "I think I could die better sadesfide if I could see you and the children one more time on erth and talk with you. But my time is so short I donte exspect to ever see you and my dier little children eny more on erth."

While Redmon faced the anguished possibility of never seeing his loved ones again, his unit's commander, Major Alfred H. Baird, wrote a hastily written appeal on his behalf to Confederate president Jefferson Davis. As the cousin of North Carolina governor Zebulon Vance, Major Baird's intervention on behalf of Redmon carried immense political weight. After slowly working its way through the decrepit Confederate mail system, Major Baird's missive finally reached the desk of the Confederate president. Opening the envelope, Davis quickly noticed that Private Redmon's name was mysteriously scratched through and, in its place, was written "Obediah B. Jarret"—Redmon's friend and fellow deserter.

Exactly who scratched out Redmon's name is not known. Regardless, Obediah went free and Redmon was condemned to his fate. Only days away from his own execution, Jobe pleaded with his wife to visit him one last time before instructing his children on how he wanted them to live in his absence. After writing his final goodbye to his children, declaring, "You cante see you papy no more on erth," his mind turned to his mother, reminding her "since I have ben in hier I have ben ingaged in seaking the lord. Dier mother donte griev for mee. I hope we will all meate in heven so farwell mother."[3] Knowing that his mother was concerned with his eternal soul, Redmon sought to soothe her anguish (as well as that of the rest of his family) by declaring his salvation and his hope for their future together in heaven. Redmon's fate is unknown, yet there are no more extant letters from him and his name does not appear alongside that of his family's in subsequent census records. More than likely, his execution was carried through and he was buried not far from where he was killed.[4]

Both Stilwell and Redmon served at different times, in two separate theaters of war, and yet both faced intense emotional need. They clearly had disparate levels of education and formal literacy and it may be that Redmon's emotions are less expressive than those of the more literate Stilwell because of this. Redmon's limited vocabulary means that he may not have been able to find the words for the depth of his feelings. Both men felt the ache of suffering wrought by the war, and both men—regardless of their different social classes and levels of literacy—clearly reached out to their wives in their desperate hour of emotional need. Both men were wrought with fear and sadness that they could not master. If prewar southern males, as many historians contend, were not emotionally introspective, then something had changed inside of men like Stilwell and Redmon—something which stretched across the educational and socio-economic divide between them. The suffering enacted on the common soldier provided an impetus that pushed pent-up emotions out of these men and on to the page. Sweethearts, lovers, husbands, and wives wrote to each other with a depth of intimacy that would have been considered culturally inappropriate only a few generations before. "Confiding to their wives, Northern and Southern men showed their emotional vulnerability," historian Peter Carmichael noted. "Such admissions would have been unthinkable before the war, but the duress of soldiering forced men to adjust how they related to the women. In other words, they became emotional pragmatists out of necessity to cope with a military world that at times left them feeling lonesome and isolated."[5]

In the prewar South, this "emotional pragmatism" was considerably less necessary as men did not face the constant prospect of their imminent death, nor did they face immense physical, emotional, and psychological suffering on the same scale as they would during the Civil War. This transition is captured in the primary source base for this book, which examined this growing "emotional pragmatism" in letters exchanged between Confederate soldiers and their wives and sweethearts. Of the two hundred soldiers that make up the sample source for this project, eighty-two were married and seven were courting (44.5 percent of the total sample). Of the 1,790 letters read from this book's entire sample of two hundred soldiers, 1,263 of these letters (70.56 percent of the entire sample) were written by these eighty-nine married or courting men. At the same time, single men represented 111 (55.5 percent) of the two hundred soldiers sampled, composing only 527 of the total of 1,790 letters (or 29.44 percent of the total sample). Clearly, married or courting men were far more likely than their single compatriots to express emotions in letters to their loved ones.

Part of the reason for this dearth of letters exchanged between single men and their loved ones is that single men, particularly among early enlisters, often enlisted in the Confederate army with their friends and family members. It is estimated that 1 million men and boys became Confederate soldiers during the war, and of that million, almost 250,000 are believed to have been teenagers.[6] Since they were single and not seen as heads of households, many of their closest family members, including their parents, brothers, sisters, cousins, uncles, and aunts, were not actively seeking their input nor were they often actively giving it. Instead, the communication between single men and their family members were often rather blasé in that they sought to reassure their loved ones of their safety and attempted to present camp life as one of tedium and boredom. Many also neglected to share the abject horror of battle with their family members to avoid upsetting them and may have felt more reticent to share their feelings as they did not experience the same emotional intimacy with these family members as husbands would with their wives. For married men, closer emotional bonds, coupled with the prevailing cultural ideal that men were heads and caretakers of families, may have impelled them to maintain a more consistent stream of communication with their wives and children. Of the 1,263 total of letters written by married or courting men in this sample, 914 letters (or 72.37 percent) evinced emotion or affection while 268 of the 527 letters written by single men (50.85 percent) expressed emotion or affection. At the same time, of the eighty-nine married or courting soldiers in this sample, eighty-seven (or 97.75 percent) expressed emotion or affection. Of the 111 single soldiers, only seventy-seven (or 69.37 percent) expressed emotion or affection.

This level of emotional expression is surprising considering that historians of the American South have often been entranced by the idea that ambition and patriarchy were the primary impetuses behind a southern man's desire to wed. Historian Stephen Berry noted that "a bid for immortality could be cold going, and a woman warmed a man in his sacrifice and his suffering. This, then, was the male project in elemental form."[7] Indeed, some extant primary source materials from the antebellum and wartime period demonstrate this, including South Carolina planter and provocateur James Henry Hammond, who wryly argued that "there are two things worth living for, love in life, immortality after death."[8] Yet Hammond and others who evinced this self-aggrandizing impulse tend to come from the upper echelons of the southern society. In the primary source documents used in the research for this book, little evidence of personal ambition or even patriarchy emanates from the less literate (and thus, less educated and less wealthy) members of the sample. This is not to argue that personal ambition and patriarchy were not important to many men. It is, however, very curious that these impetuses do not seem to jump off the page in the way that one would expect when reading secondary literature on the subject.

It is important to note that men and women of the South responded to their suffering in highly gendered ways. They also often responded according to their varying socio-economic backgrounds.[9] Among wealthier Confederate soldiers, patriarchy was inextricably linked to the concept of honor and at the heart of both was "mastery," in which male authority was seen as unassailable. To question or subvert their authority could bring dire consequences, even for wives and children. Mastery extended beyond the family to include the subjugation of African Americans.[10] Yet, in the sample study for this book, there is little evidence of substantial exertions of mastery among married Confederate men, who spent more time providing banal details of camp life or, less often but still frequently, expressed their desire to be home. The extent of their attempts at mastery was generally limited to telling their wives how to run their farms, how to conduct day-to-day business to keep their families fed and clothed, and what to teach the kids.

Historians have somewhat overstated their case for the supremacy of mastery and its connection with the male ego. While this approach fits nicely within modern feminist perspectives of male hegemony, the truth is that many men found themselves compelled by overwhelming feelings of romantic love for their wives and sweethearts. Though foreign to modern sensibilities, this romantic love was intertwined with ideals of duty to nation and honor within the community. By fulfilling social expectations of duty and honor, southern men believed that they were loving and leading their families. Duty to the nation, honor in the community, and love in the home were the ideals by which southern men lived, and during the war, these three pursuits became the reason that many southern men chose to fight. "I feel perfectly willing to sacrifice every thing save duty and honor (and I know my Darling will never ask me to sacrifice them)," Captain S. Hubert Dent of the 1st Alabama Infantry wrote to his wife in 1863, "to give you pleasure and increase your happiness would my Love that I could be with you to show you the wealth of love that overflows in my heart for you. But you know I love you above every other and all other earthly things do you not Dearest?"[11]

Southern men were pulled in many directions—toward the defense of their nation, the flourishing of their community, and the protection of their homes. In the eyes of many, to fail in any one of these pursuits was to fail in all of them, and they took this failure personally. Though historians have often couched Confederate soldiers as ideologues who fought to defend slavery and their "rights" (both of which are true), the war was often far more personal to soldiers. Their struggle on the battlefield directly correlated with their own, their community's, and their family's future safety and happiness. While historians have often argued that Confederate soldiers fought for their families' survival, relatively few have argued that they fought for their families' emotional betterment.

To do so would mean preferencing what historian Page Smith calls "symbolic history" over traditional "existential history." Symbolic history is a creation of the historian's mind that has no existence outside of his or her created mental model. Scholars give names to certain individual periods or epochs, which then act as symbols. They do not correspond to any particular identifiable reality, but instead come to symbolize styles, values, or ideals, such as the Industrial Revolution, the Middle Ages, or the Reformation. These themes are demonstrative of progressive developments that show human trends that encounter and then react to successive crises. Because of the intrinsic slowness and complexity of these epochs, they are beyond the immediate comprehension of the actors involved. It is this form of history that raises human consciousness and reveals to the historian and society at large their own understanding of the self, as well as of human nature's limitations and potential. With the resultant expansion of the consciousness and potential of individuals and societies, human progress is inevitable.

On the other hand, "existential history" consists of more sharply defined and dramatic episodes of the past, such as the American Revolution or Civil War, which exist outside of the historian's mind. In existential history, historical actors are conscious of the periods in which they live. This approach to history is heavily dependent upon historical actors' accounts, and writers present them with a heightened degree of personal self-consciousness not seen in those who write symbolic history. Usually based around crises, existential histories of groups, states, nations, or classes are typically more developed and require deep introspection on the part of their participants in explaining why or how events are happening. Thus, the historian finds their imagination fenced in by the reality presented by the historical actors. As a result, artificial constructs are largely absent and existential history is resistant to almost any type of reinterpretation because it is a form of history largely devoid of the historian's influence.[12] As the seminal "scientific" historian, Leopold von Ranke, remarked, this is history *wie es eigentlich gewesen* ("as it actually happened")—history devoid of the abstract definition of principle.[13]

Page Smith did not believe that either feeling or the "spirit of history" *alone* moved history, but he did surmise that certain "intangibles" could bridge the chasm between the distant past and the modern historian. He argued that the scientific and reason-based approach to history is only as valuable as the historian's ability to also connect with the emotional and intangible aspects of the past. Smith saw both reason and feeling as a binary that undergirded the larger metanarrative pieced together by historians of race, class, gender, politics, and economics.[14]

Approaching the Civil War in the manner that Smith suggests reveals the structural weakness of patriarchy and paternalism among southern men. Though they may have bought into and promoted this ideology, white southern men were often unable to live it out. In fact, single, courting, and married men readily relied upon their sweethearts or spouses to meet their physical and emotional needs both before, during, and in many cases, after the war. The relationship between southern men and their sweethearts and wives was often one of mutual reciprocity in which each leaned upon the other for physical and psychological strength. Southern men were not emotionally distant, as they have often been painted by those who privilege social expectations over actual lived experience. They were not two-dimensional figures restrained by these expectations. In reality, whatever the social norms of southern society, war broke these restraints and many men freely expressed their feelings in letters to their wives and sweethearts.

This chapter examines the romantic relationships of Confederate soldiers and whether the masculine ideals of emotional reticence and self-mastery were actually practiced by them. Next, it will explain how these relationships exerted an emotional "push" factor that spurred men to enlist and fight while also exerting a "pull" factor that encouraged desertion. When nationalist sentiment and syrupy dreams of battlefield glory were crushed by battle, men unashamedly turned to their wives and sweethearts. The love of a woman gave their struggles a purpose that had little to do with states' rights, patriarchy, or white hegemony. To understand this, first we must examine the inner world of white southern males at the outbreak of war.

The American Civil War opened a floodgate of change in the inner emotional world of white southern males. Much of this change was rooted within southern family dynamics and the emphasis on sentimentality and emotional bonding which arose in the period leading up to the outbreak of war. It has been argued by historian James McPherson that while personal conviction, ideology, courage, duty, honor, group cohesion, and self-respect all provided both sustaining and combat motivations for soldiers, "without a firm base of support in the homes and communities from which these citizen soldiers came, their morale would have crumbled. Even the solidarity with comrades in arms was insufficient to sustain their commitment if it lacked sustenance on the home front."[15] In the source sample for this book, southern men repeatedly looked toward their wives and sweethearts for emotional and physical support.

Some historians have asserted that the relationship between the home front and the battle front was so potent that a loss of morale at home spilled over into a loss of morale along the battle front. It was a sense of invincibility, argued historian Jason Phillips, that instead persuaded many soldiers to keep fighting, and by 1864, "when reports of civilian despair reached the front lines, soldiers felt betrayed by the millions they were fighting and dying to defend." It was, Phillips contends, "the unprecedented suffering and carnage [that] convinced many troops that they alone sustained the nation. Soldiers from across the South believed that the armies remained hopeful and patriotic while the home front sank into despondency and corruption." He went on to argue that "camaraderie fostered this cliquish notion that soldiers deserved more praise than civilians" and that "the milieu of army life reinforced the ethos of invincibility in ways that civil society did not."[16]

Yet the primary source documents read for this project do not indicate a widespread ethos of invincibility. Most of the individuals in this sample instead wrote far more about the banal comings and goings of camp life than they did expressing notions of ideology or duty. Among the eighty-nine married or courting men in this sample, only twenty (22.47 percent) made ideological statements about the Confederate cause. In total, married or courting men wrote 47 out of 1,263 letters (3.7 percent) expressing ideology or duty. Among the 111 single men for this study, only thirteen (11.7 percent) expressed ideological statements about the Confederate cause. Of the 527 letters written by single men, only fifteen (2.8 percent) did the same. While these statistics do not undercut Phillips's argument, they do indicate that at least in writing to their loved ones, white southern men were far less ideological than historians may have previously supposed. Instead, this emphasis on the plain, everyday goings-on of life does not indicate patriotic zeal or a nearly religious fervor about the South's invincibility but rather a preoccupation with wanting to return to a sense of normalcy and familial comfort. It could be argued that, if anything, instead of teaching them about their own invincibility, war taught men how truly vulnerable they were.

The letters exchanged between Confederate soldiers and their wives and sweethearts represent the primary link between the home front and the battle front. But exactly how much influence did the home front have on morale on the battle front and vice versa? Recent work by historians of twentieth-century wars may provide some appealing answers. In her study of Australian soldiers who served in the Vietnam War, historian Effie Karageorgos noted that the influence of the home front on the battle front was not monolithic but rather symbiotic.[17] Soldiers' experiences along the battle front stirred up emotions which often led soldiers to write home. Likewise, their experiences along the home front stirred up emotions which induced civilians to write to their soldier-husbands, -fathers, and -brothers. In these letters, both expressed their emotions and drew their loved ones into their own inner worlds.[18] Psychologists have noted that in treating post-traumatic stress disorder, those who experience feelings of fragmentation benefit from writing, which "provides a safe arena for integration. Review and reenactment [of the events] can take place continuously and with some sense of containment. The page becomes that holding environment for pieces of feeling that otherwise would evaporate, leaving the sufferer in puzzlement."[19] In other words, those who suffer trauma find a safe way of dealing with, and better understanding, their emotional states. This act of vulnerability, particularly when shared with others, provides a medium of healing and personal growth. It is no wonder then that married and courting men wrote over twice as many letters as their single comrades, even though they represented less than half of the total sample of two hundred men. For single men, their most intimate relationships were typically with their parents or comrades—many of whom enlisted with them. For married or courting men, their most intimate relationship was typically with their wives or sweethearts.

⌇

The letters used for this book were written by individuals of all social classes and it was abundantly clear from the style and prose who was probably wealthier and, by extension, more educated. Letters from officers were generally clearer and the spelling errors far less egregious than those from enlisted men. Though not always the case (some privates bordered on lyrical rhapsody in their letters), individuals who were more educated and had a greater vocabulary seemed to express their emotions more often. Less literate individuals seemed to write less and their letters are extremely difficult to decipher. This limitation in the sampled sources for this book is unfortunately an insurmountable one. Compared to much of the rest of the world, however, the United States was one of the most literate nations in the world, and the vast quantities of extant letters from Civil War soldiers would not have existed were it not for a broad educational movement that swept the country in the decades leading up to the war.

For most of Western history, rates of literacy among women were far less than those of men. The same was true for American women in the decades leading up to the American Civil War. By 1850, this trend changed as girls achieved literacy rates nearly on par with those of boys. The United States was the only country in the world where this was true.[20] In America, the overall rate of illiteracy peaked in 1840 at 11 percent and thereafter fell until 1860, when the rates of illiteracy again increased until 1870 as a result of the shuttering of many schools during the war. Nonetheless, the generation that fought the Civil War was one of the most literate generations in American history, up to that point. In terms of the sample used for this study, the percentage of literate residents in North Carolina in 1840 was 72 percent—the lowest of all the states for which we have data—while the rate in Alabama was significantly higher at 82 percent. The literacy rate may have been much higher than indicated by the data; since the Census Bureau counted both enslaved and free individuals, the literacy rate was lower in southern states with large slave populations. This statistic, however, does not distinguish between writing or reading literacy. By contrast, the first national report on literacy in 1840 in Britain estimated that only 67 percent of males and 50 percent of females were literate for an overall average literacy rate of 58 percent.[21] As a result of this movement toward universal literacy in America, by the outbreak of the war letter writing and reading were common and well-established practices that were open to almost every member of society regardless of their gender or age.

According to McPherson, the Union and Confederate armies that followed "were the most literate in history to that time . . . and more than 80 percent of Confederate soldiers were literate."[22] Scholar Christopher Hager believes that approximately half a billion letters were exchanged between soldiers and their families during the Civil War. That correspondence, he argues, was "authored by ordinary Americans who used letters to hold their families together during a time of great trial." On average, Hager concludes, soldiers on average wrote close to seventy letters over the course of their service, which represented "at least triple the number, if not ten times the number, of letters the average American had been writing before the war." Those to whom they wrote—primarily their families—wrote about the same number of letters.[23] Though the vast majority of Confederate soldiers used in the sample were considered literate, this does not mean that they had an advanced vocabulary and were able to better express their emotions.

For this project, the lowest number of extant letters per Confederate soldier was one, while the highest number of extant letters from a single soldier was 123. In this sample, soldiers from North Carolina wrote on average 7.59 letters while soldiers from Alabama wrote 10.31 letters over various periods represented in the letters. This dearth of letters no doubt is due to many factors. Some soldiers died without having spent very long in service, many letters did not survive the war, and some of the archives referenced only contain collections of letters from certain years of a soldier's service. Nonetheless, of the Confederate soldiers surveyed, approximately 29.5 percent wrote one extant letter, 10.5 percent left two extant letters, 9 percent three extant letters, and onward in descending order.

The most prevalent topic of conversation between soldiers and their loved ones was scuttlebutt from home or camp, followed by a recitation of their daily activities. Often, letters were virtually devoid of any real news at all, indicating that many were written to maintain an open line of communication with loved ones. Private William Addison Tesh of the 28th North Carolina Infantry Regiment wrote to his father and mother days after the battle of Chancellorsville that "I havent any thing new to write that will I terest You but I thought I would Write a little to Say," before asking about a pair of shirts and pants, describing his captain's sickness, and wondering whether anyone has heard from their uncle.[24] The mundane nature of Tesh's letter was representative of hundreds of letters referenced in the sample for this book. The reasons for the banal nature of many of these letters are unknown as soldiers, at least in this sample, did not offer any explanations. However, it can be surmised (as stated before) that soldiers simply wanted to maintain a sense of normalcy. Staying up to date on the happenings at home made soldiers feel as if their former lives were not so distant even as their circumstances were far different.

In camp, life often *was* boring and mundane, and apart from battle or the death of a comrade, there was often little to discuss. Soldiers still wrote to their loved ones with regular rapidity, thus indicating that continued communication with loved ones mattered even as the war progressed. Not surprisingly, when the flow of letters ceased, individuals on the home front and the battle front often panicked. In a November 1864 letter, North Carolina resident Ann L. Bowen wrote to her husband, Henry Bowen of the Confederate States Marines, that "I want you to rite often it has bin so long since I heard from you I want to hear bad."[25] Interestingly, many of the more emotionally expressive letters pleading with loved ones to write or expressing panic over a lack of letters came from soldiers.

Widespread literacy and technological changes made letter writing possible, but those factors alone do not explain the wartime mania for letter writing, particularly between lovers. The devotion to letter writing between romantic partners had deep historical roots and the changes wrought by evolving views on marriage had much to do with the plethora of extant letters that were romantic in nature. Since the Middle Ages, the traditional European view of marriage was that it was a utilitarian institution for elevating one's social status. This perspective followed many immigrants who streamed across the Atlantic to the New World in the seventeenth century. Yet by the late eighteenth century, the influence of evangelicalism and the Romantic Movement, as well as the emphasis on individual liberty, meant that husbands were frequently expected to focus more on their families. Rather than defining marriage or children in terms of their use, family was increasingly seen as an individual's emotional sanctuary.[26]

As male dominance began to wane, a growing individualism began to untether sons and daughters from the nearly dictatorial influence of their parents over their romantic lives. Before the American Revolution, parents still held immense sway in picking their children's potential marriage partners. Yet the influence of the Romantics, who believed that children should be free to "become themselves," in part led to the flowering of individual self-expression and autonomy that had been hitherto considered socially unacceptable. Though this burgeoning "hands off" approach to parenting was unevenly applied across America, many children found themselves able to make life's most important decisions for themselves. The emphasis on sentimentality, emotional bonding, and mutual support may have provided Victorian children with healthy attachments, and by extension, feelings of self-confidence. It may also have provided internal working models that would be used to develop other healthy attachments later in life. Seeing the self-confidence of their children and watching their development of sound attachments may have helped some parents let go of the belief that they alone could pick the best mate for their children. At the same time, the growing emphasis on sentimentality, romance, and the passions certainly hastened this cultural change. In fact, by the nineteenth century, the decision to marry (as well as the choice of whom to marry) was generally reached by the two romantic partners rather than their parents. This was particularly true among the lower classes. Moreover, love and mutual admiration were expected to exist *before* marriage rather than *after,* as was often the case in previous generations.[27]

In a sense, this period witnessed an "emotional revolution" that dramatically altered the traditional practice of courtship in Victorian America. The groundwork for a couple's future relationship was laid during the period of courtship in which a man and woman explored each other's psyches and emotional inner worlds through a guided process of discussion, letter writing, and communal leisure time. Though the Victorian age was one marked by a greater freedom in individual decision making, it was not marked by looser sexual standards. Courting couples (particularly among the upper classes) were expected to have chaperones, which protected them from acts of sexual and emotional impropriety. These same chaperones also often acted as relational guides, though marriage decisions were generally left to those courting. Even in cases where parents attempted to handpick courting partners for their children, the ultimate decision of who to marry and whether or not to marry was left to the individuals engaging in the courting process. Rarely, however, did southern women seek mates outside of their social class. In the years leading up to the war, many southern elites began to go even further in distancing themselves from the bounds of propriety by eschewing chaperoned courtships and tacitly allowing courting couples to spend time alone together.[28]

Therefore, the grand vision of self-aggrandizement on the part of men, coupled with deeply entrenched ideals of romantic love, sometimes became intertwined. Particularly among the upper classes, white southern males were expected to be ambitious and to embrace expansive visions for their future. These visions, often rooted in men's own insecurities, were often unachievable apart from great wealth or connections and, most importantly to many southern men, the supporting arms of a loving wife. For many who were unable to fulfill these visions, they were left only with feelings of melancholy or personal inadequacy. The solution, it would seem, was to shore up one's lack of self-worth by winning the tender love and affection of a woman of virtue. To depend upon a woman was, for the male, "to validate and make meaningful their struggle or success, to aid, comfort, and believe in them, even and especially when their self-belief began to fade or fail."[29]

Much of this is rooted in the idealism of womanhood in the nineteenth century. From birth, they were expected to cultivate within themselves a higher moral virtue and, later in life, were expected to help their husbands pursue the same. Because of this expectation, men often sought out women who fit neatly within societal rules that elevated femininity and modesty over beauty.[30] When Harvey Black, a surgeon in the Army of Northern Virginia, wrote wistfully of his days of courtship, he did not recall his wife's youthful beauty. Instead, he remembered her "maiden modesty, so much to be admired."[31] In a grander sense, women were supposed to be virtuous and men were to be both ambitious and virtuous. Through companionate marriage, a virtuous man and woman could build a happy and fulfilling life.

In his study of soldiers from Virginia, historian Aaron Sheehan-Dean confirmed that one of the most important contexts for understanding the widespread support of the Confederacy among Virginians was the rise of companionate marriage from the eighteenth through the nineteenth centuries. Men increasingly valued intimate family relations as one of the highest goals of life. This relational "success" was on par with political and economic success and Sheehan-Dean believes that it was based upon the emphasis of evangelical churches in sanctioning domestic families as the cornerstone of society. Within these intimate familial circles that men made their decisions to enlist, serve, or desert. At least in Virginia, "the pressures of military service encouraged men to identify their families' immediate and future well-being as the most important reason to participate in the war."[32]

The prevailing historiography surrounding nineteenth-century southern masculinity, marriage, and courting couches southern men in terms of the traditional emotional norms of the early to mid-twentieth century. "Men of the nineteenth century were encouraged to cloak their hearts and stifle their doubts," historian Stephen Berry notes, and "because gentlemen of the Old South were encouraged to swallow half of these emotions and exaggerate the remainder, we get a skewed picture of their lives."[33] Such feelings were not unusual. "Throughout American history," sociologist Michael Kimmel maintains, "American men have been afraid that others will see us as less than manly, as weak, timid, frightened." In response, he believes, "American men try to *control themselves;* they project their fears onto *others;* and when feeling too pressured, they attempt an *escape.*"[34]

However, the letters that comprised the bulk of the research for this book present an altogether different portrait of male emotions. Regardless of social expectations, white southern men were seemingly less concerned with social norms than one would imagine. Instead, they sought emotional connection with their comrades and their family members. Moreover, they were not necessarily timid in their expression of these emotions and as the war progressed and the body count rose ever higher, the more pointed their emotional neediness became. Although they made up less than half of the sample size for this project (89 out of 200), the men who could be identified as either married or courting wrote the greatest number of letters and were far more emotionally effusive than their single counterparts. Of the 1,263 total letters written by married or courting men in this sample, 914 letters (or 72.37 percent) were laden with emotion or affection while of the 527 letters written by single men, 268 (or 50.85 percent) expressed emotion or affection. At the same time, of the 89 married or courting soldiers, 87 (or 97.75 percent) of them expressed emotion or affection. Of the 111 single soldiers, only 77 of them (or 69.37 percent) expressed emotion or affection. Clearly, married or courting soldiers were far more likely to be expressive of their emotions. But why?

While soldiers' letters do not explicitly state the reason for this greater emotional expression, modern psychology and our current understanding of emotions and human development may offer clues. To be sure, the trauma of facing one's human demise and that of others rubbed the feelings of most soldiers raw to the bone. As has been the case in every war, young men do not actually expect to die. For southern men, society had taught them that they could control their own worlds and overcome the impossible through virtue and an iron will. As a result, though many soldiers held onto their patriotism and believed in the rightness of their cause, they quickly discovered their own limitations. If the war taught them anything, it was that they would achieve victory only through their collective efforts. This collective effort not only included men on the battle front but also the women and children back home. Letters became the tethers that connected these two seemingly distant worlds and soldiers craved the connection. One soldier, Cornelius Morris, reminded his wife to tell a friend of theirs "to write often for it is a great consolation to a weary soldier to hear from those near and dear to him."[35]

Likewise, Alabamian John T. Scott, an officer in the 45th Alabama, demonstrated this tendency. "To you who are in the city surrounded by friends, acquaintances and admirers with pleasures and amusements to beguile the hours that otherwise might pass wearily—the frequent arrival of my poor letters can not detract much from your happiness," he wrote to his sweetheart Philoklea Mitchell in 1862, "but to me, shut up within the circumscribed lines of a camp; cut off from all communication with the outside world, and with but few to think of or care for me, the protracted absences of the little messengers of my dear Miss Philo's affectionate remembrance, is some depressing in the extreme. I do hope then you will not suffer anything to interrupt the correspondence, which to me is the only pleasure of a soldier's life."[36]

Scott's feelings of loneliness and isolation are remarkable when one considers that he was surrounded by thousands of other men in camp. For men like Scott, war offered an escape from the banality of life on the farm. In camps of instruction, soldiers-in-training sometimes boasted of their excitement at the prospect of looming combat. On the field of battle, they would test their manhood and as is the case with most young men, many wanted to face death with a steely determination. As historian Dillon J. Carroll noted, "Before fighting their first battle, Civil War soldiers were very idealistic. They believed combat would be ordered, courage would be rewarded, and cowardice would be punished. They believed that individual men were just as important as generals, capable of shaping the outcome of a battle."[37] Before ever seeing combat, in August 1862, Private Joseph Kinsey of the 61st North Carolina Infantry Regiment proudly wrote to his sister that "no death is more honorable than one on a battle-field, especially when waving the sword or charging the steel bayonette into the steady and advancing columns of an inveterate enemy. . . . It makes me feel almost ecstatic when I think of being on a bloody battle-field."[38]

Early in the war, men like Private Kinsey flooded enlistment offices throughout the Confederacy before being transported to distant battlefields from those they loved. The anxiety of this separation, coupled with youthful impulse, heightened emotions, and an obsession with romantic love and sentimentality, led to a wave of "marriage mania" which swept across the South during the war.[39] Historians J.

David Hacker, Libra Hilde, and James Holland Jones noted a distinct pattern in their statistical analysis of southern marriage patterns throughout the war in which "a flurry of marriages occurred early in the war, whenever men went on furlough, and then again at the end of the war."[40] Anecdotal evidence supports the belief that marriage was prominent in the minds of many young white southern men and women. "I believe that neither war, pestilence, nor famine could put an end to the marrying and giving in marriage which is constantly going on," civilian Judith W. McGuire wrote in 1863. "Strange that these sons of Mars can so assiduously devote themselves to Cupid and Hyman; but every respite, every furlough, must be thus employed."[41]

Moreover, while the antebellum period was marked by the marriage of men and women *within* their social class, the travail of war and the real possibility of a lonely life cut short led many to look outside of their class for companionate partners. Overwhelmingly, women preferred men in uniform.[42] A shrinking courtship process coupled with decreasing parental influence over marriage decisions opened the floodgates for men and women rushing into marriage and many did so with little discernment in their choice of a spouse.[43] Others eschewed traditional social mores, opting instead to follow their emotions and operate independently of traditionally gendered social expectations. Not long after the attack on Fort Sumter, Elodie Breck Todd, the sister of Mary Todd Lincoln, wrote to her sweetheart, Nathaniel Henry Rhodes Dawson, a captain in the 4th Alabama Infantry Regiment. Her parents did not approve of their potential marriage. "Mother seemed to think I was to be depended on to take care of her when all the rest of her handsomer daughters left her," she wrote, "but as this is the age when Secession, Freedom, and Rights are asserted, I am claiming mine and do not doubt but I shall succeed in obtaining them as I have some one to help me in my efforts."[44]

There is little evidence that the marriages studied emerged from feelings of loneliness rather than romantic interest. Indeed, the level of emotional outpouring in the cache of letters for this study demonstrates that most soldiers did *feel* a deep and intimate connection with their loved ones back home. When husbands and beaux marched off to war, the physical distance between themselves and their wives and sweethearts raised feelings of profound anxiety. These feelings were further compounded by months and then years of material and social deprivation punctuated by moments of sheer terror from combat. In the early months of the war, men expected the conflict to rage for months, not years. Many young men, acting more out of impulse than reason, were too focused on the potential excitement that lay before them to even think about the possibility of an indeterminate war.[45]

While love for one's wife or sweetheart exerted a "pull factor" on Confederate soldiers—something that drew their minds and emotions toward home—these same relationally induced feelings could also exert a "push factor" that encouraged many men to continue fighting as the war dragged on. In December of 1861 John T. Scott of the 45th Alabama again wrote to his sweetheart "Miss Philo" that "my heart is with you, my thoughts turn to you. I constantly think of you and count the weary days that separate me from you . . . and draw fresh inspiration from the reflection that while I am far away, suffering the severities of a winter's campaign, you dearest one, are sage and surrounded by the comforts of home."[46] Loved ones back home did indeed provide, in the words of Scott, "fresh inspiration" to keep fighting. The love that a soldier felt for his beloved and the peace given by the knowledge that she was safe and secure at home encouraged him to keep fighting. In effect, he was fighting for her. As the war's destructive power steadily increased over time, and its destructive force stirred up even more feelings, the potency of the love felt by soldiers for their wives and sweethearts was an impetus for emotional resiliency.[47] Their love made men feel secure. This need for security was particularly prevalent when, as soldiers, they faced the possibility of certain death.

To participate in war is to surrender one's security. Though many men believed that they could face death, most naturally felt great fear in the face of their own mortal fragility. As a result, many looked for comfort and strength from their wives and sweethearts back home. Indeed, many longed to survive the war so that they could once again embrace them. I never new what pleasure home afforded to a man before," Private John Cotton of Hilliard's Legion, Alabama Cavalry (later the 19th Regiment Confederate Cavalry), wrote to his wife less than a year after the war began. "If it were not for the love of my country and family and the patriotism that bury in my bosom for them I would bee glad to come home and stay there but I no I have as much to [fite] for as any body else but if I were there I no I could not stay so I have to take it as easy as possible."[48] Though some soldiers eschewed ideology, soldiers like Cotton conflated patriotism and family into one overarching motivation for fighting. Similarly, in a letter to his sweetheart and future wife, Private Harrison Hanes of the 4th North Carolina Infantry Regiment wrote of his fellow soldiers not long after the First Battle of Manassas, "I think for they hav left ther homes all redy for the purpos of kepin the invaders of our soil and I think a man that will take care of his country will take care of the women."[49]

Not only did battle induce feelings of dread, anxiety, fear, and fragility, but recounting the battles later meant reliving the horror. Writing letters to loved ones allowed men to process their feelings—albeit in a safe and controlled manner. Others resorted to recording their feelings in private diaries that were often later passed down to their families. In his diary, Private Louis Leon of the 1st North Carolina Infantry Regiment recorded the sheer horror of the third day's fighting during the Battle of Gettysburg. "It was truly awful how fast, how very fast, did our poor boys fall by our sides . . . you could see one with his head shot off, others cut in two, then one with his brain oozing out, one with his leg off, others shot through the hear," he wrote; "you would see some of your comrades, shot through the leg, lying between the lines, asking his friends to take him out, but no one could get to his relief, and you would have to leave him there, perhaps to die, or, at best, to become a prisoner."[50]

Soldiers' families represented a traditional source of emotional stability. Defense scientist Anthony Kellett in his book *Combat Motivation: The Behavior of Soldiers in Battle* recounted a study of Israeli soldiers that found that those who had "combat reactions" suffered from a variety of personal and interpersonal issues such as low self-esteem, issues with spouses or children, and issues with other soldiers in their units. Surprisingly, these same individuals came from a broad swath of personalities and often served with bravery in combat. Likewise, stable family and community backgrounds had a buffering effect on soldiers who tended to suffer from fewer combat reactions. Thus, healthy relational attachments helped soldiers cope with their war weariness.[51]

Deep bonds of human affection—particularly in the form of romantic love—became one of the primary bulwarks against the erosion of a soldier's meaning and purpose. Romantic love imparted meaning to a war in which the disorienting vortex of violence and animal-like brutality dissolved much of the ideological and political motivations for fighting. After complaining about the Confederate army's demoralization and drunkenness, Captain S. Hubert Dent of the 1st Alabama Infantry Regiment wrote to his wife that "your letters are so full of love and affection Darling that it makes the tears come in my eyes. Tears of happiness Darling when I read them and little Eddie too."[52] For married and courting soldiers, the love of their wives and sweethearts gave them emotional wherewithal while also reminding them of the reason for their military service.

After the Battle of Chancellorsville, Private John Futch Jr. of the 3rd North Carolina Infantry Regiment wrote to his wife that while fighting, he "thought that every man would be killed and there would not be enough to tell the tale," and that he was worried that he had seen his wife "for the last time but God brought me through saft and I feel very thankful to him for his kindness to wards me." Rather than extolling his own bravery, Futch went on to write that "I hope we will not have to fight another battle this year and if we do I hope I will not have the pleasure of being in it again."[53] Private Futch's fear of not seeing his wife again, his gratitude for God's protection in battle, and his desire to avoid further combat stood in sharp contrast to the prewar masculine ethos of self-sufficiency and emotional mastery. Now in 1863, it is clear that Futch doesn't care about any of this. He doesn't even argue that his courage or virtue was responsible for his survival. Rather, seeing his survival as God's will, Futch wants to avoid combat so that he can come home to his wife. Proving himself no longer seems to be a priority. Many letters read for this project indicate similar feelings.

In the sample for this book, the number of married or courting men who wrote descriptions of battle is about even with that of single men (31 married or courting vs. 32 single). Likewise, when one looks at the percentages of men who described battle in the sample, the difference isn't much. Of the 89 total married or courting men, 31 provided descriptions of battle (or 34.83 percent) while of the 111 single men, 32 (or 28.83 percent) did so. Although a higher percentage of married and courting men described their actions in battle than single men, only 58 out of 1,263 (4.59 percent) total letters from married and courting men described battle while single men wrote 46 out of 527 letters (8.73 percent) that described battle. These statistics demonstrate that many men refused to talk about battle or, at the very least, that letters describing battle have not survived the past century and a half.

Yet the unwillingness on the part of Futch and many others to evince ideolog-ical and social constructions of duty, valor, and mastery serves as a microcosm of the larger change in male emotions during the war. Though historians have writ-ten extensively about the importance of social constructions of duty and honor in motivating Confederate soldiers to fight, the sample for this project indicates that far fewer were willing to express such motivations. Moreover, there seems to be a distinct difference in the willingness on the part of married and single men to express such motivations. In this sample, out of 89 total married and courting men, only 20 (or 22.47 percent total) expressed what could be interpreted as notions of ideology or duty while out of 111 single men, 13 (or 11.71 percent) expressed ideas of ideology or duty. However, married and courting men wrote 47 out of 1,263 letters (or 3.72 percent) that contained ideas of ideology or duty while single men wrote 15 out of 527 letters (or 2.85 percent). Thus, more married men expressed notions of ideology or duty, which was probably fueled by the fact that many conflated the protection of country with the protection of their families. Yet more importantly, 77.53 percent of married men in this sample and 88.29 percent of single men did not express notions of ideology or duty in their letters. These statistics suggest that southern males were not as ideologically driven, or at least not willing to express their ideological principles as often as historians may have previously suggested. Likewise, if bravery in battle was an important facet of southern masculinity and ideology a primary motivator for fighting, then why did so many men say nothing about their participation in battle or their ideological convictions? Evidence sug-gests that the masculine and ideological motivations of Confederate soldiers that loomed so large at the beginning of the war may have waned over time.

Historian Eric T. Dean Jr. points to a hierarchy of psychological suffering ex-perienced by soldiers during the war. The greatest source of psychological trauma was the terror of battle—particularly from artillery which killed randomly and with immense violence. Likewise, infectious disease was an invisible threat that soldiers could not protect themselves from. Witnessing the gradual and often pain-ful deaths of their comrades from battle and disease only compounded feelings of hopelessness and alienation. Finally, on the bottom rung of this hierarchy, the effect of marches and bivouacs in rain, snow, damp, and mud left soldiers in serious physical and psychological discomfort. Though it is debatable whether soldiers "got used" to combat, what is known is that after battle, many noted the phenomena of feeling physical exhaustion followed by feelings of depression and vulnerability.[54] Dean found a pattern in which "one often sees a progression in each life from an initial carefree optimism about 'soldiering' to a growing weariness and sense of vulnerability."[55]

This weariness and vulnerability could become a source of self-actualization in which soldiers, realizing their need for others, drew closer to their spouses or sweethearts. For others, the inability or unwillingness to face their own neediness could destroy their romantic relationships. In every major American conflict war has exerted a detrimental effect upon marriages. Divorce rates typically skyrocket at their conclusion. But this does not tell us as much about the relationship between combat exposure and marital dissolution. Sociologists Cynthia Gimbel and Alan Booth studied the effect of combat experience on marital quality—including divorce, marital separation for reasons other than divorce, infidelity, and abuse—what they call "marital adversity." Using data from 2,101 Vietnam veterans, the authors found that "combat itself does not have a direct relationship with marital quality and stability. Instead, combat creates stress and antisocial behavior, but only antisocial behavior has a direct effect on marital adversity. The effects of combat-related stress are through antisocial behavior." Moreover, they found that "combat directly increases violent and unlawful (antisocial) behavior and stress, which then affects marital quality and stability, and that this process is both mediated and moderated by premilitary stress and antisocial behavior. . . . Posttraumatic stress symptoms play only an indirect role in the combat-marital adversity fellowship."[56] The only antidote to this antisocial behavior was healthy attachments with one's comrades, spouses, or parents—all of which provided physical and emotional safety and security.

Psychiatrist Theodore Nadelson noted that "war is inherently traumatic because it dehumanizes its participants. The soldier loses meaning, that is, a sense of purpose, goals to strive for, principles (such as respect for life) to protect. The soldier cannot afford to give weight to anything outside of the immediate, which is to survive."[57] Private Jesse Hill of the 21st North Carolina Infantry Regiment provided a useful example, describing the aftermath of the Battle of New Market in 1864. He wrote to his "dear companion" that during the battle "tha was lots of our men kild I don't see how I ever com out safe for the bullets and grape and shel come so thick and tore up the men the pecs of flesh few all over me and the men fel all a round me thek dead lay thick for bout 4 miles long and 2 miles wide."[58] Hill's own words do not paint him as a man of valor or self-mastery. Rather, he was another soldier who was forced to face his own vulnerability and mortality. Unlike the many comrades whose flesh he was now covered in, Hill somehow survived. Experiences like this are inherently traumatic.

Military service was a source of immense suffering that turned the thoughts of many toward home. Home was a place of comfort and solace while camp life was often considered the polar opposite. "When we lay on the ground to Sleep," Private Silas Stepp of the 7th North Carolina Cavalry Battalion recounted to his wife in June 1864, "the frogs is gumping over us when wee go through the brush wee get full of ticks when wee go to eat wee cant hardly keap the flys out of our mouth you never saw the like of such things in your life I tel you my dear you don't now how bad I want to see you."[59] So psychologically scarring were the undulating waves of combat terror and the boredom of camp that some men simply broke. Sergeant Horace McLean of the 59th Alabama Infantry Regiment wrote to his wife, "One soldier road in to the River + Drowned himself I think he was from Pike," he wrote. "One Soldier shot another + wounded him mortally all of them belongs to the Cavalry at camp Stone. I heard that they were both Drunk Down Town at a little Eating house it seems to me that so soon as men get in camp the they loose all manner of respect for themselves + every body Else + it is much to be regretted."[60]

War amplified the dark emotions that many felt. It also threatened to destroy their motivation for fighting. Not only did soldiers witness the death of their comrades from combat, but some events were so harrowing that it struck men to their emotional core. Captain S. Hubert Dent of the 1st Alabama Infantry Regiment wrote to his wife of the looming prospect of witnessing the execution of a deserter. "I do not wish to see it," he recounted to her. "Men grow callous enough at best in the army and I do not wish to witness any more of such sights than are absolutely necessary. There is a very great difference between shooting down men (enemies) (at least in one's feelings) when the blood is warm and we are excited to the highest pitch & witnessing the shooting of one of our own men by our own men."[61]

Letters like Dent's represented attempts at connection with a world outside of war. Soldiers often did not understand how much the home front had changed because of the war. Many still had sentimental visions of their homes and families as they were before the war. Letters from home reminded soldiers of a place that many fantastically believed was untouched by the war. At the very least, it wasn't a place of terror, moral depravity, or tedium like the battlefield or camp. Letters from home also served as consistent reminders to soldiers of what awaited them if they survived. They believed that home was a better place because they wanted to believe. They were sentimental about home in much the same way that they became sentimental about their marriages and courtships. It was a distant, far-off place, removed from the hell in which they found themselves. Thus, it was better. Even if they were told that things at home were not well, it still represented a place of love and comparatively more peace. If they wanted to get home to the love of their wives and the peace of civilian life, the only way to do so was to keep fighting and bring the war to a swift end. They could not do so without emotional support.

While the depth of emotional expression in soldiers' letters could range from shallow recitations of the monotony of camp life to breathtaking declarations of love, the most emotionally charged letters in the sample for this project took place during periods either before, during, or immediately after high-stress situations. These could include the first few weeks that a young enlistee was away from home, their experiences of combat, personal sickness, witnessing the execution or punishment of a deserter, the death of a family member, or as was often the case in the second half of the war, the growing realization that the end was seemingly further and further away.

The majority of letters read for this book said nothing of battle. Of the 1,790 letters read, only 104 (or 5.81 percent) said anything about battle. Most covered such humdrum subjects as the cost of food, what a soldier ate that day, humorous stories and scuttlebutt from camp, daily routines, and more. The mundane nature of these letters represented a comforting reenactment of life before the war when husbands and wives shared even the most prosaic of information. Private John Marcus Hefner of the 57th North Carolina Infantry Regiment wrote to his wife Keziah that "I want you to rite to me as Time may Soot things to Soot I want you to give me satisfaction I would like to hear from home the best in this world to hear from you all one time more it is great Satisfaction to hear that you are all well and doing well I want to hear how you ar getting on with your work."[62] Likewise, Private James W. Watkins of the 3rd Georgia Cavalry wrote to his wife that "I hav no important nuse to wright to you this time I want to you to wright to mee how you come on a geathering the corn and hoo is a geathering hit for you and whether you hav got hit geatherd or not."[63] By inviting each other into the boring details of their lives, husbands and wives mimicked their lives before the war pulled them apart.

Unable to communicate with their spouses face to face, soldiers and their spouses depended on the transmission of letters. Whatever the subject matter, letters represented the only physical links with each other, and even the most monotonous discourse was better than none at all. Everything about a letter—from the distinctive writing style to the choice in words—reflected the individual's personality and feelings. Some soldiers even took the time to trace their hands in their letters, signifying an attempt to touch the hand of their loved ones. "Houdy my dear wife," Silas Stepp wrote to his wife Eleanor before tracing a picture of his hand, "when this you see remember mee though many miles apart wee bea."[64] This desire for touch represented the biological need for physical closeness as well as the Victorian longing for interpersonal intimacy. Some soldiers even went so far as to request locks of their wives' or sweethearts' hair so that they could carry these distinctive and tangible links to their loved ones everywhere they went.[65]

Letters represented the most common form of interpersonal connection between a soldier and those he loved. Of the 1,790 letters studied for this project, virtually every letter followed a similar pattern, regardless of one's level of literacy. Letters often began with a salutation followed by a report on their health. After that, the letter's author would ask questions about the conditions at home or in camp. The rest of the letter was typically devoted to conditions on the battlefield, physical needs, camp life, discussions of religion, opinions of officers and comrades, or the weather. Soldiers and civilians alike both recognized the limitations of written communication. "I could rite a heap," Private John W. Cotton wrote to his wife, "but when I go to rite I can think of half I want to rite if I could see you all I could tell you a heap."[66] Letters often concluded with sentimental thoughts and, in some cases, poetry.[67] The frequency of letters was very telling. Letters sent from the battle front to the home front were far more frequent than those heading the other direction. Soldiers often complained of the lack of letters from the home, and their anxiety over the possible reasons for this often led to them writing more frequently.

Men chastised their wives and sweethearts for writing less often in the hopes of evoking a response. Captain John Samuel Shropshire of the 5th Texas Cavalry complained to his wife in 1861, "I came to town today expecting to find aleast two letters from you but nary letter was there for me. . . . Please write often if you are able, if not let some one write to me how you are. I can not endure such suspense, every body sick & nobody to let me know how you are getting."[68] Most resorted to flattery and exhortation. "Your sparkling blue eys and rosey red cheeks has gained my whole efections I hope for the time to come when we shall meet again," Lieutenant William Testerman of the 8th Tennessee Cavalry wrote to his sweetheart. "I want you to rite me as soon as you can for I will be glad to hear from you any time. Direct your letters as before and don't forget your best friend."[69] Echoes of Lieutenant Testerman's reminder to his loved one not to forget him were frequently found in the letters read for this book. While it is well known that soldier-fathers often worried that their children would forget them, husbands and beaux also worried that their wives and sweethearts had forgotten them. Certainly, soldiers who were prone to frequent bouts of downtime between drills and who frequently found themselves on the march often thought of their spouses. The anxiety of physical separation and the inability of men to fulfill their socially prescribed roles as husbands and fathers led to a desire for greater communication with loved ones. This desire did not seem to abate as the war progressed. Financial hardship, sickness, and death affected the home front just as much as it had before the war, and these men were not home to care for their families. Later in the war, as Union soldiers snaked their way across the South, their anxiety only increased. Worse yet, if unsettling news did arrive, soldiers were virtually powerless to do anything about it.[70]

Likewise, soldiers' letters were often far more verbose than those from home. This could be due to a variety of factors including post-battle mental duress, feelings of loneliness or disconnection from others, yearning for the comfort of one's spouses and children, or boredom—the latter being a common complaint in the letters read for this project. The Confederate mail system did not evoke great confidence that any letter would reach its destination, either. Professor Christopher Hager asserts that "rank-and-file soldiers and their families used a lot of ink writing about their health, the weather, and what milk or butter cost. They repeated themselves . . . because they never had complete confidence any given letter would reach its destination," and more importantly, "because the source of their feelings wasn't going away: *I wish you would come home, I wish I could come home, I can't come home.*"[71]

By and large, "family" and "home" were the two major themes of soldiers' letters. Sometimes the exchange was so intense that it crossed the boundaries of propriety as spouses expressed their sexual desires—though often obliquely. "You told me to prepare for kisses," Susann Cloer reminded her husband Private William Cloer of the 62nd North Carolina Infantry Regiment in 1862. "You may fix your mouth too."[72] Others eschewed Victorian values of sexual propriety by being more direct. After pining over how much she missed her husband, Mary Bell wrote to him in the summer of 1864 that "if you would come riding or walking up I would give you some nice light bread, butter, and milk, for supper, and then invite you to sleep with me, do you suppose you would take the invitation as an insult?"[73] Though expected to be sexually demure, both Mrs. Cloer and Mrs. Bell stepped outside of prescribed feminine boundaries. Over time, the longing induced by their spouses' continued absence may have loosened any inhibitions they felt to be sexually coy. Likewise, soldiers often felt little compunction to hide their feelings, and their letters tended more often to be flirtatious in nature.[74]

⁕

Soldier-husbands were pulled taut between serving their families and serving their government. Soldiers' letters are replete with justifications for why they *had* to leave their families behind to serve in the Confederate Army. Much as she was expected to support her husband's ambitions, it was also a wife's patriotic duty to sacrifice her own happiness by encouraging her husband to enlist. Throughout the war, it was expected that women would continually encourage their husbands' sacrifice. But as the war progressed and the economic situation on the home front deteriorated, many wives pleaded with their husbands to desert and fulfill their masculine duty of taking care of their families at home. Whereas the former letters exerted a "push factor" on soldiers, the latter exerted a "pull factor." In response to letters pleading for their return, soldier-husbands often exhorted their wives to continue sacrificing for the war effort. They often did so by using gendered language that belied their socially constructed belief in their wives' inherent weakness. "Carrie let me persuade you to be a brave little woman," Sergeant Hiram Holt of the 38th Alabama Infantry Regiment wrote to his wife, and "show yourself one of power one that can endure anything."[75]

Likewise, some wives actually threatened to dishonor or "unman" a soldier for deserting. As was the case before the war, women exerted immense emotional power over men. Though some exerted a "pull factor" by encouraging their husbands to desert, many others exerted a "push factor" by encouraging them to keep fighting. They too saw the war as a tectonic struggle for the future of their families and children. Historian James McPherson argues that desertion rates were probably higher among married men than unmarried soldiers. Yet the evidence for the idea that large swaths of women encouraged their husbands to desert is scant. Even McPherson admits that "most evidence of women who encouraged their husbands' or lovers' commitment to duty, honor, and country is lost to history, for most collections of soldiers' letters home do not include letters coming the other way."[76] Historian Peter Carmichael has argued that McPherson's conclusion that more married than unmarried men deserted "has value," but also that "the methodology behind the conclusions is problematic. Any attempt to measure loyalty privileges the written sources of the elite over those of the poorly educated." Carmichael notes that rooting a soldier's decision to desert in the exhortations of his wife ignores the personal agency of a soldier. Civil War soldiers were pragmatic individuals who shifted their notions of duty and honor to meet their own immediate needs rather than rigidly adhering to a political and ideological social baseline.[77] In other words, more soldiers probably deserted because they wanted to, rather than because of their wives' demands. This assertion is supported by the evidence for this project. Soldiers repeatedly expressed their desire to go home with little prodding from their wives. Many soldiers simply did not like military service, particularly after the first year of the war. When the Confederate government extended early enlistees' for the duration of the war, many Confederate soldiers soured on military service. The act of extending their service only deepened their despair as they realized that returning home was now far less likely. The farther away that home *seemed,* the gloomier soldiers became. The grief and frustration felt by many soldiers is palpable in their letters. For others, however, their feelings about the matter barely seemed to register. Yet many soldiers repeatedly reassured their wives that this was a struggle worth fighting for. Indeed, though soldiers repeatedly grumbled about life in the military, they said relatively little about deserting or giving up the fight. This was a time in which soldiers' letters were not screened before being sent home and may be indicative of the fact that many soldiers either believed in the cause, saw it as essential for the protection of their families, or didn't want to believe that their service was in vain.

Historian Ted Ownby argues that Civil War soldiers fell into two major categories of emotional expression: the "Stoics" and the "Romantics." The contrast between the two may have initially been strong but the lines between them tended to blur as the war stretched on. "Stoics" tended to minimize the emotional impact that separation from their families had on them. They most often stressed their devotion, and the necessity of their loved ones' devotion, to duty and patriotism. In their case, emotional expression may have represented weakness, and they often looked down upon their homesick compatriots. "Romantics," on the other hand, had little reservation about expressing their feelings toward their family members. "I believe I love you better and that you are dearer to me," Captain S. Hubert Dent of the 1st Alabama Infantry Regiment wrote his wife Anna; "every day you and I are separated I count the days when I expect to see you and be with you and I often speculate about how happy the meeting will be. . . . This war has made a great change in my calculations and perhaps in some ways my feelings about these things—learning to wait is a hard lesson."[78]

Ownby argues that the brutality of the war, and its inordinate length, led to an increase in the number of "Romantics" as compared with the "Stoics" who made up most recruits in 1861. He finds that over time, the war caused men to tell family members about "the softest emotions" as "male letter writers wrote that they were changing or wanted to change due to new realizations they made during wartime."[79] In his study of later enlisters, however, historian Kenneth Noe found that Romantics had existed in large numbers from the very beginning. Married men, who made up a far higher number of later enlistees, were often surprised by how much they longed for home and their loved ones after arriving in camps of instruction. As the war progressed, the expressions of lovesick feelings in later enlisters' letters decreased, Noe argues, through death, attrition, the loss of morale, and their adjustment to new circumstances.[80]

Adding to the confusion, historian James Marten found the opposite to be true, arguing that "correspondence between soldiers and their families suggests that wartime absences prompted more intense relationships among family members. High postal rates and an unreliable delivery system turned letters between southern husbands, wives, and children into precious emotional commodities."[81] Meanwhile Noe's study found that whether or not husbands expressed greater emotion, 80 percent of his sampled soldiers who were married wrote faithfully to their wives and children throughout the war.[82]

The source base for this project does not indicate whether the majority of soldiers were either Romantics or Stoics. What it does indicate, however, is that letters were precious commodities in which men and women opened their inner emotional worlds to others. Moreover, these letters provided emotional tethers between soldiers and their wives and sweethearts. These women encouraged men in their martial pursuits as well as the cultivation of personal virtue and self-sacrifice. In effect, letters from home were a reminder of why men fought and the frequency with which their loved ones wrote, coupled with the potency of their words, encouraged men to keep fighting. Some historians, such as George Rable, go so far as to argue that "communication with families, rather than male bonding with other soldiers, satisfied most men's emotional needs during the war."[83] Though many struggled to express their feelings, even the most illiterate would make the attempt. Soldier Armistead L. Galloway of the 34th Alabama Infantry Regiment wrote to his wife Eliza in June of 1862, "if you can read this bad wrighting wright ne word for know one els can wright mi feelings nor neither can I[.] I must close[.] Right every few weks to me[.] I wish I cold spend all my time in trying to wright to you."[84]

The act of writing is a symbolic method of restitutive creation for survivors of trauma. As psychologists Susan C. Feldman, David Read Johnson, and Marilyn Ollayos note, "To the victims of trauma, the act of writing calls forth the realization, 'I exist; I am not gone.' Once written, the piece acquires its own autonomy; it is no longer in the victim" and "recording on paper propels ambiguous and fleeting inner states into the consensual world, in a language that is not personal but collective."[85] In other words, writing pushes the emotional burden of trauma outward toward others. By doing so, trauma's effects are ameliorated as loved ones help bear the burden. Likewise, writing is an inherently private act that allows for careful editing, giving the writer a sense of control—a feeling often lost in the wake of trauma. Because they were able to think through their feelings, letter writing provided a safe conduit for the transmission of emotions without the pressure of face-to-face interaction and the prospect of immediate humiliation or judgment.[86]

Husbands and wives as well as beaux and sweethearts were not the only ones who craved emotional connection through the written word. Unmarried men, many of whom were in their late teens or early twenties, also craved emotional affection from women. If military service represented the apex of masculine ambition and sacrifice, then young men looked for women who would both encourage their grand ambitions and backfill their insecurities. As one young soldier wrote, they often wished "to go corting and squeaze some of the girls, for I no that they would like to be squeazed a little."[87] The prospect of imminent death and the lack of female companionship in camp meant that many single men frantically corresponded with women that they had known before the war, hoping to fan the embers of romantic interest. Others felt so lonely in camp that they would write to women who, as members of women's auxiliary groups, had provided food or homemade goods such as socks and uniforms to soldiers. Out of these letters, two individuals who had never physically met would sometimes become romantic partners. Many women on the home front themselves lacked male companionship as so many had been swept into Confederate Army. Through the exchange of these letters, men and women explored each other's psyches while also tacitly interviewing each other for possible future matrimony. Women celebrated male ambition and sacrifice while men celebrated a woman's modesty and femininity—characteristics seen as more important than physical beauty.[88] Though seemingly superfluous, these flirtatious letters reminded soldiers of a loving world beyond their own narrow, battle-scarred existence. To soldiers who had witnessed so much horror and suffering, the idea of a world of affection and romantic interest gave them hope.

Letters were almost of existential importance to soldiers and, by extension, to the Confederate war effort. Though prone to frequent breakdowns and thousands of undelivered letters, the value of the Confederate mail system to soldier morale cannot be overstated. Confederate soldiers *needed* the reassurance of their wives and sweethearts. Confederate authorities recognized this, with some even going so far as to bring local women into camp to maintain morale and remind men what they were fighting for.[89] As the war stretched on, the deterioration or capture of an already languishing and relatively miniscule railroad system meant that mail increasingly either never reached its destination or arrived weeks and months after it was sent.[90] Soldiers did not always understand or even care for logistical reasons behind the dearth of letters from their loved ones.

Civilians, too, reacted angrily when their letters were not reciprocated. Writing to her soldier-husband, Ann Bowen exclaimed that "I would be glad to hear from you every week or every day if I could but I no I cant we could hear from each other every week if those that carryes the letters would not be so carless but it don't concern them and they don't care for it is next thing to seeing you and having a long talk with you to get a new letter."[91] Wives and sweethearts treasured the letters that they received. They could be read and reread again when they wanted to "converse" with their loved ones: these letters were consistent reminders that one's husband or beaux was alive and that those who remained at home were not forgotten. The anxiety generated by the sense of potential loss was multiplied by the contradictory and often inaccurate casualty reports published in newspapers across the Confederacy. Family members often learned of a loved one's wounding or death *months* after the fact. Sometimes the most reliable method of learning about a soldier's status was through his comrades.[92] "On the way to the battlefield," Private Spencer Welch of the 13th South Carolina Infantry Regiment wrote to his wife, "I met a negro who recognized me and told me that your brother Edwin was wounded in the breast and had gone to Richmond. I fear there is some truth in it."[93]

A letter's delivery could lift the spirit of a soldier or civilian or pull them down to the depths of despair. Because husbands and wives felt deeply for one another, letters were instrumental to maintaining morale on the home front and the battle front. One expert on modern militaries, Roger W. Little, noted that "letters represent the soldier's major contact with the social unit that reinforces his desire to serve faithfully and under great hardship."[94] Lieutenant Edmund Patterson of the 9th Alabama Infantry Regiment echoed this sentiment, writing that "letters from home or the immediate neighborhood of home have more to do with keeping up the spirits and morale of the army than is generally supposed. When each individual member of a company or regiment feels that his labors are appreciated by his friends and neighbors at home, he asks no other recognition of his serves and is cheerful and contented, and the spirit becomes general and animates the command as a body."[95]

In a world marked by alternating extremes of stress, boredom, and terror, soldiers found that writing letters soothed their anxiety. Some even went so far as to write them during battle. On August 17, 1864, Private Samuel King Vann of the 19th Alabama Infantry Regiment wrote to his wife: "I hear a ball pass by me every syllable I make, and since I have been writing there has been two men shot through the body right here in camp. Poor fellows, I think they will die. I am sitting behind a tree to prevent being shot until I get this letter wrote, and the balls are constantly striking the tree that I am behind, but just so they don't strike me I will not stop writing." Sensing that it might be his final moments on earth, he continued: "I may be writing to you for the last time, but I truly hope not, for I don't want to die just yet awhile, but alas, serious times with me for life is so precarious that a man ought to feel so, for in a moment he may be shot through as one poor fellow is out there on the ground crying to God for help." Even in the torrent of battle, Vann reminded his wife that "I want you to write to me often for this will be the only comfort and consolation now. . . . Please do not wait for me to first, for I will surely write, and if you do not get any letters from me, do not indulge the idea that I have quit writing for I never expect to so long as you will write to me, for I expect to write one lady only and that shall be you, for I love you more than all the rest."[96]

Letters were conduits for the safe expression of one's innermost feelings. As the war dragged on and soldiers faced ever-greater stressors, the mask of self-mastery fell from the visages of many battle-hardened men. The prospect of permanent separation from their wives and sweethearts led these men to embrace dark thoughts and at times, even darker dreams. "My cheaks is very ofen wet with tears a bout you and darling Child to think that wee are so far a part and cant Get to See each other faces," wrote Private William Irby Box of the 3rd South Carolina Infantry Regiment to his wife Margaret and daughter Rachel, "I can study a bout you and see your sweet fase and dream of you very ofen and when I wake I cant rest all day."[97] Women too often dreamed of their husbands. "It is no use to say to you I want to see you for you now that but I never did want to see you as bad I dreamed last night of see ing you," Nancy King wrote to her husband Private Jasper King of the 18th South Carolina Infantry Regiment in March 1863; "I thought you was at home I can see as well how you looked I thought you looked sweet and prety as ever I wish my dream would come to pass."[98] According to historian Jonathan W. White, dreams provided a sense of solace that "may have contributed to the sense of closeness that endured between men and their families despite long separations." Though soldiers dreamed of everything, in their letters, the most common dreams recounted were those of home.[99]

Historian James McPherson estimates that between 700,000 and 800,000 married men enlisted in both Union and Confederate armies during the American Civil War.[100] Men and women who were romantically involved haunted each other's thoughts when awake and, as has been demonstrated, even their dreams when asleep. Historians of the American Civil War have often argued for a divide emerging between soldiers along the battle front and civilians among the home front.[101] The evidence for this project indicates that if there was a divide, it wasn't an emotional one. Soldiers and civilians alike expressed their frustrations with the war and, more often, with the living conditions at home or on the battle front. Yet husbands and wives generally seemed bound together by their love for each other and could often find a common bond in their mutual frustration with the war. Rarely did they speak out against Confederate leaders or the Confederate cause. Many did not seem to want to waste precious paper or ink complaining when they could instead be sharing news or their own private feelings. Sadly, each letter had the possibility of containing the last words of a husband to his wife.

Men who marched off to war understood that death was a possibility. The imminence of combat and the ravages of disease meant that the once-distant possibility of death drew closer. The prospect of separation magnified the feelings that soldiers and their spouses felt for each other. Emotions that may have grown dormant in times of peace could be violently awakened by the looming specter of eternal separation. So powerful were these feelings that some men wrote to their wives in poetic terms. This was particularly true in the face of battle. Sometimes, the very thought of loved ones back home gave men the strength to face combat. "At dead of night when the enemies guns are roaring around me, I still take time to think of you all and my home!" Private Hiram Talbert Holt of the 38th Alabama

Infantry Regiment wrote to his wife, "Oh! how I think of thee and it lifts my soul almost from out of my body to think of you so far away. . . . And for the present let it satisfy you that I have acted nobly, that I am where the brave die, that whether on the tented field or mixing in the carnage of battle I still will love & think of thee."[102] Likewise, Private Thomas Inglet of the 28th Georgia Infantry Regiment wrote to his wife, "Oh when I am on the Battle field an think of you how Shall i feel you so many a mil from me What Would I Give Could you I See."[103]

In fact, so intertwined was emotion with home that medical professionals believed that longing for home could cause immense physical distress. Today, we understand many of the physical effects of "homesickness." Those experiencing homesickness tend to be obsessively preoccupied with thoughts of home that often leave one wracked with feelings of anxiety, nervousness, and sadness. Today, psychologists argue that homesickness is not only rooted in the instinctive need for love, security, and protection (which are rooted in the home) but also in the loss of routine, normality, and social space.[104] Some individuals can become so impaired by homesickness that they become emotionally crippled. In some cases, it can also cause physical debilitation. "It afforded me no small pleasure to hear from you and my little ones, and to know that you are well," Private Edward T. Broughton of the 7th Texas Infantry Regiment declared to his wife. "But it would afford me to bear our separation as best we can. My physician said my disease from which I am recovering was produced by homesickness."[105] For homesick soldiers, letters provided some relief as conduits for emotion and interpersonal processing, which helped ameliorate some of the psychological distress caused by homesickness.

"Letters are not intended merely to convey intelligence," one soldier informed his sister, "they are more precious as a medium for carrying on a silent conversation between those who have thoughts and affections & sympathies & hopes alike."[106] These "silent conversations" acted as girders that provided stability to a soldier's life. Confederate soldiers faced almost daily reminders of life's uncertainties and their own vulnerabilities. The uneasiness of their lives stood in sharp contrast to the stability of home. Men who at one time thought of themselves as masters of their emotions found that much of their self-confidence emanated from the approval of their wives or sweethearts. War crippled self-confidence. Facing the imminence of death and the erosion of their self-confidence, men relied upon the words of their wives for strength and motivation. As Peter Carmichael noted, letters "moved the war from political abstractions to reminders of their past lives at home, where pure feelings of sympathy, compassion, and familial love made life sacred and worth dying for."[107] Wives represented one of the strongest emotional reservoirs upon which soldiers drew. Moreover, many soldiers saw this war as one waged to protect their families' economic futures and emotional happiness.[108]

Seeing the war in these terms was a source of immense personal stress for Confederate soldiers. Many felt that they could not simply abandon the war, as doing so was tantamount to abandoning their families. Repeated pleas for help from home reminded men that the war's tentacles stretched beyond the battlefield. Stuck between two impossible positions, at times even the most stoic soldiers allowed their emotions to bubble to the surface in their letters home. In the sample for this book, the two periods most marked by emotional effusiveness were those in which letters were written immediately after battle or around the holidays—particularly Christmas. "Mother I have been in A battle sence I wrote to you it was the hardest fight that I ever heard tell of before," Private John Wesley Williams of the 35th North Carolina Infantry Regiment wrote in July 1862. "I never saw before I have been on two battle fields besids the one that I fought in two men got shot down wright by me an the canester balls I never witchnest the Like before . . . not A haire of my head got hurt I thought I Loved you and my god before but I did not Love you Like I do now."[109] Likewise, after his brother and comrade was captured after the Battle of the Wilderness in May 1864, Private John A. Everett of the 11th Georgia Infantry Regiment was in an extremely heightened emotional state. From a hospital, he wrote to his mother four days after the battle, "Well ma I am hear alone I have no Brother with me now I am in hops that he is not Dead if he is you know that Iam in abad condision no one to Care for me it Seames to me lik I Can heare Him Calling me I hear his voice all the time," before writing, "I feel like I have not got afriend in this world my Only Companion is Gone and left me alone in this trublesom world."[110]

Although southern males had often witnessed violence on a much smaller scale in their civilian lives, few had witnessed Minié balls or cannon balls tearing human bodies to ribbons. After the adrenaline of battle wore off, soldiers were left to process what they had just seen and experienced. "The soldier's privilege to kill," psychiatrist Theodore Nadelson writes, "is unlike anything most other individuals have ever experienced, and the soldier who kills is permanently changed, fixed to the death he has made."[111] Modern clinical research indicates that psychological trauma from combat does not stem from the fear of death or injury. Rather, the natural "resistance to over aggressive confrontation, in addition to the fear of death and injury, is responsible for much of the trauma and stress on the battlefield." In other words, the natural human inclination toward the *preservation of life* and war's demand to the contrary constituted the basis for much of the soldier's psychological trauma. "Fear, combined with exhaustion, hate, horror, and the irreconcilable task of balancing these with the need to kill," Dave Grossman writes in his seminal book *On Killing: The Psychological Cost of Learning to Kill in War and Society,* "eventually drives the soldier so deeply into a mire of guilt and horror that he tips over the brink into that region that we call insanity. Indeed, fear may be one of the least important of these factors."[112]

When human beings experience trauma, their stress hormone system triggers, sending a cascade of signals through the central nervous system. Generally, a "fight or flight" response is triggered but then returns to equilibrium once the threat has passed. For those who experience post-traumatic stress disorder,[113] the stress hormone system fails to return to equilibrium. Signals of an impending threat continue to be sent through the central nervous system long after the traumatic event has ended. For some individuals, the central nervous system becomes overwhelmed, and the "fight or flight" response is stuck in the "on position." The constant secretion of stress hormones leads to lingering feelings of agitation, panic, and, eventually, the degradation of an individual's physical and psychological health.[114]

A soldier's response to battle varied. While most soldiers felt abject horror at the sights and sounds of the battlefield, others found combat innervating and exciting. For most, even fighting for a "just cause" did not necessarily equate to feeling justified for their actions in combat. Soldiers often felt a sense of guilt and shame that would become overwhelming. "The combat soldier appears to feel a deep sense of responsibility and accountability for what he sees around him," Grossman writes. "It is as though every enemy dead is a human being he has killed, and every friendly dead is a comrade for whom he was responsible. With every effort to reconcile these two responsibilities, more guilt is added to the horror that surrounds the soldier."[115]

Soldiers who experienced battle were often torn between their devotion to duty and country and the emotional toll of taking human life. In combat, sentimentalism and idealism beat a steady retreat in the face of torn bodies and random killing. Communicating what they saw, as well as what they did to others, was a difficult task for many soldiers. "I will try to describe the battle field to you but I hardly know how," Private Lewis Sylvester Branscomb of the 3rd Alabama Infantry Regiment wrote to his father in June 1862, "Just imagine yourself walking over a large field half leg deep in mud scattered all over with dead men and horses wounded men lying all about groaning in the agonies death begging you for assistines and you will have some idea of a battle field."[116] Individuals under stress who have only a vague understanding of what their feelings are and why they feel that way are far more likely to ruminate on them. "Being able to clearly understand one's feelings (that is, having greater emotional insight) enhances one's ability to regulate these feelings," noted psychologists Eileen Kennedy-Moore and Jeanne C. Watson. "In contrast, poor understanding of one's feelings increases the chances of being caught in an aversive ruminative process, trying to figure out one's internal state."[117] This rumination could lead to a dramatic emotional spiral that could leave soldiers reeling. Communication with loved ones was vital for their emotional processing and healing.

Studies of trauma have consistently found that a strong emotional and physical support network is the most powerful way to fortify one against trauma. Healthy attachments are vital to one's feelings of safety and emotional equilibrium. After surviving acute trauma, survivors are encouraged to see familiar faces and to communicate with loved ones as their love and support can often help pull individuals back from the brink of emotional collapse. The human brain is wired to connect with others and recovery from traumatic episodes requires these connections. In contrast, attempts to manage the stress of combat or PTSD on one's own can easily lead to "dissociation, despair, addictions, a chronic sense of panic, and relationships that are marked by alienation, disconnection, and explosions." This need is evident from infancy as human touch and emotional attunement constitute the most natural methods for calming an infant's distress, diminishing its natural arousal response due to perceived trauma.[118] In the absence of physical touch, Civil War soldiers used physical letters to process their grief with their wives and sweethearts.

Romantic relationships were in fact a major part of a soldier's emotional healing that helped them to endure the dehumanizing effects of war. Though most men longed for the lives they lived before the war, these longings were inflamed by physical distance. Such feelings led to even bolder declarations of love and affection that ran contrary to prevailing prewar expectations of male emotional expression. Writing to his wife, Confederate Surgeon Harvey Black reminisced about their blissful days of courtship. "I don't know how much pleasure it affords you to go over these days of the past," he wrote, "but to me they will ever be remembered as days of felicity. And how happy the thought that years increase the affection & esteem we have for each other to be love & be loved. . . . May I make you happy and in so doing be made happy in return. A sweet kiss and embraced to your greeting."[119] For Black, as for hundreds of thousands of other white southern enlisted males, the prospect of returning to his beloved wife was all that he had to hold onto. Their love was vital to their survival.

CHAPTER 3

PHILIA
AND
FRIENDSHIP

HOW HOMOSOCIAL BONDING
SUSTAINED THE SOLDIER'S MORALE

With the outbreak of the American Civil War in April 1861, twenty-two-year-old James R. Montgomery was a promising young law student at the University of Mississippi. Not long after the attack on Fort Sumter, Montgomery and his classmates eagerly enlisted for twelve months of service in the Confederate army. Swept up in the *rage militaire* of the early war period, the young Mississippian was mustered into Company A of the 11th Mississippi Infantry Regiment (known as the "University Greys"). Over the next many months, the lives of these men were woven together through the collective experience of fear, suffering, and loss. The idealism that had emboldened them early in the war was long gone. In 1863, Montgomery was captured and sent to the Old Capital Prison in Washington, DC. He was soon paroled and returned to his unit just in time to participate in the Battle of Gettysburg. In the ensuing battle, his regiment suffered a staggering 100 percent casualty rate.[1] Montgomery miraculously survived.

In May 1864, Private Montgomery lay prostrate in agony from a shoulder wound after the Battle of Spotsylvania Courthouse. Flitting between fear and resignation, he penned his final letter. "This is my last letter to you. . . . I know that death is near, and that I will die far from home and friends of my early youth," he wrote to his father in Camden, Mississippi, "but I have friends here too who are kind to me. My friend Fairfax will write you at my request and give you the particulars of my death." As pen scratched paper, rivulets of blood dripped down his arm, permanently staining the fragile paper. The cruel hand of war had snatched all that he had once known and hoped for—his bright future as a lawyer, the friendship and camaraderie of his fellow classmates, the comforting presence of his parents and loved ones. "My grave will be marked so that you may visit it if you desire to do so, but it is optionary with you whether you let my remains rest here or in Miss. I would like to rest in the grave yard with my dear mother and brothers but it's a matter of minor importance. Let us all try to reunite in heaven," he wrote before his final agonizing goodbye: "My strength fails me. My horse and my equipments will be left for you. Again, a long farewell to you. May we meet in heaven."[2]

Four days later, Private Montgomery succumbed to his wounds. Heartbroken over the loss of his friend and comrade, Private Ethelbert Fairfax wrote to his own mother of Montgomery's death: "I don't think I ever witnessed such an exhibition of fortitude and Christian resignation as he showed. Although so far from home (he lived in Mississippi) and his early friends, no words of complaint escaped his lips. He wrote a beautiful letter to his father soon after he received his wound. I have just completed a letter to his poor father enclosing it to him, announcing his death."[3] Fulfilling the wishes of his friend, Fairfax wrote to Montgomery's father, "In this sad bereavement you will have the greatest of all comforts in knowing that he made peace with God and was resigned to his fate."[4]

The letters of Montgomery and Fairfax represent a broader emotive archetype that characterized homosocial relationships between the approximately 800,000 and 1.2 million men who enlisted in the Confederate army during the war.[5] Most had never traveled more than a few miles from home and many did not know each other. Yet the war wove together the lives of thousands of strangers who would eat, fight, drill, live, suffer, and in some cases, die together. Their close physical proximity bred emotional connection as soldiers' identities and affections became inextricably bound to their comrades.

These emotional connections are not tangential to our understanding of how and why Confederate soldiers fought. They are *fundamental* to understanding how soldiers endured a war that historian Michael C. C. Adams argued was "neither sharply delineated nor fought by combatants bonded together in defense of clearly enunciated positions and universally held ideologies."[6] The traditional motif of soldiers bound together through political ideology, shared cultural heritage, or military training provides only part of the answer to the question of why soldiers fought. They also fought for each other. Moreover, they were able to fight *because* of each other. Theirs was a bond of mutual suffering which united individuals of all genders, classes, religions, and geographical boundaries.[7] According to psychologists Ervin Staub and Johanna Vollhardt, the experience of violence "often shakes the very foundations of a person's beliefs and can create, in individuals and whole communities, a sense of living in a meaningless and threatening world." Individuals who face violence often "reclaim meaning and turn toward others, becoming caring and helpful, a phenomenon that has been referred to as *altruism born of suffering.*"[8]

Union and Confederate soldiers exhibited altruism toward their comrades and, in some cases, their enemies. The emotional bonds forged between soldiers were sometimes so strong that they carried through to the postwar period, which witnessed the emergence of soldiers' societies and fraternal orders that were designed to care for veterans and their families. By tracing the genesis of these wartime friendships from enlistment through their development in camp and their actualization in battle, this chapter demonstrates that comradeship and friendship filled an emotional void wrought by soldiers' separation from their families. Furthermore, it argues that these relationships provided an emotional bulwark against the demoralizing effects of war.

To understand the emotional power of comradeship and friendship, it is first important to understand society's views of these relationships. As previously noted, the century leading up to the war witnessed a growing acceptance of heightened emotional expressionism among southern white males. Though masculine stoicism was a powerful social expectation, the American Civil War provoked widespread emotional, psychological, and even physical trauma that shattered many prewar cultural restraints. The war thus marked an important turning point in the cultural expectations of emotional expression in male relationships. According to historian Stephen Berry, men went into the war with a "prickly sense of self," as they were "constantly on their guard, watching each other for signs of respect and disrespect, competing with each other for mates, honors, and distinctions. Even in friendship, there was a standoffishness, an unwillingness to appear weak, vulnerable, or emotionally needy."[9]

However, the source base for this project indicates that white southern males were not as emotionally "standoffish" as previously asserted. The overwhelming topic of conversation in the 1,790 letters written between 200 soldiers and 366 family members and 15 friends between 1861 and 1865 was not battle, religion, children, or even ideology or duty. Rather, it was the daily minutiae of a soldier or family member's life. Nestled within many of these mundane letters were scattered declarations of emotion and affection. Of the 1,790 letters for this project, 1,182 (66 percent) include emotional or affective expressions toward the letter's recipient. One hundred and sixty-four out of 200 soldiers (82 percent) in the sample expressed emotion or feeling. References to children came in second, with 524 letters (29.27 percent) and 64 out of 200 soldiers referencing them (32 percent); religious declarations third, with 332 letters (18.55 percent) from 90 out of 200 soldiers (45 percent); descriptions of battle in fourth, with only 104 letters (5.81 percent) from 63 out of 200 soldiers (31.5 percent); and only 62 letters that expressed ideology or duty (3.46 percent) from 33 out of 200 soldiers (16.5 percent). Amongst literate white southern males, feelings were the things most expressed in their letters—at least compared to ideology, religion, and battle. While many of the letters do obliquely reference relationships in camp, the majority contain expressions of emotion directed toward family members and, in a few cases, friends at home. Thus, it is from oblique references in their letters home and as well as their own extant diaries and remembrances that we come to understand the depth of feeling that Confederate soldiers held for each other.

In August 1863, not long after participating in the Battle of Gettysburg, Private W. L. Jones of the 26th North Carolina Infantry Regiment described the emotionally jarring effects of combat to a friend: "Just staying out here to fight Just for the fun of the thing if that is the case I can say for myself that I never have seen any fun in it but to the reverse for God knows that I saw enough of at Gettyesburg to make any man shed tears. . . . I shall have to stop saying any more about that bloody field for the thought of it allmost makes me shed teares."[10] Jones's description is telling in that his depiction of the battle—and the feelings that cascaded from recounting his experiences—represented cracks in the psychological dam of his masculine stoicism. The war often left its participants with deep feelings of powerlessness. There was no way to know where the bullets would fly or the cannonballs land and survival seemed to be the result of mere chance. The anxiety could at times be overwhelming. Many men tried to ignore these feelings—to avoid their sense of powerlessness. In the case of Private Jones, this may have been the case as he refused to further describe the gory scene on the battlefield. It is telling that the person he shared these feelings with was a male friend with whom he clearly felt a sense of interpersonal intimacy.

What is also striking about Jones's description is that when he wrote his letter, he had already served for two years, and yet did not seem to lose his sensitivity toward the suffering of others. Bearing witness to, and participating in, the destruction of human life could make soldiers more emotionally effusive as they tried to process what they had seen and done. The weight of suffering during the Civil War was often too overwhelming. Like clockwork, soldiers' letters written after battle were often replete with feelings of fear, anger, loss, and grief. This observation flies in the face of historians such as Gerald Linderman, who argued that "courage served to detach the soldier from the sights that might otherwise unnerve him."[11] Tangential to Linderman, many others argue that soldiers underwent a process of "hardening" that over time enabled them to become emotionally inured to taking life or losing comrades and friends. As historian Reid Mitchell notes: "Part of masculinity was achieving a self-discipline within the institutional discipline of the army" and "part of the transformation necessary to become a soldier was hardening."[12]

These arguments are not necessarily wrong. It is true that through repeated exposure to suffering, human beings can become numb to, or detached from, their emotions. According to psychologist Bessel van der Kolk—one of the foremost experts on trauma—there are three responses to a perceived threat. The first stage is when the Ventral Vagal Complex (VVC) or "social-engagement system" of the brain, which is responsible for registering and responding to other's actions (that is, smiling in response to other's smiles or nodding one's head in agreement with others), is triggered when one feels threatened. In this stage, human beings' facial expressions become reflective of their inner turmoil and their tone of voice changes to beckon others to come to their assistance. If no one responds, the limbic system kicks in and begins mobilizing the muscles, heart, and lungs for a fight or flight response. If there is no hope of staving off the inevitable, the Dorsal Vagal Complex (DVC) begins to "disengage, collapse, and freeze." Individuals often become unresponsive to their environments.[13]

Trauma can induce a phenomenon called "alexithymia" which is characterized by an inability to understand or describe one's emotions. Often, survivors of trauma thereafter struggle to identify felt physical and emotional sensations. "They may look furious but deny that they are angry; they may appear terrified but say that they are fine," van der Kolk notes. Unable to understand what is going on inside of them, they may ignore their own needs such as sleeping, eating, or taking care of themselves. By suppressing overwhelming emotions, sufferers of alexithymia eventually find that they are no longer able to recognize their feelings. Some Confederate soldiers experienced alexithymia but many more probably experienced a phenomenon known as "depersonalization" in which an individual loses a sense of self. In this state, victims of trauma feel disconnected from their bodies.[14] In 1928, German psychoanalyst Paul Schilder gave the most succinct description of this phenomena, writing that "to the depersonalized individual, the world appears strange, peculiar, foreign, dream-like. Objects appear at times strangely diminished in size, at times flat. Sounds appear to come from a distance. . . . The emotions likewise undergo marked alteration. Patients complain that they are capable of experiencing neither pain nor pleasure. . . . They become strangers to themselves."[15] Yet the experience of alexithymia or depersonalization was not universal among Confederate soldiers, and the experience of trauma does not always lead to a process of hardening or self-detachment. The source base for this book indicates that though many soldiers probably struggled to deal with their emotions, they nonetheless clearly felt them— even after years of service. "Trauma victims cannot recover until they become familiar with and befriend sensations in their bodies," Van der Kolk argues. "In order to change, people need to become aware of their sensations and the way that their bodies interact with the world around them. Physical self-awareness is the first step in releasing the tyranny of the past." To do this, victims of trauma must find ways to relax and feel safe. It is only in this state that they are then able to connect the physical manifestations of trauma to psychological events and then reconnect with themselves. The most natural way to calm oneself and develop a sense of safety, in the words of Van der Kolk, "is by clinging to another person."[16] The act of clinging to others is reflective of the infant's dependence upon his or her parents. Physically and emotionally vulnerable, an infant's healthy development is partly dependent on the touch, attention, and expressed love of his or her caretakers. Trauma, in part, involves a realization of one's own vulnerability and it is not surprising that survivors often find themselves reaching out to others to restore a sense of safety and self-confidence.

One way of connecting with others is through letter writing. Psychologists Susan C. Feldman, David Read Johnson, and Marilyn Ollayos, all of whom instituted a PTSD program for Vietnam veterans, found that writing was integral to a soldier's recovery. They noted that writing integrated "the experience of Vietnam into the entire life sequence, thereby widening the veteran's narrow focus on Vietnam as the only significant life experience" and that "sharing one's life history with empathic and interested veterans and staff becomes a healing counterpoint to the disinterest and rejection previously signaled by society and family."[17] In the same way, sharing their experiences with their comrades and friends, whether through written or verbal communication, is integral to their healing. Critical to the healing process is the ability to share with those who understand, or at least who are empathetic to, one's experiences. In the case of Confederate soldiers, this generally included their comrades.

For this study, only fifteen recipients of letters from the soldiers sampled could be identified as friends not actively involved in military service. The reason for this paucity may be twofold. First, paper and pencils/pens were in short supply in the Confederacy and were relatively expensive. Confederate soldiers tended only to expend these precious resources on their immediate and extended families—people with whom they were more emotionally close and for whom they had a responsibility to stay in touch. While only fifteen friends received letters in this sample, 366 identified family members received letters—primarily wives, followed by parents, and then children. The second reason for the lack of letters between soldiers and their friends is that many enlisted with their friends. From 1861 to 1865, the Confederate States of America mobilized more than 80 percent of its draft-age military men. Soldiers from the same hometown were usually mustered into the same company or regiment. Thus, there was little need to exchange formal letters.[18] Because of the critical lack of letters exchanged between soldiers in camp, however, modern historians' best primary sources dealing with homosocial relationships in the military are soldiers' diaries published during and after the war. The few extant letters and many extant diaries indicate that the American Civil War was a catalyst for the development of male friendships that, at least for those four years, reached a depth of intimacy that ran contrary to prevailing sociocultural norms. However, it is important to understand the gradations of homosocial relationships during the war.

Definitions at this juncture are crucial. Historians of the American Civil War make sharp distinctions between two words that seem almost interchangeable but are in fact very different in historical parlance. The difference between *comradeship* and *friendship* is of vital importance, although the average soldier in the American Civil War often experienced them concurrently and in overlapping ways. American philosopher Jesse Glenn Gray roots this distinction "in a heightened awareness of the self in friendship and in the suppression of self-awareness in comradeship." He argues, "Friends do not seek to lose their identity, as comrades and erotic lovers do," but rather "friends find themselves in each other and thereby gain greater self-knowledge and self-possession."[19] Friendship preserves individual identity while comradeship means the absorption of one's self and one's identity into the greater whole of a military unit.

Dutch philosopher Desiree Verweij argues that "strong bonds are of the utmost importance in the context of war. . . . The mutual love of comrades and their dedication towards each other are necessary for survival." She further argues that "friendship gives comradeship an extra dimension . . . it contributes to a flourishing life, and in doing so it helps the friend to refrain from behavior that will disrupt his/her humanity and thus his/her human flourishing."[20] In the abstract, soldiers needed each other to maintain connection with their own humanity while, in the physical sense, they also needed each other to survive materially. Whether that was through absorption of the self into the larger unit through comradeship or the individuality of friendship, soldiers often learned to skillfully navigate these interpersonal relationships. They drew from each category what they deemed necessary to survive.

The intimacy that developed between men, either in the form of comradeship or friendship, reached levels that would have been surprising before the war. Soldiers often wrote home with great poignancy of their experiences that seemed emotionally incommunicable to civilians back home who did not experience battle or the homosocial intimacy of camps. Lieutenant Wayland Dunaway of the 47th Virginia Infantry Regiment recounted that during the Second Manassas campaign in August 1862, a "Lieutenant Ball" and "[Ball's] most intimate friend Mordecai Lawson" were found dead from mortal wounds to the head. "With bayonets and hands a grave was dug," he wrote, "in which we laid them side by side, and spreading over them a soldier's blanket, we heaped above them the turf and clods. In neither army could there have been found two braver men. Boon companions in life, in death they were not divided."[21] Likewise, First Lieutenant George Booth of the 1st Maryland Cavalry Regiment (CSA) witnessed the death of his friend who took a mortal wound to the head in June 1864. He recounted that before taking "the last leave of this dear friend," he "stooped to kiss his brow, now covered by his life's blood." Years after the war, Booth noted that whenever his mind drifted back to the loss of his friend, he and his comrades felt "an overpowering sense of the great personal loss we had sustained. Few men were ever so loved, none more deservedly."[22]

Likewise, in her study of suicide among Confederate soldiers, historian Diane Sommerville noted that soldiers often responded with empathy toward comrades' psychological or emotional struggles. Even those who deserted were sometimes met with great sensitivity if these actions were the result of severe psychological or emotional strain. This empathy is demonstrative, she asserts, of "a redefinition of martial courage and a relaxation of attitudes towards suicide."[23] It is also representative of a larger emotional turn during the war—one which placed more emphasis on intimate homosocial relationships that were far less prevalent before the war. The shared experience of their unique suffering bound them together in ways that class, politics, or social interests never could. These bonds were instrumental to a soldier's survival and, by extension, the continuation of the war.

What formed these emotional bonds? Moreover, how did these bonds motivate soldiers to fight? According to historian James McPherson, "for Civil War soldiers the group cohesion and peer pressure that were powerful factors in combat motivation were not unrelated to the complex mixture of patriotism, ideology, concepts of duty, honor, manhood, and community or peer pressure that prompted them to enlist in the first place."[24] In the prewar period, the communal consensus held an almost dictatorial power over the behavioral norms expected of white males. Men were expected to master themselves and others but never to allow themselves to be mastered. Suffering changed this as men discovered their need for each other. Private Carlton McCarthy of the Richmond Howitzers recounted of the soldier: "the romance of war charmed him, and he hurried from the embrace of his mother to the embrace of death. His playmates, his friends, and his associates were gone; he was lonesome, and he sought a reunion 'in camp.'"[25]

The stories shared by Lieutenant Dunaway, Lieutenant Booth, and Private McCarthy indicate a depth of emotional bonding that goes much deeper than mere companionship. The rigid masculine ideals that emphasized individuality and emotional restraint in the prewar period are clearly not present in their accounts. Moreover, soldiers' diaries and memoirs are replete with intimate remembrances of comrades and friends. If historians' claims of stoic masculinity are true, it is clear that during the war, white southern men began to privilege emotional survival over cultural conformity. Some stories reflect an almost marriage-like depth of feeling between these soldiers. Intimacy emerges when individuals share meaningful experiences or feelings either consciously or unconsciously.[26] The increased importance placed on these relationships provided the impetus for a subtle shift in homosocial relationships. It did not happen all at once.

Early in the war, political and social causes bound white southern males together in one purpose. Communal living and training in camps of instruction further strengthened these bonds. When the initial *rage militaire* of the war's early months eventually gave way to a fight for survival, soldiers had to look beyond ideology and politics to find meaning for their struggle. They did so often by sometimes personalizing their experiences and limiting their motivations to those around them. Particularly for single men, the war was one which was fought for their comrades with whom they had formed deeply intimate interpersonal bonds. For those who were married, it seems as if they more often saw the war as one fought for their families. Yet the disconnect between soldiers' relationships with their loved ones back home and their comrades in camp could at times be stark. For survivors of PTSD, they may have experienced what is now called a "broken connection" between themselves and society, as their traumatic experiences made them feel stigmatized or alienated from those who did not share in those experiences and thus understand their feelings.[27]

Alfred Wilson, who could not enlist due to ill health, personified much of this disconnect when he wrote to recent enlistee James Watson, "please reed this note address to all the friends I call you friends because you all stand in my defence as well as your own and I love and thank you all for it like wise all the good soldiers in the sothern confederacy."[28] Wilson could afford to maintain his patriotism. For those who actually fought, there was often little room for the idealism of those nestled in their comfortable homes. In May 1863, Private Hezekiah C. Ward of the 64th North Carolina Infantry Regiment reflected on his exhaustion with the war, writing to his brother-in-law that "I would like to see you all at home once more I never was as tired of any things in my life as I am of this old war for thare is no jestus in this old war."[29]

The traumatic and frenetic nature of Civil War combat left many men exhausted because of adrenal responses to stressors. Extended exposure to stressors often leads to prolonged feelings of physical exhaustion. War was brutal and frightening and one's life continuously hung by a thread. At the Battle of Savages Station in June 1862, Sergeant David August Dickert of the 3rd South Carolina Infantry Regiment awoke on the battlefield to "the roar of musketry and the boom of cannon, with the continual swish, swash of the grape and canister striking the trees and ground." After placing his hand on his chest, he "felt a dull, deadening sensation. There I found the warm blood, that filled my inner garments and now trickled down my side as I endeavored to stand upright. I had been shot through the left lung, and as I felt the great gaping wound in my chest, the blood gushing and spluttering out at every breath, I began to realize my situation." Dickert's brother was a field surgeon, who, upon hearing of his brother's wounds, carried him to the rear. Sitting on a tree trunk, the surgeon pronounced his brother's wound as fatal. After probing the wound with his finger, in the words of Dickert, his brother "gave me the flattering assurance that unless I bled to death quite soon my chances might be good!" Surviving his wounds, Dickert later recounted his feelings in that moment. "Gentle reader, were you ever, as you thought, at death's door, when the grim monster was facing you, when life looked indeed a very brief span?," he wrote. "If so, you can understand my feelings—I was scared!"[30]

In his hour of need, Dickert had his brother by his side. Many others did not. They would have to lean on others—many of whom were strangers before the war but with whom they now wove their lives and fortunes together—to survive. With loved ones sometimes hundreds of miles away, soldiers came to rely upon each other in ways that would have seemed inconceivable before the war. This bonding process began long before any of these men saw a battlefield. For most, it began in their own hometowns.

⁓⟡⁓

Before the outbreak of war, many Confederate enlistees had previously served in local militia units. While most were glorified social clubs, militias soon became the nuclei for the burgeoning Confederate army.[31] During the war's early months, both sides placed the onus for filling their ranks on the individual states, who were neither organizationally efficient nor ready for the massive influx of enlistees. As a result, the process of raising companies relied on either local or personal initiative. Recruitment rallies in small towns became pressure cookers of masculine bravado where would-be officers used shame to encourage potential recruits to "fight like men" rather than stay home as "shirkers."[32] The Reverend Randolph McKim, who enlisted as a private and later served as a chaplain in the 2nd Virginia Cavalry, recounted the irresistible pull of the period's zeitgeist. "Day after day the spirit of the epoch wrought in me more and more mightily," he wrote, "till I felt that I could no longer resist the call to follow the example of my kindred, my friends, and my fellow students, and enlist in the Southern Army."[33] As a result, Confederate companies were replete with men who had either grown up with each other or were at least familiar with each other.[34] "A unit was composed not of strangers but of friends and relations who had known each other all their lives," Stephen Berry notes. "The privates were all schoolmates; their captain was the local grocer, planter, lawyer, or alderman. They had joined up together; they would see it through together; they were comrades."[35] Even among later enlisters, many enlisted with their neighbors or kin and the preexisting nature of these relationships often led to stronger interpersonal bonds as the war's suffering increased and the need for a sense of safety and familiarity grew.[36]

After enlistment, men were mustered into companies before being sent off to camps of instruction where they would learn the basics of drill and discipline. For the teenaged youths and young men who made up the bulk of early enlisters, camp was their first step toward transforming into men and, eventually, warriors. Some of them probably found themselves asking the same questions as the Reverend William Broaddus, who wondered, "*Here I am,* far from home, and loving friends, and long-cherished associations: from all that makes life dear to me. And why *am I here?*" He reminded himself, among other reasons, that he had a duty to serve. "I owe all this to myself, to my friends, my country," he wrote, "and my God."[37]

Although many men had enlisted with brothers, cousins, brothers-in-law, and sometimes their own fathers and uncles, others were untethered from the familial relationships that had sustained them for years. Since states and the national War Department combined companies from the same state to form new regiments, camps of instruction were regional melting pots of men from differing backgrounds, education, experience, age, class, religion, and morality. Men who might have never wanted to associate with one another were now forced to rely upon each other. The prospects were not always so rosy. As Private George Cary Eggleston of 1st Virginia Cavalry wryly noted, "The composition of the battery in which I served for a considerable time afforded me an opportunity to study some rare characters, of a sort not often met with in ordinary life."[38]

In camps of instruction, young men who eagerly awaited battlefield exploits awoke to one of the starkest and unexpected realities of life in the military: ceaseless monotony. Captain Nathaniel Henry Rhodes Dawson of the 4th Alabama Infantry provided a blueprint for his unit's daily routine, which was like that of most units in the Confederate army: "We are roused daily at 4 o'clock by the beating of reveille; officers drill from 4 ½ o'clock to 7. Breakfast at 7 ½. General inspection at 8. Drill for companies from 9 to 12. Recess from 12 to 2 ½. Drill from 2 ½ to 5 ½. Dress parade at 5 ½. Supper at 6 ½. Roll call at 9. Tattoo at 9 ½ when lights are extinguished, and we are all required to retire."[39]

Likewise, Private Matthew Clanton of the 12th Mississippi Infantry Regiment wrote in February 1862 that the "supposition is we will have plenty of fighting to do then, I hope so, and may god speed the time. I want us to whip out the yankees and come home for I am verry tired of camp life. we have nothing to do but lye up here in camp & make fires and sit by them & that dont suit me I like something more exciting."[40] While soldiers despised the monotony of camp life and drill, their officers understood that continuous drill and harsh discipline were necessary to grind down the cultural and psychological barriers between men. Learning to move in unison through close-order marching developed a sense of collaboration and belonging that melded the individual recruit's identity into a larger cohesive whole.[41]

The physical closeness of drill and camp life also encouraged emotional bonding, which at best developed *esprit de corps* among men. This collective pride was centered on collective accomplishment rather than individual achievement, but this did not necessarily mean that a recruit lost his individuality. As stated before, friendship helped preserve individuality.[42] Carlton McCarthy noted that "the fact that men were in the same company put them somewhat on the same level, and produced an almost perfect bond of sympathy."[43] As the days whittled away in endless rounds of drill, marching, and countermarching, recruits entertained themselves with communal activities including sports, theaters, concerts, practical jokes, and even drinking and gambling. These diversions from the tedium of training not only birthed new friendships but also strengthened old ones, creating a sense of camaraderie among the men. In a letter to his wife, Private John H. Hartman of the 1st North Carolina Artillery reflected this camaraderie, referring to "J. A. Hartman, Mosses, goodman and all that I noad in the redgiment" as his "play mates."[44]

These strong relational bonds did not extend across the board, however. After complaining about the horrors of camp life including "coarse dirty food, dirty blankets and clothes; unwashed linen . . . and the ineradicable camp vermin," Lieutenant Randolph Shotwell of the 8th Virginia Infantry Regiment saved some of his worst complaints for his officers, writing that "perhaps I ought to include the bitter mortification of having to obey in silence the coarse commands of petty upstarts from corporals to captains and colonels, vulgar in speech, manner, and action, but clothed with 'a little brief authority' which gave them opportunity to domineer over men in every respect their superiors." These frustrations "far exceed the mere physical hardships and sufferings."[45]

After transferring from camps of instruction to "field service," soldiers were attached to various brigades, divisions, and armies scattered across the Confederacy. It was here in camp that soldiers spent most of their time with little to do other than drill. In September 1861, Private James R. McCutchan of the 14th Regiment Virginia Cavalry described his frustrations in a letter to his wife, writing that "I despise inaction, I want to be doing something, something that my mind or hands can be employed at. . . . This dismal routine of drilling at little going on guard occasionly & cooking day after day & week after week just kills one."[46] At times, it seems that boredom was the soldier's greatest companion. However, this boredom and the collective nature of military life meant that men had to spend their time playing games, eating together, drilling, and talking, with little room for privacy.

The communal and intimate nature of camp life bred deeply affectionate relationships. Private Sam Watkins of the 1st Tennessee once described his friend "Berry" in glowing terms as a "very handsome boy. He was what everybody would call a 'pretty man.' He had fair skin, blue eyes, and fine curly hair, which made him look like an innocent child. I loved Berry. He was my friend—as true as the needle to the pole."[47] Like Watkins, Private William Abernathy, 17th Mississippi Infantry Regiment, wrote of his friend Billie Echols: "the very thought of him brings a smile. . . . It was a comfort and a solace ever to be near him. . . . He was as ticklish as a woman, though I didn't know how I am going to explain to my wife how ticklish that was, but all the same when I got a little hot, all I had to do was to tickle Billie Echols, and then for the row of us got plenty of stir for a while."[48] While guarding the local camp hospital, Liberty Independence Nixon of the 50th Alabama Infantry Regiment met a "Lieutenant Vaughn" with whom he shared similar moral convictions. "From that time to this," he wrote, "we have been very intimate."[49]

The horizontal relationship between soldiers was also matched by the vertical relationship between soldiers and their officers. Early in the war, the relationship between officers and enlisted men was largely egalitarian. This reflected the democratic zeitgeist of the prewar period, and the relationship between superiors and subordinates was often friendly, despite many would-be martinets. George Cary Eggleston noted that "a feeling of very democratic equality prevailed, so far at least as military rank had anything to do with it . . . so officers and men messed and slept together on terms of entire equality, quarreling and even fighting now and then, in a gentlemanly way, but without thought of allowing differences of military rank to have any influence in the matter."[50] For those who were friends before one's promotion, relatively little was expected to change afterward. After Captain S. Hubert Dent of the 1st Alabama Infantry Regiment helped a friend achieve promotion to the rank of lieutenant, he wrote that his comrade "dislikes the idea of leaving me himself and I think we will still mess together."[51] Letters and diaries from officers also indicate a deep sense of intimacy and connection that developed between them. In 1863, after the death of his beloved friend Colonel Henry King Burgwyn of the 26th North Carolina Infantry Regiment, J. J. Young wrote to Burgwyn's father that "the Col and myself messed together [and] we were more intimately connected than men can possibly be in civil life and I had an insight of his whole character."[52]

In Civil War camps, the group dynamics that bound men to their units also created smaller social cliques within those units. Carlton McCarthy noted that, "as time wore on, the various peculiarities and weaknesses of the men showed themselves, and each company, as a community separated into distinct circles."[53] Men who identified with, and melded themselves into, smaller social groups developed the strongest emotional bonds. While a soldier may have been proud of his regiment, brigade, or division, his strongest bonds were with those in his mess, squad, platoon, or company. The soldier's primary social group was his "mess," which consisted of a voluntary squad of four to eight men with whom one ate, slept, lived, and fought. Individuals took turns preparing meals in rotation and they often dined and socialized together around the campfire.[54] Each member of the mess fulfilled a duty that was designed to serve the other members. Henry C. Semple of Goldthwaite's Battery, Alabama Light Artillery, made note of some of these duties, recounting that "Elmore is the head of our mess, and we live very well. We have good beef, cook Charley is cook and catches a mess of fish every day, Enoch is valet and chamber maid, dining room servant, etc. and Dick takes care of the horses."[55] The divvying up of roles helped maintain equanimity as long as men fulfilled their clearly prescribed communal expectations. In a letter to his father in November 1861, Private William Batts of the 12th Georgia Infantry Regiment recalled that "last night after Supper . . . we called our mess together consisting of 15 men and held a meeting: in which we made a great many by laws: by which the mess all decided to be govern and if we will only carry them out we will get along tolerably well."[56]

In their study of combat motivation in the Iraq War, military researchers Thomas A. Kolditz, Leonard Wong, Raymond A. Millen, and Terrence M. Potter noted that "cohesion is not just developed in training. In the long, often mundane, periods of time spent neither in training or actual combat, the bonds between soldiers are often nurtured . . . much of the cohesion in units is developed simply because there is nothing else to do except talk."[57] Civil War messmates spent considerable time in conversation around the glow of the campfire, where they complained about officers, shared news from home, and conversed about the events of the day.[58] "How good it was to be with the fellows around the fire," Carlton McCarthy recounted, "How companionable was the blaze and the glow of the coals! They warmed the heart as well as the foot!"[59] Likewise, Corporal James T. Jones of the 12th Mississippi Infantry Regiment wrote that after meal time, he and his messmates "built a large fire in front of our tent for the accomodation of our friends whitch has been crowded ever since I arrived."[60] Through conversation and preparing meals for one another, men wove their identities together. Fidelity to one another provided another telling motivation for why soldiers fought in the American Civil War. "Social cohesion is what motivates soldiers not only to perform their job," Kolditz and his co-authors noted, "but also to accept responsibility for the interests of other soldiers."[61]

This "small-unit cohesion" is fundamental to our understanding of the relationships between soldiers during the American Civil War. The mess was in some ways a substitute family where individuals took care of each other and often sought solace in each other.[62] Writing to his wife Rachel in 1862, Private John James Jefcoat of the 20th South Carolina Infantry Regiment told her that "I never can forgit the good friends I have in my mess tha have give me such kinde attention sence I have bin sick I feel greateful toward them for their kind deeds."[63] Likewise, Private Elisha Kindred Flournoy of the 46th Alabama Infantry Regiment wrote to his wife a year later that "when I am sick my mess waits upon me as good as they can and far better than I could expect."[64] In the Confederate army, the lack of proper medical care meant that one's survival often depended on the tender care of a messmate. Camp life offered men a physical and emotional closeness that compared little to most homosocial relationships before the war.

Likewise, one morning after a battle, Sam Watkins's friend Sam Campbell "complained of being cold, and asked me to lie down beside him. I did so and was soon asleep; when I awoke the poor fellow was stiff and cold in death."[65] Unsurprisingly, Campbell sought solace in the physical closeness of his friend. Captain Charles Dobbs, a chaplain in the 12th Mississippi Infantry Regiment, related the similar story of a former druggist who fell ill to violent cramps, most likely due to opium withdrawals. After receiving a bottle of morphine from the camp hospital, he returned to his tent but was soon overwhelmed with pain. His companions, the regimental surgeon, and the regimental chaplain collectively nursed the former druggist through the night. By dawn, he was dead. "It was a sad blow to his many friends," Dobbs wrote, "Those who were killed in battle, or died of disease in the army, were remembered and mourned, with the consolation left to them that they died while on duty. But how sad the reflection of his comrades was that last evening, and what could they write to his friends at home!"[66]

Men also bonded by carousing together. In a letter to his cousin, Private Daniel H. Whitener of the 35th North Carolina Infantry Regiment wrote that there was a "different kind of religion that is in our regiment" which involved "some a cursen and swering some playing cards Some dansing and all kind of foolishness."[67] Likewise, Private Benjamin L. Mobley of Cobb's Georgia Legion wrote to his sister that "Sis I enjoy my Self fine ly we have a dance evre night or two when the fiddle is at home."[68] The shared experience of dancing, playing cards, and listening to music was important in building *esprit de corps*. According to psychologists Bronwyn Tarr, Jacques Launay, and Robin I. M. Dunbar, the experience of listening to music, either passively or through active engagement leads to synchrony (otherwise known as "self-other merging") or neurohormonal mechanisms (primarily in the form of endorphins) which encourage interpersonal bonding. It is like, they note, "that some combination of endorphin release and self-other merging lead to the social bonding effects of music, although the relationship between the two mechanisms remains to be sufficiently explored."[69]

Sometimes, music shared with one's enemies promoted interpersonal connection. Private George K. Evans of the 4th Virginia Cavalry was on picket duty one night in the later summer of 1862, when he heard music coming from nearby Union ships. "I was ¼ of a mile frome any other Videt," he recalled to a friend from a hospital soon after, "and stood two hours one very dark night and listened to the music on the Yankey gun boats which kept me frome being loansome."[70] Even today, men generally build relationships through shared activities. It was no different in the mid-nineteenth century. After the Battle of Fredericksburg, Captain D. A. Dickert of the 3rd South Carolina Infantry Regiment recalled that even in the midst of camp's ennui, "troops abandoned themselves to base ball, snow fights, writing letters, and receiving as guests in their camps friends and relatives, who never failed to bring with them great boxes of the good things from home, as well as clothing and shoes for the needy soldiers."[71]

The nature of the physical closeness between Civil War soldiers has left a few historians wondering how many bled over from homosocial to homosexual relationships. The answer is unclear. Nineteenth-century social mores permitted men to sleep in the same bed together without eliciting questions of their sexuality, and homosexuality only developed as a concept in the latter years of the nineteenth century.[72] Moreover, Civil War soldiers were not prone to share their homosexual experiences with family members or spouses. Even if they had, it is likely that many family members would have destroyed these letters. Aside from the records of occasional court martials, historians can only guess how many men became lovers. None of the letters used in this study either directly or indirectly hinted at homosexual behavior in the camps, but many recount stories of men sleeping together platonically—generally due to a desire to stay warm or the lack of necessary equipment. The inability of the Confederacy to properly clothe, feed, and equip its soldiers meant that many did not have basic necessities like tents or even blankets. At times, they were forced to sleep in the open air, exposed to the ever-shifting extremes of the seasons. In winter, men "spooned" each other for warmth and survival. The idea of "personal space" was virtually nonexistent in the Confederate army from its beginnings.[73] Private Robert Pressly Boyd of the 7th South Carolina Infantry Regiment wrote casually to his family that "we have A Grat Deal off sickness hir Jams Alewine is sick he has Got the Measels & so has Jams simp son & henry Hamton and of Grat Miney outhers i expect to tak them for i Sleep with them every knight."[74] After four days of nonstop rain, Dick Simpson of the 3rd South Carolina Infantry Regiment complained to his aunt that "I have the blues so bad now that I can scarcely live. Everything seems sad and dreary. . . . The last three or four nights have been as cold as we have down South in Nov. We suffered very much with cold, but by crowding together and keeping close we managed to keep tolerable warm."[75] Near the war's end, Private Henry Bowen of the Confederate States Marines wrote to his wife Ann that "we sleep negro fashion on a ledgeing it was too hard for my bones at first but I have got use to it now I and george sleeps to gether and maks out first rate."[76]

As a result of this homosocial bonding, white southern men began to fashion a new definition of masculinity.[77] This redefinition was in part due to the shift from primary-group cohesion, in which an individual's identity is melded into the larger unit, toward small-group cohesion, wherein individuals develop much smaller groups of deeper and more intimate relationships. Men found it easier to identify with smaller groups such as a mess, squad, platoon and company. These are the individuals that they interacted with most often and upon whom their survival often depended. Together, these men took on domestic roles in camp, such as preparing food and caring for the sick—jobs which were previously considered the sole realm of women.[78]

Soldiers also took it upon themselves to support each other through sharing their material bounty. After receiving goods from home, eager soldiers often divided their treasures with those around them. Mail call provided a startling glimpse into the mutual affections that developed between these men. "Occasionally a whole mess would be filled with the liveliest expectations by the information that 'Bob' or 'Joe' was expecting *a box from home*," Carlton McCarthy wrote. "The wagon comes into camp escorted by the expectant 'Bob' and several of his intimate friends. . . . It is evident one man cannot eat the eatables or smoke the tobacco and pipes. Call in, then, the friendly aid of wiling comrades. They come; they see; they devour."[79]

⁓⊰⊱⁓

For many soldiers, religion also played a decisive role in shaping their motivations. Religion, too, provided a sense of comfort and security. Historian George C. Rable noted that "religion undoubtedly helped sustain morale and lengthen the war, a point recognized by even the indifferent and the skeptical."[80] If prewar ideals of masculinity emphasized self-mastery, war imploded this ideal. An enlisted soldier was never his own master. Life in the military was highly regimented. Men were forced to submit to the nearly absolute authority of their superior officers. Moreover, death occurred with such randomness that one never really knew if he was going to be the next one to die. Fatal disease lurked everywhere and it often struck suddenly. Private Alfred N. Profitt of the 18th North Carolina Infantry Regiment, for example, wrote to his sister Rachel on the death of their brother that "the doctor who attended him in his last hours said it was an inflamationn of the brain he had not been sick but 3 or 4 dayes and had not been bad of untill a few hours before he died he had been able to walk a bout and do his cooking untill the night before he died he complained of his head and brest."[81]

Bullets also killed indiscriminately. After the Battle of Fredericksburg, Private James C. Zimmerman of the 57th North Carolina Infantry Regiment recalled the casualties in his company, writing that "we nearly lost all our company out of fifty eight over half was killed or wounded" and that he was near death himself when "one bullet passed through my hat and one cut my blanket on my sholder."[82] Private Jesse M. Frank of the 48th North Carolina Infantry Regiment wrote the following spring of the uncertainty of a soldier's life: "life is so un certain and deth is shure we know not when it will come some die suddenly in camp some on the battle field and others are yet on the land of the living and on mercies side of eternity so let us live each day as if we expected it to be the last." For Private Frank, his relationship with God was one of his few comforts; he wrote that "we hav prayer meeting in the brigade evry day preaching evry night and preaching of Sundays it is agreate privilege we hav it strengthens me greatly against the wites of the devel and fits me more for prayer to love the name of Jesus."[83]

Many Confederate soldiers turned to God for solace and strength. In the words of historian Douglas Southall Freeman, religion "robbed the minié of its terror" and imparted "a faith that defied the battle."[84] Likewise, historian Dillon J. Carroll saw religion as a critical method of coping with combat as "the thought that an omnipotent God controlled all events—even on the battlefield—helped troopers make sense of why they survived and others died; it further helped make veterans feel safe and led them to believe that God would ensure their safety in future conflicts."[85] In the source base used for this project, 90 out of 200 soldiers sampled (45 percent) made references to God or religious declarations. Of the 1,790 total letters, only 332 made references to God or religious declarations (18.55 percent). This was far less than the 164 soldiers (82 percent) and 1,182 letters that expressed emotion or affection (66.03 percent), or the 64 soldiers (32 percent) who wrote 525 letters with inquiries or references to their children (29.33 percent). Religion seemed somewhat less important to the common soldier as compared to their families and loved ones. Religion was also referenced more often in the sample than descriptions of battle or references to ideology or duty. Men such as Hiram Talbert Holt of the 38th

Alabama Infantry Regiment epitomized the ideal "Christian soldier" who, in the words of historian Robert Partin, "carried his faith with him into the army, he lived by it, he fought by it, and he died by it; and unquestionably his faith had a profound influence upon Holt as a fighting man. . . . His personal faith had always been his chief support in time of hardship and danger and—insofar as he was sustained by religion—it became after mid-summer 1863 his only one."[86]

On the battlefield, soldiers witnessed the random destruction of human life at the hands of other men. Witnessing this inhumanity, taking part in it, and experiencing immense suffering themselves, soldiers often turned to religion, seeking hope and meaning in the midst of chaos. While Evangelicalism reshaped emotional norms before the war and during the war, its emphasis on an individual's personal relationship with, and dependence upon, God continued to erode the masculine ideal of self-sufficiency and self-mastery. Realizing that they could not control their own circumstances or possible demise, many surrendered to the will of God. Private Simeon Skinner of Cobb's Legion (Georgia) wrote to his sister in January 1862 of his nephews and the need for religion in the camp, stating, "tell them not to forgit to put thare truste in God and to remember that we all remember them at a throne of Gods grace who is able to comfort the soldier on th fielde of battle as well as those who are at home I see more cause for religion now than I ever have befor religion is almoste for gotten here it is almost as bad hear as a heathense country."[87]

Religion also offered another avenue for interpersonal development by binding men of differing personalities and temperaments together under one umbrella of belief. The individual around whom these connections were formed was typically the regimental chaplain. Unfortunately, few clerics or priests volunteered for the chaplaincy due to the low pay, physical hardship, and doctrinal issues among denominations. When present, chaplains preached weekly messages and facilitated Bible study and prayer meetings that brought men together. These services often included administering sacraments and singing hymns, reflecting their commingled feelings of uncertainty and faith in *unum unita*. When chaplains were not present, individual soldiers often took it upon themselves to lead religious meetings. Whether led by chaplains or laymen, these meetings often evinced intense emotional and spiritual fervor, the expression of soldiers' inmost thoughts and feelings, and sometimes even tears.[88] Evangelicalism normalized the expression of emotion and encouraged vulnerability. It is thus no surprise that religious revivals in the Confederate army promoted vast swaths of emotional effusion.

In her study of Italian soldiers' emotions in World War I, historian Vanda Wilcox noted that "a legitimate language for the expression of intense emotion . . . was provided by religion" and that "more often religious faith and practice acted as a source of metaphor and imagery." Tension between the fear of death and promises of faith allowed men to express how they felt without the stigma of appearing weak.[89] Faith opened the door to greater emotional expression while simultaneously encouraging soldiers to lay their lives in the hands of God; it provided a prophylactic against a soldier's emotional hardening. In this vein, the Reverend John E. Edwards of North Carolina wrote, "You are in great danger of becoming hardened under your sufferings. There is a foolish notion, too prevalent among soldiers, that it is unmanly to manifest any *feeling* under the pressure of bereavement or mental distress—that it is unsoldierly to exhibit any emotion under the most excruciating pain—that it is womanly and childish to weep. Too many have made up their minds that a profession of religion is incompatible with the profession of arms. This is all a mistake." Indeed, as Edwards later noted, this suffering would only continue as the war stretched on.[90]

⁘

War enveloped men in a world detached from many of the social mores that gave society order, decency, and security. If unchecked, this detachment could lead to dissociation and the erosion of one's sense of self as well as one's empathy toward others. Repeated exposure to killing could, at times, lead one to embrace unhealthy attachments. One night, George Eggleston and a couple of fellow officers came across two men fighting—one holding a butcher knife and the other with a deep cut in his neck. While Eggleston and his cohort tried to bind the knife-wielding man, the victim arose, picked up a brick, and tried to bash in the head of his attacker. Eggleston asked why the man had attempted to kill his friend. Pointing to the gash on his neck, the man replied: "Don't ye see I'm a dead man, captain? An' sure an' *do you think I'm goin to hell without me pardoner?*"[91]

Combat provided an impetus to emotional expression which belied a shift in the relationships between men. Historians' assertions of the preeminence of self-mastery and individualism during the war seem to be based more on prewar masculine norms rather than the period of the war itself, in which soldiers faced new stimuli and were forced to approach cultural norms with a greater sense of pragmatism. The source base for this project indicates that some of these masculine norms were eschewed by many Confederate soldiers. Though most soldiers likely never lost all of their belief in these norms, they were not often displayed in their letters. Out of the 200 soldiers sampled, more men expressed emotion, made religious declarations, or inquired about their children than those who recounted their experiences in battle. Battle was the proving ground for one's mastery of self as well as the opportunity to demonstrate one's manly courage. Why not boast about it in their letters, then? Perhaps these soldiers were simply trying to protect their families from the grisly details of battle. But the letters that do mention battles are extremely vivid and often unflinching in their exposition of the writer's nearness to death. Perhaps, soldiers preferred to share these details with those who could recognize and understand their experience, such as their comrades. Shared suffering and a mutual sense of fear drew these men closer together through experiences that their civilian counterparts could not understand. "Plenty of marching, plenty of common hardships, and not a little fighting," Randolph McKim wrote, "quickly made us good friends."[92] Likewise, D. A. Dickert of the 3rd South Carolina Infantry Regiment noted the emotional resolve that came from his comrades, writing that "the soldier is not the cold unfeeling, immovable animal that some people seem to think he is. . . . His love and sympathy for his fellow-soldier is proverbial in the army. In the lull, of battle, or on its eve, men with bold hearts and strong nerves look each other in the face with grim reliance."[93] In the smack of lead against flesh or bone, in the boom of a nearby cannon, and in the horror of every fallen friend, the rigid walls of prewar masculine individuality crumbled under the felt need to allow oneself to express one's emotions and to seek succor in doing so with others.

For Colonel C. M. Avery of the 33rd North Carolina Infantry Regiment, the Battle of Gettysburg was a moment in which his individualism and self-sufficiency imploded. Writing to the father of a fallen comrade, Avery recounted that "we advanced to within forty yards of the Enemys work and it was here that my little friend Jonny fell. I saw him but a few moments before we were ordered to fall back discharging his whole duty. You cannot imagine my feelings after reforming my Rgt to find him absent and upon being told that he was seen to fall forward on his face." This "loss of my little friend," he wrote, "is to me one of the most distressing incidents of the war. His noble nature in a short time had won from my bosom the warmest affection."[94]

During another battle, Private Sam Watkins had just finished killing two men and was reloading when a Union soldier suddenly rushed upon him, exclaiming "You have killed my two brothers, and now I've got you." Stunned, Watkins could only watch helplessly as the Union soldier leveled his musket and began pulling the trigger. Just then, Watkins's friend William Hughes grabbed the muzzle of the gun and as smoke and fire poured forth from the musket, Hughes received the full force of the blast, shredding his hand and arm. Later, Watkins recalled Hughes as "my old mess-mate and friend, who had clerked with me . . . and who slept with me for lo! [He was] a boy who loved me more than any other person on earth has ever done." As Watkins watched him die, Hughes gave Sam his weapon and his belongings before finally succumbing to his wounds. "He gave up his life for me," Watkins lamented, "and everything that he had. It was the last time that I ever saw him."[95] Remembering his dear friend "Spratling," Private Louis J. Dupre of the 62nd Alabama Infantry Regiment recounted that they relied "upon the other as confidently as upon himself, and each having often imperiled his life that the other might live; inseparable as Spratling and I had been from the hour that Jefferson Davis lighted the match at Fort Sumter that set a nation aflame; made friends by common toils and dangers and by indestructible confidence."[96]

After the first harrowing experience of battle, many soldiers confronted the fact that their lives could be snuffed out on a distant battlefield, far from their families. And yet according to the Victorian ideal of the "Good Death," one's final moments were an opportunity for family and friends to witness the deceased's eternal direction—either to salvation or damnation. It was believed that the nature of the individual's death (whether it was peaceful or not) provided evidence of the direction of one's soul after death. Those who died peacefully were believed to be entering heaven while those who exhibited terror in death were bound for hell. Either way, death was considered a family affair.

The war ripped the dying soldier from his family. The vast distance between family members meant that the ritual of the "Good Death" needed alteration. In this enactment of the "Good Death," soldiers replaced family members with comrades who were expected to be by their side in their final moments. After their expiration, one's comrades were expected to provide the details of his death to his family to assure them of his peaceful passing and evident salvation.[97] This is one of the many pragmatic approaches taken by Confederate soldiers in the American Civil War. It is reflective of their willingness to reshape cultural norms to fit the needs of the moment. Even though they were absent from blood family, they could enter the afterlife with the next best thing by their side—a sort of chosen kin.

At no point did these relationships prove to be more necessary than in the immediate aftermath of battle. After the First Battle of Manassas, Private Green B. Samuels of the 10th Virginia Infantry Regiment wrote to his wife, "The hardest trial to one's nerves is the sight of the wounded and the dead; in many cases the agony of the wounded was awful and their pitying cries for water heart-rending . . . some had evidently died in awful agony, with distorted faces, glaring eyes and clenched hands. I will write no more of this awful scene; it makes me sick to think of it."[98] After the Battle of Gettysburg, Private T. J. Hodnett of the 13th Georgia Infantry Regiment recounted the moment that his file leader was shot down in front of him during the battle: "He look up in my fase and Sed Jeffy I am hit take me way, you cant tell how it made me feel to leave him thare," he wrote, "but I was a blige to do it we wasent a lowed to S[t]op to carry of[f] the wounded after we was halted." After the battle, Hodnett lamented, "Oh what a Sene to See the wounded the dead the diing Oh my God how long Shal this wor last the lord only nows I thaut wonce that maby So it might clos this fall but now I havent no hopes of it."[99]

Intimate homosocial bonds were developed by sharing the burden of adversity. The incommunicable experience of battle gave soldiers a unique understanding that almost no civilian could comprehend. The overwhelming emotions generated by participating in and surviving combat allowed soldiers to develop empathy for one another as they were able to place themselves in others' shoes and understand each other's feelings. If manliness was equated with self-control, then the inability to control one's fears or anxieties would surely mean that you were not a man. At least, that would be the case in times of peace. Yet those who experienced combat often felt a certain tenderness and compassion for those around them who shared their fears and ameliorated their anxieties. Soldiers often formed strong attachments which provided a sense of security and gave them the wherewithal to do things that they themselves may not have had the strength to do on their own. In effect, the empathy generated by this shared burden of suffering often brought out the very best and noblest characteristics in those who, evolutionarily speaking, should have reverted to their natural animal instinct for self-preservation. After the Battle of Cold Harbor in June 1864, Private George Robertson of the 17th Mississippi Infantry Regiment received a furlough for shooting down the Stars and Stripes in the enemy's trenches. Not long after, one of his comrades received a letter from home that one of his children had died from typhoid fever, that his other two children were on the verge of death, and that his family was financially destitute. Robertson "handed his furlough to his comrade, took his place behind the breastworks," and in the words of witness William Abernathy, "acquitted himself like a man." Robertson, was like many of his fellow soldiers who, Abernathy noted, "longed for the embrace of a loving mother and to feel the fathers hand in blessing on him," but he was willing to sacrifice those prospects for a fellow soldier who understood and experienced his own suffering.[100]

Likewise, after the death of his fellow comrades at the First Battle of Bull Run, Captain Nathaniel Henry Rhodes Dawson of the 4th Alabama Infantry Regiment recounted to his sweetheart the scene in camp after battle:

> Our chaplain, Mr. Chadwick, who was in the late battle and had his clothes cut by several balls, delivered a most touching and feeling prayer, and when he alluded to our dead and wounded comrades, he was choked to suffocation, hardly able to express himself, and in the large assembly of bronzed and bearded soldiers, you could see almost every eye and cheek furrowed with big tears. It is singular how much attached we become when thrown together as we are in military life without knowing it. When I stood alone at the grave of our four killed men, I cannot express the feeling of my heart. It was akin to the feelings when I have stood at night and knelt at the tomb of one in whose existence my life has been wrapped. I prayed for the presence of the dead and desired to sink into the same grave.[101]

Modern sociological literature indicates that social cohesion born of shared experience "is positively correlated with psychological well-being and negatively correlated with psychological distress."[102] In fact, this social support may provide a stress-buffering effect that enables soldiers to endure high-stress conditions.[103] In many of the primary source materials used for this project, this certainly seems to be the case.

The empathy generated by shared experiences could also at times extend to one's enemies. At the Second Battle of Manassas, Wayland Dunaway of the 40th Virginia Infantry Regiment was reconnoitering the front when he came across a wounded and dying Union officer. Begging for water, the Union officer's plight moved Dunaway to kneel down and give the man a drink of water from his own canteen. As the light faded from the Union soldier's eyes, the officer nobly surrendered his sword to Dunaway who then warned him that he had "better retire, because our men will soon be here again." The Union officer then warned a stunned Dunaway that he himself was in danger from a Union counterattack. "He was thirsty, and I gave him drink," Dunaway later recalled, "I was in danger, and he gave me friendly warning."[104] Torn apart by politics and ideology, the two men shared what Oliver Wendell Holmes Jr. later called "the incommunicable experience of war."[105] It was this shared experience that ultimately enabled them to have empathy for one another.

In her study of altruism and suffering, psychologist Johanna Ray Vollhardt noted that in many modern social-psychological circles, there is "a commonly held view . . . that altruism and prosocial behavior originate in positive experiences and processes, whereas antisocial behavior is often rooted in negative conditions and life experiences." This view may be rooted in the fact that most research in clinical psychology has focused on the negative effects of traumatic events in order to develop new treatment methods. Fellow psychologist Ervin Staub has coined the term "altruism born of suffering," which describes "how individuals who have suffered may become particularly motivated to help others—not only despite their difficult experiences but precisely because of them."[106] This leads to a shift in perspective in which suffering becomes "a source of intense empathy/sympathy for others in need, and of an increased prosocial orientation, a central aspect of which is a feeling of personal responsibility for others' welfare."[107] In other words, trauma and suffering can often lead an individual to channel their pain into helping and caring for others.

Whether through friendship or comradery, the deepening bonds between men in the Civil War helped lessen the deleterious effects of combat on the individual's psyche by dispersing the burden of success across a much broader swath of individuals. These relationships provided a sense of security in the knowledge that each man was working for the protection of the other. Facing suffering together often encouraged this reciprocity and trust. The emotional intimacy birthed by this shared suffering was often difficult to explain to others.[108] D. A. Dickert of the 3rd South Carolina Infantry Regiment, for example, wrote, "As a guard, we watched over our friends; as a picket, we watched for our foe." Just before a Union scouting party overran his camp, he wrote, "All felt a perfect security, for with the pickets in front, the cavalry scouring the country, and the almost impassable barricades of the roads, seemed to render it impossible for an enemy to approach unobserved."[109]

Soldiers recognized early on that they shared responsibility for each other's survival. When Private Billie Echols of the 17th Mississippi Infantry Regiment heard that a friend was wounded and slowly bleeding to death in a rifle pit north of his position, Echols and his friend Jim Crawford grabbed a litter and jumped over the parapet of their trench, heading north under withering fire to find their friend. While their comrades laid down covering fire, Echols and Crawford found their wounded friend and loaded him on to a litter before rushing back to the trenches. Thanks to the love of his comrades, the man survived. Before regular medical details were established, the responsibility for evacuating a wounded soldier often rested, literally, on the shoulders of his friends. Even though officers usually tried to prevent men from leaving their ranks during battle, many privates would do so anyways to help a comrade. So strong were the bonds between men that rushing to the aid of friends sometimes depleted the ranks even more than losses from those killed or wounded in battle.[110]

The deep bonds that developed between soldiers, however, could also lead to negative mutual influences. The emotional tensile strength of these relationships sometimes drew soldiers into committing acts that would have never seemed comprehensible before the war. Soldiers who share close bonds with their comrades might take part in killing out of a fear of letting their friends down—particularly if their mutual survival depends upon each other. In his book *On Killing,* Dave Grossman discovered that by couching the act of killing in groups, members often develop a sense of battlefield anonymity that exacerbates the level of violence that they inflict upon their enemies. He found that the size of the social group, coupled with the depth of its psychological bonding and physical proximity, directly correlated with an increase in both the ability and willingness of the individual to kill.[111]

Soldiers sometimes lived with the fear that an unwillingness to kill could inevitably lead to the death of their comrades. This fear was exacerbated by the regular loss of one's friends and comrades. As Lieutenant Colonel Charles A. Derby of the 44th Alabama Infantry Regiment wrote to his sister, "The war seems to be dormant precisely at this time. How long it will be before it rouses from its lethargy, I have no idea. My intimate friends and neighbors have suffered dreadfully. Many of them have been killed and many are dangerously wounded. It makes my heart sick to think of it."[112] Derby himself would be counted among the dead just two months later at the Battle of Antietam. Although friendship and comradery often gave men psychological and emotional strength, for others the opposite could sometimes ring true. For those whose sense of right and wrong was bent by their suffering, the power of group dynamics sometimes severed the tethers between an individual and his moral beliefs. Relationships, and the emotions that they engendered, were just *that* powerful.

In most cases, however, homosocial relationships protected soldiers from the erosion of their individuality and their sense of humanity and empathy. The more dangerous the situation and the more desperate their survival, the more likely soldiers were to cling to one another. Nowhere was this more evident than in the lives of those unfortunate enough to become prisoners of war. In the sample for this project, 25 out of the 200 soldiers (12.5 percent) could be identified as prisoners of war at some point. If soldiers thought that they get a respite from the tedium of camp and the terror of battle in prison, they were sorely mistaken. A Civil War prison camp represented one of the most hellish experiences that one could endure. The sights, sounds, and smells of prison camps were often overwhelming to the point that new enrollees vomited at the sight of emaciated bodies and the stench of feces and body odor enveloped their senses. When sanitation deteriorated, often due to overcrowding or a lack of funding, few men bothered to use the latrines, opting instead to urinate and defecate just outside of their quarters.[113] Prisons crawled with lice, rats, and mice that literally fed off human subjects. Cut off from their families and many of their friends, some prisoners lost all interest in life and camp surgeons began to list "nostalgia"—that is, homesickness—as a principal cause for many of their deaths.

For those captured, separation from their comrades and friends was jarring. "Where are my most intimate friends? Those with whom I had formed ties of friendship never to be broken," prisoner William Heartsill of the 2nd Texas Cavalry wrote in his journal. "I alone am left to find other; but never truer friends." One of these friends, Charlie Carter, was one whom Heartsill "loved as a brother."[114] Languishing in the Union prison camp at Johnson's Island in Ohio, Private William Tilmon Bishop of the 16th Alabama Infantry Regiment wrote to his wife that "I have been looking for a letter from you for Some time but in vain for I have not received one from you Since I have been in prison this is the 4th one I have wrote to you you can not imagin how anxious I am to here from you. for I am verry lonesome here for there is but 2 men here that I ever Saw before."[115]

Soldiers in prison camps were stuck with nowhere to go. Rather than facing a relatively quick death from combat, many now faced a slow and agonizing death from disease or malnutrition. As was the case outside of prison, survival depended on building strong relationships with others. Sometimes, if a soldier was particularly lucky, he could find himself imprisoned with hometown acquaintances or members of the same unit. After his capture at the Battle of Baker's Creek, Mississippi, Lieutenant William J. Samford of the 46th Alabama Infantry Regiment was imprisoned at Johnston's Island. He was delighted when William J. Slaton—a Confederate officer and his old college professor—arrived at Johnston's Island as a prisoner. While in prison, William continued his studies under Professor Slaton until his eventual release in 1864.[116]

For most men, imprisonment represented the shattering of old relationships and the construction of new ones. Without these relationships, the individual's will to survive greatly decreased. At Elmira Prison, Private Berry Benson of the

1st South Carolina Infantry Regiment complained that "the bunks were made of unplanned pine boards, and as we had no blankets, they were left bare during the day, and at night occupied simply by ourselves. Later Baxter [his friend] was given a blanket and piece of cloth by a friend, and these he shared with me."[117] Not only did comrades provide emotional support, but they also provided physical support as well. Men like William Heartsill had not lost their humanity and their concern for each other. "It is heart rending to listen to the moans and supplications of the sick during the long cold hours of the night," he wrote, "and to know that it is out of our power to relieve them." And yet Heartsill awoke one night to a scene of incredible tenderness between his fellow prisoners. "About one oclock last night I was awakened by a cry of distress," he wrote; "a man was freezing to death; his comrads done all they could for their suffering fellow-soldier, but disease and cold have done their work."[118] Likewise, as a prisoner at Johnson's Island, Wayland Dunaway of the 40th Virginia Infantry Regiment noted that "the nursing was performed by the patients' more intimate friends, who took it by turns day and night." As he stayed up one night with his captain to administer medication, he remembered that "the ward was silent save for occasional groans, the lights were burning dimly, and there was no companion watching with me." At midnight, the "emaciated sufferer" died. Dunaway recounted that he "closed his eyes and remained near the body until the grateful dawn of morning. Guarded by soldiers we went to the cemetery without the walls, and committed the body to the ground, far away from his family and native land."[119]

Those who eschewed traditional masculine norms of male individuality and self-sufficiency instead became members of surrogate families that worked for each other's survival. If one member of a social clique was assigned to a work detail, he would often ask for special privileges or obtain positions for friends. This could be as small as "sneaking extra bread back home if he worked in the bakery, an extra stick or two of wood if he was in a gathering detail, or a clothing item if he worked in the burial detail."[120] Sociologists Dora Costa and Matthew Kahn studied the potential benefits of social networks on Union prisoners of war in Confederate prison camps. They postulated that the primitive nature of prison camps, with their lack of law enforcement, property rights, formal markets, and subsistence income, rendered social networks vital to survival. In numerous diaries they found that prisoners' friends provided moral support that helped them to avoid depression, meet material needs, care for the sick, and discourage suicide. Their study proved conclusively that friendship greatly increased one's chances of survival and that the closer the friends became, the greater their chances of surviving imprisonment.[121]

As was the case in camp, prisoners resorted to entertainment as a distraction from their mundane existence. They formed makeshift debate societies, local governments, created classes, held dances, hosted music performances, played dice, marbles, ball games, backgammon, checkers, and more. Most of all, as in camp, they wove their identities together through conversation. The "meeting of old friends and comrades, and the making of new acquaintances," wrote prisoner James Williamson—a pro-secession civilian from Maryland—"is a source of great pleasure to use and a relief from the monotony of what could otherwise be a dull routine of prison life."[122] In their conversations, men told stories, reminisced about home and good food, plotted their survival, and debated the possibility of exchange, the war's end, or escape.[123]

<hr/>

Whether in camps, on the battlefield, in a hospital, or trapped in a prison, Confederate soldiers looked to each other to endure the most cataclysmic war the young Republic had ever known. In 1861, many men marched off to war with visions of battlefield glory that soon melted in the heat of combat. The desire to prove one's masculinity instead gave way to the more basic will to survive. By "outlasting the war," soldiers could return to their parents, their wives, their sweethearts, and their children—the very people for whom they fought. Individual effort would fail them, however. Soon, they discovered that their survival hinged on collective support and mutual aid. However, these men found that they needed much more than mere physical support from those they loved. With the support of their wives, sweethearts, and comrades, soldiers found the emotional strength to keep serving and fighting. But for many men, the will to fight found its strongest basis in the love that they held for their children. In the minds of many, they were fighting for a better world for their children. To give up and go home would be to betray the very individuals who they were tasked, as men, with protecting.

CHAPTER 4

STORGE
AND
STEADFASTNESS
HOW FAMILIAL LOVE ENCOURAGED
CONTINUED CONFLICT

On a hot, muggy day in August 1861, Private Asa T. Martin of the 12th Alabama Infantry Regiment felt deep anguish over being separated from his wife and children. "I wood like to sea you and the children very much," he wrote. "I want to know if William and sis has forgotten me or not I would like to sea them[.] I saw a little girl in richmond before we left there it made me think of home."[1] Longing for the comforts of home and the embrace of his family, Martin's mind was not focused on the battlefield or even the Confederate cause. Instead, Martin's sorrow was rooted in the anxiety produced by the separation from his family and by his latent fear that his children had forgotten him. One of the most common fears evinced in Confederate soldiers' letters is that their children would not remember them. Many were very young when their fathers marched off to war and, understanding the fickle emotions of children, soldier-fathers often feared that they would not be remembered or, even worse, that their children would not care that they were gone.

In August 1862, Sergeant Isaac Lefevers of the 46th North Carolina Infantry Regiment arrived at his new camp outside Richmond, Virginia. Union forces under Major General George B. McClellan had almost captured the city during the Peninsula Campaign before Confederate general Robert E. Lee assumed command of the Army of Northern Virginia. Quickly repelling Union forces during the Seven Days Battles in June and July, McClellan was soon forced to retreat. Though Lefevers would be expected to bask in the glow of his army's great victory, his letters indicate that his mind was instead turned towards his wife and children. "It gave mee great sattefacton for all to hear you & the little children was all well and that buds pig was getting fat," he wrote. "I want him to keep it up till I come home & feed it good & make a big hog till paw comes home & then we will kill it." Lefevers then described his unceasing thoughts of his children and his longing for home, writing that "I Dremp of Bud last night I thought I saw him as plane as ever I did in my life I thout that I saw his purty little head Dear wife I have dremp of you & the childrean often since I have bin in camp but I dont now what is the Reasen I have dremp oftener of bud then enny of the other childrean & I now I would like to see them all."[2]

When Martin, Lefevers, and their fellow comrades enlisted, they could not have imagined the sheer scale of destruction to come. The size of armies and the loss of life were more akin to wars of the ancient world or the multicountry European wars of times past. In America, the colonial frontier wars, the French and Indian War, and the American Revolutionary War were comparatively smaller in scale and military service emphasized traditional European norms of martial glory, honor, individual liberty, and duty. Yet the visceral horror and scale of battle—the sickening thud of lead smacking flesh, the acrid smell of black powder, and the sight of men writhing in the last throes of their existence—turned the American Civil War from an abstract struggle for liberty into a concrete struggle for survival. The convergence of outdated tactics and relatively new technology, coupled with military commanders of questionable skill, meant that more human beings would die during the American Civil War than in all other previous American wars combined. Moreover, they would die in far more horrific and impersonal ways.

Facing this horror was emotionally overwhelming for everyone involved. Generally, only socio- or psychopaths would feel a lack of revulsion at the deaths (and manner of deaths) of those in battle. It did not matter that they were strangers. They were still human beings. But the loss of those for whom one held strong attachments was even more harrowing, and thus it is no surprise that men found combat emotionally overwhelming. Though they were supposed to be emotionally staid, the truth is that many men longed for an emotional and, in some instances, physical escape. Men sought emotional escape by sharing their experiences with each other and by sharing their feelings with those back home through letters. Others sought physical escape through desertion. Either way, soldiers faced the insatiable pull of home and the desire for physical and emotional connection with their loved ones.

In particular, it seems that fathers may have felt the emotional pull of home more strongly than their wedded but childless comrades. The deeper the emotional connection, the harder the pull towards home.

For Confederate soldier-fathers, letters exchanged with their wives are replete with questions either directed toward, or about, their children. Of the 200 soldiers sampled for this project, 82 were married (41 percent) and, of these, 65 were identified from their letters as having children (representing 79.27 percent of those who were married and 32.5 percent of the whole sample). All 65 fathers expressed emotion (100 percent), 64 made references to their children (98.46 percent), 50 made religious declarations (76.92 percent), 23 described battle (35.38 percent), and 18 expressed notions of ideology or duty (27.69 percent). Out of a total 1,790 letters sampled, 524 included inquiries or references to their children (representing 29.27 percent). In my sample, the 65 soldiers who were identified as fathers wrote a combined 1,055 letters out of 1,790 (58.94 percent), which indicates that married fathers were the most communicative group in the sample. Or at the very least, that their wives were most likely to preserve their letters. This statistic may represent survivor bias as those with children may have wanted to preserve the letters for their progeny. Additionally, of the 1,055 letters written by soldier-fathers, 777 (73.65 percent) expressed emotion or affection, 524 (49.67 percent) made inquiries or references to their children, 235 (22.27 percent) contained religious declarations or references to God, 45 (4.27 percent) included descriptions of battles, and 40 (3.79 percent) contained expressions of ideology or duty. Clearly, much like soldier-husbands, soldier-fathers were far more expressive of their emotions than their single counterparts, and much of this was directed toward their children.

The letters written by fathers to their wives and children for this project indicate that Confederate soldier-fathers felt deeply for their progeny. Though it is commonly thought that "gentle parenting" or "emotional tenderness" is a relatively recent phenomena, the reality is that in the letters for this project, nineteenth-century American fathers were often extraordinarily tender toward their children. The love that they felt for their offspring was so strong that many saw their military service as an extension of their masculine duty to protect their families and children. The world that they were creating—albeit one rooted in white supremacy and the protection of the institution of slavery—was one in which protecting the old pre-industrial racial and economic order would enable their children's flourishing. This, many believed, was worth the sacrifice of their own lives.

In the summer of 1862, Private Asa T. Martin of the 12th Alabama Infantry Regiment lay dying in a Richmond hospital. Mortally wounded at the Battle of Seven Pines, he discovered that the amputation of his arm left him unable to write to his family. He had to rely upon his nurse, Mrs. B. F. McGruder, to write to his wife and children. Eventually, as his health deteriorated, Mrs. McGruder began to write to Martin's wife on her own volition. In one letter, she wrote that "he would talk to me of you all and said he could not bear the idea of going home with one arm and his eyes would fill with tears spoke of his mother and a tall sister he had of his parents and yours." Though Martin had probably participated in, and witnessed, the taking of life, he clearly was not emotionally hardened to the point of becoming unfeeling. His unique position as a husband and father may have helped keep his heart tender. Mrs. McGruder recounted that, lying in bed suffering from "chills and fever," Martin "heard a child crying on the street," and "he asked me if it was possible he could hear one cry again said it had been so long since he had seen one or heard it cry one little one came in to the hospital and up to his bed he put out his arm and drew it to him that was enough to soften the heart of stone. I know he was a kind affectionate husband and father."[3]

Private Martin lived within a paradox faced by all soldiers during the American Civil War. On the one hand, they witnessed and often partook in the extremity of human violence and moral degradation, while on the other they sought to maintain their own tenderness toward those whom they loved. These relationships provided a safe arena in which they could express these emotions and thus keep the tender part of themselves alive. One soldier, ruminating on the future, wrote to his sister: "Society will not own the rude soldier when he comes back, but turn a cold shoulder to him because he has become hardened by scenes of bloodshed and carnage." But this was not the whole story, as he explained to her, "I tell you, dear sister, there are feelings, tender feelings, deep down in the soldier's breast, which when moved will prove that all that is good is not quite dead."[4]

In the Union and Confederacy combined, historians estimate that almost 40 percent of military-age (age 13 to 43 in 1860) white males served in the armed forces.[5] In his sample of the Army of Northern Virginia, historian Joseph Glatthaar found that in the 1860 census, "3 of every 8 (37.5 percent) soldiers in the sample were married, and 5 of every 8 (62.5 percent) were single" and that "a bit more than 3 in 10 (30 percent) men had children at home. By the time they entered the army that proportion would have increased slightly as well."[6] These numbers are slightly lower than the sample for this project, which reveals that 82 out of 200 (41 percent) of the men sampled were married (compared with 37.5 percent of Glatthaar's), 7 out of 200 (3.5 percent) were courting, and 111 out of 200 (55.5 percent) were single (compared with 62.5 percent for Glatthaar's). If one counts those who were courting along with those who were single, the number is much closer to Glatthaar's figures, with 118 out of 200 (59 percent) being counted as single. Of those who were married, 65 out of 200 total soldiers had children, representing 32.5 percent of the overall sample size—a number very close to that of Glatthaar's, which was 30 percent. Thus, in terms of sample sizes, the source base for this project closely mirrors that of Glatthaar's much larger sample from the Army of Northern Virginia. Thus, the findings of this study may be applicable on a much larger scale.

In this sample, one of the most striking findings was the large number of letters in which fathers openly lamented the absence of their children. "I waunt to See you and the children verry Bad But I am two far off to Come to See you," Corporal Ebenezer Coggin of the 47th Alabama Infantry Regiment wrote to his wife in June 1862, "though I havant forgot you Nor I Never Shal my heart is fild with greif and my eyes with tears to think that we ar so far apart that I Cannot see you and my Sweet little children."[7] In an age of masculine stoicism, soldier-fathers often went against the grain of social expectations. "I hope that God will give power to Conquer our enama and we will all return home to our wifes and dear little Children on harmed," Private Wilburn Thompson of the 56th Georgia Infantry Regiment wrote to his wife; "I want you to wright to me whether you did get aney of mi oates saived or not dear wif you dont no how bad i want to sea you and the Children I wish i was thar to kiss that sweat little babe i want you to kiss the Children for me tha ant minut pases mi memory be what i think of you and the Children."[8] "I want yo to take car of al yor pervisians take car of the children and yor Self and never forgit me," Private James E. Wesson likewise wrote to his wife Rachel in January 1863. "I Se a hard time her I rit these lines with tears in my eyes if eny of the children gits Sick I want yo to rit to me as Son as yo can. I Want yo to rit to me as Son as yo can I want to hear from yo So bad that I dont no what to do I have shed meny tears since I left yo."[9]

These examples are reflective of the increasing acceptability of emotional expression during the war. Though anecdotal, in the light of the statistics for this project, it is clear that emotional stoicism was much easier to abide by in times of peace rather than war. Moreover, the expression of these feelings did not seem to evince any perceived degradation of an individual's manhood. Civil War soldiers were pragmatic and willing to shift normative standards, especially when it came to protecting those that they loved. Perhaps no other motivation spurred these soldier-fathers more than the belief that they were making a better world for their children. The letters exchanged between soldiers and their families were often emotionally intense (by Victorian standards) and they may have grown stronger as the war stretched on. The war should have torn families apart. The negative psychological and physical ramifications of combat coupled with the economic destruction wreaked by the war sometimes severed emotional ties and left families virtually destitute. But in the sample for this project, it seems that most found themselves wound more tightly together as their survival depended on collective shouldering of the war's burdens. The growing emphasis on emotional intimacy in the decades leading up to the war sowed the seeds for this wartime blossoming of emotional expression and emotional intimacy. Paradoxically, though the brutality engendered by the war reached unimaginable heights, it also stoked a depth of male emotional expression that had not hitherto been seen on such a scale in America.

❦

This notion of the emotionally effusive white southern male runs contrary to an idea prevalent among many historians of the antebellum South: that white men of the period were emotionally repressed. This oft-invoked image of the sexually and emotionally repressed Victorian was largely a creation of liberal reformers and political radicals around the turn of the twentieth century. Scholars in the 1960s adopted this stereotype as a negative commentary on what they saw as the draconian and outdated social mores of the present day. They argued that Victorian marriages were "as characteristically cold as the relations between husband and wife were emotionally distant and formal."[10] In their view, that stereotypical coldness extended horizontally from husbands to wives as well as vertically from fathers to children. Historian Anthony E. Rotundo echoed this sentiment, writing that "the nineteenth-century father often lay outside the main emotional currents that flowed within his own home," and that "in middle class families of the nineteenth century, the emotional lives of fathers and sons simply did not become so entwined."[11] However, the research for this project indicates that nineteenth-century southern fathers did not fit within this mold.

The relational intimacy between fathers and their children in the nineteenth century represented a dramatic shift from the relationships between fathers and their children in the colonial period. Up until the early to mid-nineteenth century, American fathers were expected to be involved in the lives of their children, though they were often seen as "emotionally distant." A father's primary role was to meet the physical needs of his children, apply discipline, and lend a guiding hand toward marriage and future success.[12] Most white southern colonial males were subsistence farmers. A family served as a basic economic unit that worked together to meet each member's physical and economic needs. At the head of this unit was the father who served as the chief of production. As such, fathers held immense power over the family's finances, behavior, spiritual growth, and standing in the community. Their ability to exert discipline and project their power ranged from verbal persuasion to corporal punishment, and this model of fatherhood has been termed "Patriarchal Fatherhood."[13] This framework became the primary model embraced throughout the country leading up to the outbreak of the American Civil War. By the time of the American Civil War, the relationship between the father and his family had shifted.

Some historians have rooted this change in the social ripples of the Industrial Revolution, where the twin-headed hydra of urbanization and industrialization pushed middle-class men out of the home and into the workplace, thus establishing separate spheres between home and work and eventually deconstructing the family as the basic economic unit of American life. In this view, the movement of the father out of the home meant that husbands became less involved with their families and thus the patriarchal model of fatherhood slowly deteriorated. This, they argue, is concurrent with the rise of nineteenth-century mothers' involvement in the care of children and the creation of the "Cult of Domesticity."[14] Domesticity represented a value system that couched ideal womanhood in terms of one's ability to achieve the virtues of purity, domesticity, and submission. In terms of purity, women were to maintain their chastity and were expected to be more religious and virtuous than men. In terms of domesticity, they were to bear children and inculcate them with republican values and biblical morals. And finally, in terms of submission, they were expected to submit themselves to the wills of their fathers or husbands. The degree to which women were expected to, or were able to, achieve these goals relied largely on a woman's socioeconomic status. For example, in some social circles—particularly those of the upper classes—women did not work outside of the home, as they were considered too pure for such work. Meanwhile, a man's value lay in his ability to provide for his family so that his wife would not have to work.[15] Most women of lower socioeconomic classes would have to help their families on their farm, by making goods at home, or, in some rare cases, by going out into the workforce.

Either way, women who did work typically worked in and around the home and those who did not work were still expected to tend to the home. This model of parenting applauded the consistent presence of women in their family's lives and emphasized the importance of maternal affection and interpersonal bonding. While the mother's role in the emotional development of her children increased, many historians have noted that antebellum fathers continued to assume the role of a strict disciplinarian who was less concerned with the emotional well-being of his family and more concerned with his family's honor, morals, and economic future.[16]

However, this framework is largely the result of historians' studies of fathers from northern states, on whom urbanization and industrialization had a far greater impact. Southerners resisted industrialization and they saw its intense capitalistic focus on profits at the expense of people (that is, white laborers) as the antithesis of their idyllic pastoral world. Of course, their distaste for the exploitation of northern workers did not generally translate to a distaste for the exploitation of Black workers in the South. Nonetheless, the traditional masculine motifs rooted in an industrialized North were seemingly far less potent in the South. For southern men, land ownership equaled independence and self-sufficiency. Direct participation in the market economy—as an employee at a factory for example—meant that a man was now dependent on his employers—a position tantamount to slavery. Though the effects of the Industrial Revolution spread unevenly across the United States, in the South, white yeoman farmers generally worked on their family farm and thus intentionally avoided being pulled into the industrial marketplace in the same numbers as their northern counterparts.

That southern fathers spent much of their time at home meant that they spent much more time near their children. Though this does not mean that they were always deeply involved in their children's lives, as demonstrated earlier, physical closeness often led to the development of deeper emotional bonds. This aligns with the work of more recent historians who have shown that by the outbreak of the American Civil War, parents viewed children as sources of emotional comfort and personal happiness. Children, one historian notes, "became a haven from stress, a conduit of moral values, and a prominent component of what their descendants would call 'quality of life' whose disruption was to be avoided at all costs."[17] Fathers contributed toward, and reaped the rewards from, this new perspective of children and family. This was a trend that spread from Europe to the Americas by the outbreak of the Civil War. In their study of middle-class Victorian British fathers, historians Eleanor Gordon and Gwyneth Nair found "that there were many different ways of being a father in this period because Victorians had complex and ambiguous notions of what constituted a proper paternal role. . . . They could be strict but could also be indulgent. They stressed duty and deference but could be informal and intimate."[18] Mothers also partook, and historian Suzaan Boettger noted that their devotion to their families' emotional well-being increased as a reaction to the horror of the Civil War. Amid the war's tumult, women were seen by contemporaries as a stabilizing social force within the home.[19]

Though soldier-fathers marched off to war to defend their families, their political rights, and for many, the institution of slavery, they understood little of the great sacrifice that would be demanded of them. Many echoed the sentiments of rabid secessionist A. W. Venable, who, while speaking to voters in North Carolina in February 1861, pulled a handkerchief from his pocket and, waving it around, declared "I will wipe up every drop of blood shed in the war with this handkerchief of mine."[20] Southerners were steeped in the romantic and idealistic belief that their own masculine courage could overcome the Union's material and numerical superiority. In part, this was the result of their own cultural isolation from the rest of America and the belief that their agrarian and rural way of life was inherently superior.[21] This attitude was reflective of a wider belief that white southern men were of more noble character and that, as historian Dillon J. Carroll noted, "they could shape and even control events by their attitude and their character . . . men believed that they would be able to survive the war simply by their courage and daring."[22] In October 1861, one soldier from Alabama boldly declared that the South would win, "because we are going to kill the last Yankey before that time if there is any fight in them still. I believe that J. D. Walker's brigade can whip 25,000 Yankees. I think I can whip 25 myself."[23]

This sense of patriotism and inflated belief in their own moral and martial superiority may have drawn many men into the war, but reality tempered this *rage militaire* as the war progressed. If patriotism and belief in their own superiority could not sustain them, their love for their families (and their families' love for them) could. Regardless of how involved they were in their children's lives, it is clear that white southern men deeply loved their children. In the sample for this book, soldier-fathers consistently sought information about their children and were more likely than others to express their emotions. To shirk their responsibilities on the battle front was tantamount to abandoning their children to a bleak future.[24] This fear does not seem to have waned throughout the war and there is anecdotal evidence that it may have increased as the Confederate war effort faltered in the final year of the conflict. As noted earlier, soldier-fathers saw their military service as an extension of the masculine role that they had always played as protectors of their families' honor, health, security, freedom, religion, emotional health, culture, and economic wealth. Even during the war, when wives complained about the burden of maintaining their homes and farms in their husbands' absence, husbands often reminded them to remember their familial duty as wives and mothers and, by extension, to their nation. Soldier-fathers found themselves stuck in the painful nexus between duty to their country and duty to the needs of their families. In some sense, it gave them empathy for their wives, who also found themselves pulled between their duty to their families and their republican duty to the preservation of the Confederate cause. Soldiers and their wives had to pragmatically navigate these competing loyalties and social expectations. Private John W. Cotton of Hilliard's Legion, Alabama Volunteers, wrote to his wife in May 1862, "I would bee glad to see little ginny and give her a kiss and see the rest of the children frolic around and play on my lap and see babe suck his thum if it had not have bee the love I have for them and my country I would have been ther now."[25] Likewise, in a letter to his wife Eliza, Quartermaster Sergeant R. E. Corry of the 11th Alabama Cavalry complained of his commander, Major General Nathan Bedford Forrest, of being "a rash man and fond of going into danger," adding that "if Gen. Forrest does say that he will give the Alabamians transfers & whenever they become dissatisfied with him for one I would give up all my interest in the Spoils and Glory for the priviledge of being near my dear wife and little ones, but we may do our Country better Service here and it is the duty of a good soldier to obey orders and not Complain."[26]

As the conflict stretched the physical, economic, and emotional limits of its participants, soldier-fathers repeatedly reassured their wives of the importance of their service while also assuring their children that they would one day come home. Though historians of gender have made great strides in uncovering the lengths to which mothers went to maintain the stability of their families during the war, fathers' contributions to the emotional stability of their families have been less researched. Fathers too bore the burden of familial stability, and unlike most of their single comrades, soldier-fathers were saddled with the responsibility of continuing to lead, provide for, and care for their families from far away. At the same time, fathers were expected to participate in, and maintain their intimacy with, their children. The horror of war and the vast distance between themselves and their children may have actually made this easier—at least as the imminence of their own demise and the growing fondness created by their absence sharpened fathers' feelings towards their children. Often, this took the form of offering advice, counsel, and stories, etc., which were traditional fatherly acts which they continued to fulfill through the written letter. The letters for this book indicate that many did so with deep affection and kindness and little air of superiority—something that runs contrary to the belief that nineteenth-century males were somehow emotionally repressed or distant. As historian James Marten noted, "The affection that leaps out of their letters to their children transcends Victorian rhetoric and indicates how important to their self-image were their roles as fathers."[27] In a letter to his wife and children, Private Daniel Murphy of the 1st North Carolina Infantry complained that "you say you [see] a great of trouble and I expect you do but cant See the trouble that I do you can see your children and friends but I am draged away from you and my dear babes in to a land of Stranger and heathens where there is any thing but peace or comfort."[28]

The importance of the written letter cannot be understated. It was the method by which family members maintained communication, shared their feelings, and kept each other updated on the news from the home front and the battle front. Even as the Confederate mail system fell into disrepair and paper and ink became more difficult to procure, fathers proved themselves to be hungry to know that their families were safe and experiencing some modicum of stability. After all, this was a large part of their motivation for fighting. "I have bin looking for a letter from you som time though haven't receive it yet," Private George A. Williams of the 7th North Carolina Infantry Regiment wrote to his children in June 1864, "and I want you to write as soon as this comes to hand and give me all the neuse I want to know how you all ar getting on Dick is well and hearty tell Mrs Martha Trice to write to me and let me know how the children is getting on."[29]

Moreover, soldier-fathers wanted to know that they were not forgotten by their families, particularly by their children. This fear was not wholly irrational as many soldiers had marched off to war with children who were too young to even remember their fathers. As the war progressed and the number of furloughs decreased, some soldier-fathers worried that their young children would never truly know them. Writing directly to his children in March 1864, Private Franklin Setzer of the 1st North Carolina Cavalry wrote "a few lines to you children i want you to do all you can and make all the corn and watermelons you can tel i get home i would be glad to see you all but i dont no when that will bee so i must close by saying dont forget me."[30] Likewise, in a letter to his wife Eliza in November 1863, R. E. Corry wrote, "Don't let my sweet little girls forget me and tell them a great many things to make them love me."[31] Immersed in a culture in which one's name and honor was considered a man's legacy, the fear of being forgotten was palpable in many of the letters for this project. For many, this fear was deeply rooted in the feeling that the love that they had for their children would not be reciprocated. Unreciprocated love can be the most painful experience in human existence. Thus, it is no surprise that soldier-fathers repeatedly reminded their loved ones in letters home to not forget them. Feeling insecure, many soldier-fathers worried that the comforts of home lulled their loved ones into a state of forgetful indifference. This perceived affective imbalance was jarring. Whereas before the war women were expected to support the grand visions of men in their lives, during the war they were now responsible for ameliorating their husbands' insecurities. One of the most important ways that they accomplished this was by reminding their husbands that their children had not forgotten them. Some would even tell their husbands that their children had mentioned them by name, just to prove that they were not coaxed into remembering. Other mothers took it upon themselves to help their children to get to know their fathers by telling them old stories that illustrated their fathers' characters and lives.[32]

Likewise, wives also worried that their husbands would forget their children or feel little connection to them because they were not physically present. More often, though, the anxiety seemed to lay in the minds of soldier-fathers, perhaps due to the fact that they were frequently confronted with their own mortality. In response to his wife's worry that he would forget their child, Private Asa T. Martin of the 12th Alabama wrote to her in January 1862 that "I want to sea you and the children very bad you wantid to know of me if I ever thought much a bout the baby or not I dont know what made you amagon that I never thought much a bout her I want to sea her as well as I dwo eney body I want you to send me a loc of her hair if it is loing a nought I want som of williams and sises hair and a brade of your hair."[33] Thus, husbands and wives sought to soothe each other's insecurities and anxieties, much as they had done before the war. However, now the physical distance wrought by war and the anxiety surrounding their mortality exacerbated the anxieties and increased the need for mutual comfort. For both husband and wife, much of their anxieties centered on their children.

The impact of the war on parent-child relationships followed a similar course to that of husbands and wives. During the war, the only contact between a father and his child was a hastily written letter or a few words scrawled on a page. Yet with each passing year, as the prospects of permanent separation grew ever more stark, soldier-fathers sometimes became apoplectic waiting for news from their families.

In February 1863, Private Benjamin Mason of the 60th Alabama Infantry Regiment wrote to his wife, "I have waited as long as I have patience to wait for a letter I have written four times since I have recd a letter from you and have no patience to wait any longer I want to see you and the children worse than I ever did in my life and if I cant see you I must hear from you oftener than I do (so you see if you dont write I will just get me a wife that will) there is plenty of girls in this country and them that is pretty and want to marry too."[34] Likewise, to his daughter, Lieutenant W. V. Fleming of the 3rd Battalion Alabama Infantry Reserves wrote that "I have written home four time and have not heard one word from home Daughter I want you to write to me Every week as long as you can git paper and ink I never was as anxious to hear from home in my life give my respects to your granney & Grancer tel them I want to see them all tel son ny must learn to write So he can write me a letter."[35]

Positive news from home often provided temporary comfort which buffered their anxiety and, by extension, probably helped prevent many from deserting. "Our Regiment have now a little breathing time. I have been thinking much of my poor wife and children. I have not heard from them since I left them," Lieutenant Colonel Charles A. Derby of the 44th Alabama Infantry Regiment wrote to his sister in July 1862. "If I could hear from my family, I would be satisfied."[36] The anxiety that soldier-fathers felt was also often rooted in the mindless nature of drill and the long periods of boredom in which they found themselves, with little to distract them. Therefore, soldiers were desperate to receive news from home in the hopes of ameliorating these anxieties.

Throughout their time in service, fathers wrote letters either directly to their children or, more often, to their wives with asides or parentheses about their children. These letters unlock our understanding of the relationship between fathers and children during the war. Roger W. Little, an expert on modern armies, explained the importance of communication, writing that "letters represent the soldier's major contact with the social unit that reinforces his desire to serve faithfully and under great hardship. The conception of his role as a citizen of a community or member of a family was enhanced by the letters written him by persons whose evaluations of him were very important."[37] In other words, what his family thought of him was extremely important to a soldier's morale and letters were the mode by which these sentiments were exchanged.

While letters written to children from fathers far exceeded the number of letters written by children to their fathers in this sample, children who did communicate with their fathers generally did so through their mothers, who recorded their statements or wishes in their regular correspondence. Recognizing the mother's primacy over the family as well as the greater importance placed on the marital union, fathers often likewise responded to their children through their wives. Private Armistead L. Galloway of the 34th Alabama Infantry Regiment wrote to his wife, "my Dear tell cole to right to me how he is getting a long tell them all to right to me I wold wright to them all if I cold but all the time I hav I must giv it to you Eliza."[38]

Historian James Marten—the foremost expert on paternal relationships during the American Civil War—saw three broad conceptions of fatherhood in his study of soldiers' letters. First, letters displayed fathers' interest in their children's everyday lives. This included events that might have been banal at home but took on greater significance when families were apart. Fathers asked about their children's daily lives because they wanted to be invited into their child's lives much as they had been at home. To converse with their children and to inquire of their activities was demonstrative of the fact that they cared for, and wanted to draw close to, their children. It also demonstrated to their children that they were not forgotten. These are not the actions of the emotionally repressed or relationally standoffish.

Second, fathers were emotionally torn. On the one hand, they understood that their place was on the front lines, defending the honor of their nation and their families. On the other hand, they were still expected to take part in the development of their children's character and moral standing in the community. Fathers were supposed to raise their children to become honorable men and, in the case of boys, to become self-sufficient men as well. This was problematic due to their absence. On the one hand, fathers were absent because they believed that they were fighting for their children and their future. On the other hand, their lack of physical presence meant that they were unable to model proper behavior for their children as often as they would have liked. Confederate soldier-fathers were pulled taut between these two positions. In the moments before he marched into battle, Private Liberty Independence Nixon, of the 50th Alabama Infantry Regiment, pondered the possibility of his impending demise, whether or not he was truly a Christian, and whether he was ready to take the life of another, recalling that in that moment, "the thought of my little children would rush to my mind then the burden of my heart would be spared my life O Lord for my little children's sake. But not my will but thine be done."³⁹ Nixon marched into battle and survived another day. Faced with the possibility of his own demise, who would teach Nixon's sons to become honorable men? Faced with the destruction of the Confederacy, would his sons even be *free* to become an honorable man? These were the questions that reverberated in the minds of many soldier-fathers.

Third, Marten noted that there was an insistence on the part of soldier-fathers to fulfill their duty to provide authoritative wisdom and instruction to help their children transition into adulthood. Much as they had before the war, they sought to project both their authority and their love on their children. Only now, it consisted of words on a page—words that defined what was right and wrong, good and bad. In their eyes, father truly knew best. Through letters, Confederate fathers remained "fathers" in function as well as in name. But for many, it was not enough. They longed to be with their children and to carry on with them much as they had before the war. Though soldier-fathers tried to raise their children as best they could through letters, this method of parenting proved insufficient. Fathers wanted to be physically close to their children and now because of their absence, mothers would have to take on many of the duties once relegated to the male head of household.⁴⁰

Some may wonder, if children were so important to their fathers during this period, why was so little of their communication devoted to them? Why was most communication with their children either through their wives or in direct asides in their letters? Furthermore, why did fathers not communicate more often with their children? First, paper and ink were in extremely short supply, particularly as the war progressed and the Union blockade cut off imported paper and ink from Europe. If soldiers were going to write to one individual, it would be those with whom they were closest—their wives. Most letters written by married Confederate soldiers were directed toward their wives—a fact which is demonstrative of the supremacy that romantic relationships held in a man's life. Second, mothers were considered the locus of family life and as such they were the gatekeepers of the family. Their primary role was to nurture the family while a husband's primary role, at least before the war, was to provide a link between the family and the broader community. The war altered the father's role as men were forced to spend long periods away from home and thus could no longer be directly involved with their local communities. Now, fathers seemed to focus more on the inculcation of honor, discipline, and character within their children. Just in case they did not survive, these letters would serve as a legacy of moral instruction that could help guide their children in the future. Finally, many of these soldiers had the misfortune of either having children who were very young or who had been born after their father's enlistment. Many children knew nothing of their fathers and, in some cases, their fathers knew almost nothing of them. The only way to get to know each other was through the exchange of letters.

⁓⁂⁓

The emotional pain that soldier-fathers felt in the absence of their children was deepened by what they saw on the battlefield. Combat pierced the veil of human propriety. Captain Frank M. Parker of the 30th North Carolina wrote to his wife after the Battle of Gaines Mill: "What can make people go to war? To witness the destruction of life on the battlefield is enough to put a stop to all such arguments in the future. I mean such arguments as war."[41] One of the most frightening aspects of war was the uncertainty of when and how one would die. Soldiers never knew when the next bullet or contagion would come for them. Moreover, they were powerless to prevent them. Soldier-fathers not only struggled to protect their families, but they also had to reconcile themselves to the prospect of their own imminent death. This uncertainty impelled fathers to make a more concerted effort to connect emotionally with their children.

In his study of the 154th New York Infantry Regiment, historian Mark Dunkelman found that "uncertainty—endemic in the army—plagued the men. They were helplessly afflicted by a typically military myopia. . . . If active campaigning put them incommunicado, they had no idea of current events at home or in the nation at large. . . . The unrelenting passage of time induced war weariness in the soldiers."[42] Confederates were no less affected. While his unit was exposed to intense bombardment at Spotsylvania Courthouse, Virginia, in 1864, Sergeant Isaac Lefevers of the 46th North Carolina Infantry Regiment wrote a letter to his wife. In the uneasy silence between bombardments, Lefevers ruminated on his own mortality and the prospect of never seeing his family again. Because of his love for them, Lefevers reached out to his family in the midst of battle. "I tel you my Dear wife nothing gives me so much pleasure as when I can hear from you and Rite to you," he wrote; "my Dear wife I could not tel you how glad I would be to See you and the Dear little childrean this morning I most tel you that I Dremp of seeing the Sweat little babe last night and how glad would I abin If it had bin sow but I stil trust and pray to the good lord that I may See you all before long." Even after years of military service, Lefevers did not lose his compassion or empathy. He still ached to see his children and he still hurt when he witnessed suffering. After surviving the Battle of Spotsylvania Courthouse, he looked over the battlefield and saw "lots of Dead bodes Burnt in to a crips and I have no Eyedea but what some of the wonded was burnt of both sides but the most that I saw was of the enemy." "I saw one man that was burnt that had the picture I suppose of his little Daughter in his pocket," he recounted; "it was all burnt only the glass it loocked to be the Sise of Ida a very sick little girl I neaver saw enny thing that made me feel more sorrow."[43] For this Union soldier, his final gaze would be upon those whom he loved dearest. Seeing a father who, like himself, longed to be back with his children sparked a flicker of empathy in Lefevers who may have seen in his vanquished foe the possibility of his own future. At the very least, he saw in his enemy a man much like himself. No doubt, this scene only exacerbated Lefevers' feelings toward his children. In his study of northern soldiers, historian Stephen Frank argued that "in particular, war as a masculine endeavor may have accentuated—and exaggerated—whatever bonds existed between fathers and sons," and that "the father-son relationship emerged most prominently in these letters at five moments in soldiers' lives: the time of enlistment; the time of blooding or baptism by fire; the time of resignation and mustering out; the time of wounding; and the time of death."[44]

Soldiers also sought the aid of their families through their families' prayers. Religion not only bound soldiers to one another, but it also bound soldier-fathers to their families. In war, everyone feels powerless. In God, soldiers and their families had access to the One they believed reigned supreme over all of the universe. In this way, they were no longer powerless. At the same time, through their prayers, family members supported one another. In December 1864, Private Francis Marion

Poteet of the 39th North Carolina Infantry Regiment wrote to his wife and children that "if I cant git to see you I want you to still pray for me and all the balans of the soldiers and tell all of my friends to pray for me and to pray to god to spare my life to live to git home to raise my littel Children I have agrait desire to see you all one more."[45] By asking for prayer, Poteet recognized his loss of control. He was no longer a master of himself or his circumstances. Rather, he and his family were dependent wholly upon the will of God. Apart from this, they may never see each other again on this side of heaven.

The possibility of permanent separation could be as formidable for wives and mothers as it was for husbands and fathers. Overwhelmed by the anxiety generated by the possibility of losing their husbands, a growing war weariness, and a sense of isolation and loneliness, soldiers' wives could at times experience emotional detachment from their children. Exactly how often this occurred will never be known, but it does represent an important aspect of the emotional development of children during the war. Already struggling from the emotional pain of an absent father, children's emotional health now mostly depended upon the ability of the mother to manage her own anxiety and emotions alone. Women were particularly burdened by the need to put their children before themselves in a way that their husbands did not often understand.[46]

The immense toll that the war took upon soldiers' wives is evident in many of their letters, particularly in its latter two years. When Kezia Stradley Osborne received a letter from her husband, Private Roland C. Osborne of the 25th North Carolina Infantry Regiment, her insecurities were inflamed by his lack of information. "I felt like there was something wrong when I saw so much blank paper, and as I read it down tears gathered thick and fast in my eyes but I forced them back until I went to my bed by my self where I lay for hours studying and crying," she wrote. The blank page was a visual reminder of the growing void between herself and her husband, wrought by the war. Kezia further worried that by communicating her needs, she was adding to her husband's distress and only deepening their marital turmoil. She was overwhelmed and wanted him to help bear the burden. After sharing her thoughts, Kezia's feelings shifted away from the sins of her husband to what she perceived as her own failings in expressing pain. "I am only sorry that I did not bear all with out complaining; can you forgive me for distressing you with my little troubles," she wrote. "If I were never to see to you again I never would forgive my self for giving you so much pain. . . . I know you have troubles enough of your own and I would rather try to lighten them than to add to them so I try to bear all in silence."[47] Kezia's honesty about her insecurities, fears, and disappointments are indicative of the fact that she felt secure enough with her husband to share the truth of her feelings. Like millions of other southern women, she was overwhelmed by the burdens of caring for her family's needs at the expense of her own. Kezia may have wanted to "lighten" her husband's burdens, but by expressing her feelings, she too was hoping that he would help carry hers. In effect, Kezia's outburst was indicative of the fact that she felt like she needed to hear from her husband as she longed for emotional connection with him.

Even from a distance, fathers often stepped in and provided emotional support for their children when their spouses were overwhelmed. For the sake of their family's health, mothers and fathers had to be regularly involved in the emotional development of their children. For fathers, this was particularly difficult considering the vast geographic expanse between themselves and their progeny. One review of longitudinal studies of fathers' involvement with child development found that "*cohabitation* with the mother and her male partner is associated with less externalizing behavioral problems" and that "active and regular *engagement* with the child predicts a range of positive outcomes, although no specific form of engagement has been shown to yield better outcomes than another. Father engagement seems to have differential effects on desirable outcomes by reducing the frequency of behavioral problems in boys and psychological problems in young women and enhancing cognitive development."[48] Letters and the occasional furlough were the only methods by which soldier-fathers could engage with their children. Though sparse, these haphazard interactions were crucial to a child's healthy development.

Much as the loss of a father could hinder the healthy development of a child, the loss of a mother could also hinder a child's growth. Though civilians may have been spared the horror of the battlefield, they too felt uncertainty about the future. The always looming specter of disease and financial collapse elicited feelings of helplessness which left many women clinging to their distant husbands even more. In effect, while both husband and wife suffered along the battle front and the home front, they often grew more emotionally needy for each other, to a depth they may not have in times past when they were at peace and physically close. In a letter to his wife Eleanor in May 1864, Private Silas Stepp of the 6th North Carolina Cavalry wrote:

> I tel you my dear you dont now how bad i want to see you and the children itel you it is hard for aman to bea drag away from his family i wood give any thing i have got to get home and stay with you the rest of my days . . . iam sorry to here the wimmen and children is Suffering for bread tel mee if you have got enough and how your truck look i am sow oneasy about you i can see now peace here that is any satis faction to mee i often think of old times that wee have had to gether i wood bea glad if i was there to day.[49]

Though not serving on the battle front, wives and children were not passive participants in the war. They participated directly by maintaining the morale of their soldier-husbands and -fathers through regular letter writing. These letters reminded men of why they fought and what they could potentially lose, in their own minds, if they lost the war. At the same time, children imbibed the prescribed imagery and heroic stories of Confederate military service through newspapers, books, word of mouth, and letters from their fathers. In this way, adults invited children to participate in the war by stirring up feelings of honor, sacrifice, and patriotism in future sons and daughters of the Confederacy.[50]

In this regard, children came to see their fathers' service as a necessary evil for the protection of their family and nation. By the spring of 1861, many schools throughout the South were shuttered as older students and their teachers enlisted in the Confederate army. Those educators who remained were expected to support the war effort by publishing materials favorable to the Confederate cause. Military service was painted as a profession of honorable sacrifice. Yankees were portrayed as sniveling weaklings who were easily conquered by the moral and martial superiority of white southern men. These instructive texts heavily downplayed the ethics and martial spirit of Union soldiers and civilians.[51] An 1863 textbook called *The Geographical Reader for the Dixie Children* explained the war this way: "In the year 1860 the Abolitionists became strong enough to elect one of their men for President. Abraham Lincoln was a weak man, and the South believed he would allow laws to be made, which would deprive them of their rights," and that "Abraham is unable to conquer the 'Rebels' as he calls the South."[52]

Children were thus turned into participants in the war and though they may not have often shouldered a musket or marched into battle, the South would not allow them to remain unwitting bystanders. Children were not shielded from their role in the conflict. Instead, they were politicized and expected to be willing to sacrifice their parents and their own future happiness for the good of the country.[53] At the same time, if their fathers fell either in battle or from disease, the South's educational system was expected to step in and provide the moral development which had previously been the father's purview. Many thousands of children would be subject to this. Moreover, southern education portrayed the wartime service of children's parents in stark terms of sacrifice and honor. As such, the children of Confederate soldiers could become their fathers' biggest cheerleaders, often reminding them of how proud they were of their service and how desperately they needed to keep fighting. By doing so, it was implied, these soldier-fathers maintained the honorable stature of their children and families within the broader community. Yet more than that, this system tapped into a far deeper and far more personal aspect of human motivation. By training children to see military service and sacrifice in such terms, soldier-fathers would be motivated by something far more potent than their families' standing in the community—the adoration and approval of their own children. Much like today, fathers longed to be their children's heroes, and military service represented an important avenue to accomplishing this. This system had a price, however. The war forced family members into uncomfortable new roles which required immense interpersonal support. In their father's absence, sons were forced to "grow up" rather quickly while assuming responsibilities that were once the domain of their fathers or older brothers. Likewise, wives and young daughters assumed new roles that were once the purview of their husbands and fathers. Women and children now plowed and harvested, bought and sold property, negotiated the price of crops, slaughtered animals for sustenance, and worked in the fields or factories to survive. The average pay of a Confederate private rarely covered his family's expenses. In taking on these new responsibilities, wives and children were themselves sacrificing for the war effort and they were often cheered on by their soldier-husbands and -fathers. Wives and children too wanted to make their husbands and fathers proud. Without this mutual exhortation, the Confederate war effort would not have lasted as long as it did. Everyone had to sacrifice and the mutual bonds of affection and adoration from those that one loves made it worthwhile and endurable.

The constant barrage of news of the war and of the economic and material deprivation of the home front ignited a level of emotional effusion rarely seen on such a broad scale during times of peace.[54] Though family members were expected to take care of each other at all times, the lengths to which the war would force them to care for each other could not have been foreseen when it began. Now, not only did wives and children participate in the war *physically,* but they also took part *emotionally.* Husbands craved communication with their children, and it was these missives that reminded them of why their struggle was worthwhile.

❧

In the source base for this book, it is clear that soldier-fathers often felt pain, frustration, and guilt because of their absence from their children's lives. Soldiers were not tone deaf to the struggles of their wives, children, and families along the home front. John T. Scott of the 45th Alabama Infantry Regiment wrote to his sweetheart in 1863 that "it is no wonder that the poor soldiers have become dispirited, when every letter reaches them from the loved ones at home bring the unpleasant tidings that the children cry for bread and the rich lend them no assistance. It is not to be wondered at that God has not favored us when in the short space of three years our people have become bankrupt in morals, bankrupt in religion and bankrupt in everything that should elevate us as a nation."[55] Even though many loved their comrades, this love did not replace or supplant the love that they had for their wives and, particularly, for their children. The emotional weight felt in the absence of one's children could be overwhelming. In their waking hours, the thoughts of home and the fear of never seeing their families again could become overwhelming. Even in the unconsciousness of sleep, these fears stalked them. "We was allowed to lie down & sleep if we could som slep soundly I did not sleep much my mind being on my Dear Wife & little wons at home, I dream of them often of being with them, you do not draw any ida how I feal being compeld to stay from them," Private

Isham Simms Upchurch of the 16th North Carolina Infantry Regiment wrote to his brother; "5.00 chances to 1 wether I ever shall see them a gain on earth if I do not I feal that I shall meet them in heaven."[56] Dreams often reflect one's anxieties, and according to historian Jonathan W. White, "Home was the most common dream theme for soldiers both North and South."[57] Some dreamed so vividly of their children that upon awakening they felt emotionally crushed by the cruel illusion.[58]

Children were an extraordinary source of anxiety for fathers—particularly anxieties over their safety. On average, mothers in the early nineteenth century gave birth to an average of seven children. In 1850, the average life expectancy was 39.5 years for whites and the infant mortality rate was 216.8 deaths per 1,000 births annually (or 21.68 percent). By 1860, life expectancy rose to 43.6 years with 181.3 deaths per 1,000 births annually (18.13 percent).[59] "Before 1850, infant deaths were commonly accepted as a part of everyday life, a reflection of the natural order in which the strong outlived the weak," developmental psychologist Jeffrey P. Brosco wrote. "In the latter half of the century, however, families began to value children as more than an economic resource, and infant deaths no longer seemed acceptable."[60] Realistically, the death of one's child was never seen as acceptable, but it is true that by the outbreak of the American Civil War, it was less expected. In his study of childhood death in the Old South, historian Craig Thompson Friend argues that the commonly held belief that Victorian parents' familiarity with death left them resigned to the loss of their children was false. Moreover, he argues that the idea that parents were expected to restrain themselves emotionally in the wake of the death of their progeny was false as well. The loss of a child, he notes, "elicited a great range of emotional responses from parents," which included grieving "deeply over deceased children, expressing guilt, confusion, and frustration at their helplessness." They would not hesitate to express their anger or even, at times, question God and His will.[61] Thus it is no surprise that soldier-fathers felt immense anxiety at the prospect of losing their children, nor should it be a surprise that they were willing to openly express this anxiety in their letters.

Although Victorian ideals of masculinity dictated that men were supposed to suppress their emotions and master their fears, the war brought about such immense emotional distress that throughout the conflict, masculine norms went out the proverbial window—particularly when one lost a child. Though fathers may have made fewer *public* displays of emotion, this does not indicate a lack of concern or a willingness to elevate cultural standards over one's emotional needs. Some individuals are naturally less expressive of their feelings and would prefer to mourn in more private ways and with only select individuals with whom they could entrust their feelings. This has less to do with cultural norms and more to do with a natural predisposition towards being taciturn, a desire to withhold emotional expression for fear that it would overwhelm them, or a belief that emotions were equated with vulnerability and thus should only be shared with those with whom one felt safe. As noted earlier, this is a pattern that men had engaged in before the war. "Given the opportunity to express themselves in private diaries," Craig Thompson Friend wrote, "men were often more tender and as grief-stricken as their wives."[62] Indeed, even when not facing the loss of a child, men were extraordinarily tender when it came to their children. While recovering in a Richmond hospital for "infmmation of the bowles," Private Jesse H. Everett of the 11th Georgia Infantry Regiment wrote to his wife Patience, "my darling if i only cold tell you had bad i want to see you an my dear little children i no that you would bee Sorry for me tears dims my eyes so i can hardley write," before ending his letter with a request to "pleas write Soon an Send me Som of the babes hair."[63] These are not the words of a father who mastered his emotions, refused to express his feelings, or sought to assert his patriarchal authority. Rather, Everett's expressions of emotion were indicative of thousands of other soldier-fathers who deeply loved and missed their children and were not ashamed to say so.

⋯⟡⋯

War rips apart every beam that undergirds one's sense of stability and security. Husbands were torn away from their wives and fathers were separated from their children. Life simply could not carry on as it once had, and yet soldiers and their families tried their very best to make it do so. Wanting to provide security and stability for their children, soldier-fathers sought to share advice and wisdom to guide their sons and daughters, much as they would have at home.[64] They accomplished this through letters, which could be referenced repeatedly if a child's father were not to survive the war. Many soldier-fathers hoped that their words and actions would not only bring honor to the family but also stir their children to become honorable adults in their absence. Private George A. Williams of the 7th North Carolina Infantry Regiment reflected this impulse when he directed his children "to be Smart and all ways have respect for olde peples dont gave them any provication of corsecting you I want you to be smart and take good advise from a friend who is capable of advising you."[65] Likewise, Private William T. Presley of the 1st Alabama Cavalry reflected this sentiment by writing to his wife, "If I could only see you and them Dear little Babies I would be Proud but there is no telling when I will see you . . . try to improve the Children all you can in Education and in manners and tell them to be Smart Boys So that Papa can brag on them when he comes home."[66]

Fathers became wells of written paternal advice as they felt powerless to impart these values in person. Facing the uncertainty of their own mortality, they also feared that if they did not communicate these life lessons to their children now, they might never have the opportunity again. While wanting to leave a legacy of sacrifice and courage by defending their country (and thus their children's futures), soldier-fathers also desired to leave a legacy of wisdom. At a critical junction in his daughter's life in which she had just begun her teenage years Private Benjamin Mason of the 60th Alabama Infantry Regiment wrote to her that "I hope my daughter that as you grow in age and size that you will try to improve in wisdom and prudence that you may be a sorce of pleasure and comfort to your friends and usefulness to your self do all you can to help your Ma to take care of your little brothers and sisters."[67] Mason's words represented his best attempt at fulfilling his socially prescribed duty to lead his daughter toward becoming a woman of virtue. Mason clearly wanted to guide his children through life as he would have were he physically present.[68] In the absence of touch, these letters were the only physical link between children and their fathers.

Soldier-fathers often found themselves particularly tender toward other children in the absence of their own. The physical distance between themselves and their progeny, and their longing to be reunited, made many battle-hardened soldier-fathers very sentimental towards other children that they encountered. One of the most famous examples of this tenderness was that exhibited by Major General Thomas "Stonewall" Jackson. Married and with one daughter, Jackson had seen little of his family by the winter of 1862. In the gloomy gray of a Virginia winter,

Jackson struck up an affectionate friendship with six-year-old Jane Corbin, who lived near his winter quarters. Corbin and Jackson were inseparable. Known for his odd behavior and particularly stern opinions, in the young girl's presence Jackson exhibited "a degree of joy and lightness that not only surprised, but astonished observers who thought they knew Jackson well."[69] Historian W. G. Bean explains this behavior by adding, "Doubtless, his love for his newly-born daughter, whom he had not yet seen, overflowed to little Jane Corbin." When the young girl passed away unexpectedly from scarlet fever, the normally stoic Jackson received the news through a veil of tears.[70] Likewise, soldiers less famous than Stonewall Jackson often relished the presence of children, particularly as the war stretched on and the prospect of a bright future with their own families seemed to dim. When the children of strangers or comrades entered camps, soldiers often abandoned all sense of propriety and eagerly played with them.[71] Communicating with their own children or playing with other people's children provided soldiers with much-needed relief from the stress and tedium of military service.

Though the presence of innocent children could be soothing for many soldiers, war cruelly destroyed the innocence of many children. During the siege of Vicksburg, local resident Mary Loughborough's two-year-old daughter befriended a young Confederate soldier named Henry who showered the little girl with flowers, apples, and even pets. Loughborough's daughter awoke one morning to see Henry perched upon his horse and riding toward a body of water in the distance. "O mamma, look at Henry's horse, how he plays!" she exclaimed to her mother. As Henry and his horse moved closer to the home, the Loughborough's saw a black cylindrical object in his hand. Not long after, the object exploded, tearing off Henry's hand at the wrist and embedding a piece of shrapnel in his head. It was an unexploded piece of ordnance. As the Loughboroughs watched helplessly, Henry cried out for his comrades "Where are you, boys? O boys, where are you? Oh, I am hurt! I am hurt! Boys, come to me!—come to me! God have mercy! Almighty God, have mercy!" while the young girl clung to her mother's dress, screaming "O mamma, poor Henry's killed! Now he'll die, mamma. Oh, poor Henry!" before being carried away, never to see Henry again.[72]

Literature examining the psychological and emotional effects of war on children emerged shortly after World War II. Much of it found that children who came into direct contact with war's sights, sounds, and even smells often exhibited symptoms of post-traumatic stress disorder on par with those of soldiers. Many experienced symptoms such as intrusive memories of the events, reoccurring nightmares, and hypersensitivity to sensorial reminders of war. Some were affected more than others, generally depending on their temperament, age, gender, capacity to cope with emotional distress, and level of exposure to violence. In addition to this direct trauma, children could also experience the indirect trauma of being separated from their fathers, something that psychologist Emmy E. Werner argues was "often more distressing than the violence that surrounds them." Though many attempted to suppress their memories of the war, others found healing by either talking or writing about their experiences. In the Civil War, they often did so through written letters to their fathers or face-to-face with their mothers. In this way, family members processed their emotions within the safe confines of their nuclear unit, and this mutual support provided an emotional buffering effect against their own emotional degradation. At the same time, these relationships promoted resiliency and imbued children with a self-confidence born out of their increased responsibilities to the family and their ability navigate the treacherous shoals of adulthood without a present father.[73]

The emotional potency of familial relationships is best demonstrated by the rates of desertion among Confederate soldiers. Of the approximately 880,000 Confederate soldiers who served during the war, official statistics from the period indicate that 103,400 soldiers officially deserted—representing 11.75 percent of total Confederate enlistments. Some historians argue that the number of Confederate deserters may have been much higher.[74] However, if these numbers are correct, 776,600 Confederate soldiers (or 88.25 percent of total enlistees) did not desert. So why did so many Confederate soldiers refuse to desert? After all, those who deserted generally did so because they believed that the Confederate government was either unwilling or unable to protect and provide for their families. In the minds of many, the best way to protect their families was to return home and help out on the farm. If the Confederate government would not help provide for their families, then many men took it upon themselves to fulfill their masculine duty to provide by deserting and returning home. Of course, others deserted for a variety of other reasons, including disillusionment with the war, cowardice, and more. For many single men, their reasons for desertion could at times be less noble than those of their married counterparts. Yet most soldier-fathers continued to serve in the Confederate army, even as the Confederacy unraveled toward the end of the war.

In his study of desertion among soldiers from Buncombe County in western North Carolina, historian Scott King-Owen found that most followed a pattern of temporary desertion in order to visit with their families or help out with the harvest before returning to duty. He argues that "most absentee soldiers seemed to have considered loyalty to family paramount to their conditional loyalty to the Confederacy."[75] This runs contrary to much of the historical literature, which argues that soldiers' ideology, commitment to the cause, or their own personal or familial honor were paramount to the unwillingness of so many to desert. In this way, families exerted a "pull factor" in which desperate pleas from wives and children for the return of their husbands and fathers resulted in increased desertions. "For most residents of western North Carolina," King-Owen asserts, "neither slavery or its social system, nor particular political preferences, played a large role in shaping desertion."[76] On a much larger scale, historian Mark Weitz noted that "the South faced the same problem the colonies had encountered during the American Revolution: the inability of the common citizen to recognize a duty higher than family and community" and that "Confederate patriotism found its basis within a duty to local peoples and places. Abstract notions of democracy involving states' rights lost their relevance if taken beyond the immediate context of family and community."[77] In effect, in the minds of married soldiers, the war was always inextricably tied to family.

However, what some historians have ignored is that families also provided a "push factor" that encouraged Confederate soldiers to keep fighting. They did so beyond verbally exhorting their husbands and fathers to continue the fight; rather, many did so tacitly by helping their husbands and fathers bear the emotional weight of military service. They provided a "listening ear" for men to process their feelings while also reminding them of why they were fighting. The love of their families compelled them to fight and gave meaning to their service. Abstract political ideals alone were not enough to motivate soldiers to fight, as evidenced by the letters for this project. Soldiers rarely discussed ideology or political reasons for their service with their families. Out of 200 soldiers, only 33 (16.5 percent) expressed notions of ideology or duty connected to "the cause." Out of 1,790 letters read, only 62 (3.46 percent) contained expressions of ideology or duty. By the last two years of the war, the Confederate war effort was probably motivated more by family than by political principles. And without these families, the war could not have continued.

In recognizing this as a war for family, husbands and fathers often felt immense pity for those whose loss left their families defenseless and in the lurch. In a letter to his wife in April 1863, Private Eluctius Treadwell of the 19th Alabama Infantry Regiment wrote that the death of his friend Luke Aubury "is sad news I presume to his wife and an irreparable loss to his little children who are now left without a kind father's protection. God bless the fatherless and keep them with a fathers hand." As Treadwell's mind turned from his friend toward his other comrades, he was shaken to his core, both as a husband and father. "I now look away to the top of yonders knole and see the mounds that mark the last resting places of many who no doubt have left many dear little ones behind to mourn their loss," he wrote; "they have fell victims to disease and are now done with the cares of Earth. Nothing marks their resting places Except a mound of clay." The possibility that his own future lay buried beneath such a mound of clay impelled Treadwell to appreciate the moment. "Mattie to day's Sunday tis quite a lovely day indeed the Bluebirds are singing beautifully around me," he wrote, and "the sun shines warm and now and then I hear the innocent dove cooing in the top of some distant tree. Tis pleas-ant for a moment to be thus situated." Surrounded by the beauty of Spring's first blush, Treadwell noticed that "around me I see the earth coverd with green grass and the trees that a few days ago looked as though they were dead now are putting forth their green foliage." The surge of life around him reminded him of happier times. "The present time seems to me to be one which could not fail to carry my mind back to days and hours more pleasantly spent," he wrote, before recounting the "hours that were spent in the presence of all that was dear. Will it ever be that I may be allowed the privilege of dwelling in Peace with thee and hour little ones again. God grant that the time may come when peace will again through out the land reign." Before signing off, Treadwell assured his wife that "I am tolerable well and hope this will find you and our dear little ones well. Kiss them often for me and Reserve a full portion of my love to your self."[78]

Though Treadwell survived the war, many soldier-fathers never saw their wives or children again. Thousands moldered in hastily dug graves scattered across the country while others died emotionally after losing their children to wartime disease or accidents. Facing this agony, soldier-fathers did not master their emotions. They were overwhelmed by them. Many, even if they survived the war, wondered: what was the point of fighting now? Their only hope lay in the future prospect of being reunited in heaven. After receiving news of the death of his son Slocumb, Private Daniel Webster Revis of the 64th North Carolina Infantry assured his grief-stricken wife Sarepta that "he is gon to rest bles his sweet little soal he is gon to heaven to sweet Jesus whar he wil never suf fer no more hecan not come to us but we can go to him sereptia I want you to prepair to meet me and little slocum in heaven." He went on to remind her that "I may never se you hier any more but stil I hope I wil but if it was gods wil that I shold not I hope I wil meet you in heaven whair we shal hav to part no more."[79] Private Revis was captured in Petersburg, Virginia, in February 1865, and sent to the Union Prison at Point Lookout, Maryland. Like most of his comrades, Revis held on to the prospect of seeing his family once again and his love for them compelled him to keep going. In June 1865, he was paroled and not long after, made his way back home where he once again felt the embrace of his beloved wife Sarepta and his last remaining son, Daniel.

CHAPTER 5

ETHNOS
AND
AUTHORITY
RACE, EMOTION, AND THE BOLSTERING
OF MALE MOTIVATIONS

Up to this point, I have examined the relationships and emotions between white southerners and their families and friends. I have argued that these relationships, and their emotional power, are one of the primary factors undergirding the willingness of Confederate soldiers to fight. In arguing this point, I have provided data from hundreds of soldiers' letters. But I have also said relatively little about relationships between the races, and it must be noted that the American Civil War was one that was fought for a variety of reasons in the minds of its participants. Two of the most powerful political and social motivations for the war include a desire to protect the institution of slavery and a desire to preserve what many white southerners saw as "states' rights." For nineteenth-century southerners, these two motivations were intertwined.

Recognizing this fact, modern historians have been loath to examine whether emotional bonds developed between white southerners and free or enslaved African Americans. Around the turn of the twentieth century, the rise of Lost Cause mythology sought to paint the relationship between the races in erroneous terms of white benevolence and Black obsequiousness. In an attempt to reshape the narrative around what caused the American Civil War and who was ultimately to blame, white southerners sought to justify both slavery and race-based hierarchy by arguing that white southerners "took care" of their slaves and that the relationship between southern whites and enslaved Blacks was one of tenderness and mutual reciprocity. It was northerners, they would argue, who turned the hearts of African Americans against their "masters" and who destroyed the congenial relationship between the races in the South.

This was a stunning inversion of reality, in which white southerners recast themselves as victims, rather than perpetrators, of injustice. Unlike the Old South, the New South under Reconstruction was increasingly becoming what southerners had long feared: a soulless industrial marketplace bereft of the interpersonal magnanimity of yore. To white southerners, they were the only ones willing to accept the "burden" of caring for what they saw as an inferior race.[1] Indeed, they often pointed out the hypocrisy of northerners who abhorred slavery and yet refused to hire newly freed African Americans in their factories, turning instead to cheaper immigrant labor. In southerners' corrupted thinking, this was crueler than their own system of slavery. Those Black workers who did receive jobs in northern factories would now become anonymous laborers who were discarded when they were no longer profitable. That white slave owners themselves did this often was willfully forgotten. Indeed, it was the slave aristocracy which shaped this post-war racial narrative which was designed to bring defeated white southerners back together and to instill in them a sense of pride and moral superiority. This was no easy task. Only approximately one out of four southern families either owned slaves or belonged to families that owned slaves, but still, as one psychologist pointed out, white southerners had a distinct "emotional investment in slavery, for many white men and women saw the potential of owning slaves as a means of increasing their status and worth."[2]

Few Confederate soldiers owned slaves. In his study of the Army of Northern Virginia, historian Joseph Glatthaar noted that slightly more than one in ten enlistees in the first year of the war owned slaves while one in four lived with parents who owned slaves. When combined, these numbers indicated that volunteers in 1861 were just 42 percent more likely to own slaves or live with family members who owned slaves as compared with the general population. However, the vast majority were connected to slavery in some regard.[3] Post-1861 enlistees tended to be married men who were older and wealthier while enlistees in 1861 were typically middle-class. Thus, the number of those who owned slaves who enlisted after 1861 increased to nearly one in five while those who lived in slaveholding households increased from 45 percent to 48 percent.[4] In his study, Glatthaar notes that the Army of Northern Virginia was "not so much an army of the poor with an educated and opulent officer corps. It was instead largely an army of property, primarily soldiers who either owned land or a business themselves or lived in a household where their family did. This was an army that risked everything—families, property, and slaves that had taken them and their ancestors lifetimes to accumulate."[5] In his study of later-enlisting Confederate soldiers, historian Kenneth Noe found that among his sample, only 21 percent wrote approvingly of slavery while only half of this 21 percent were slaveowners or sons of masters. The other half were nonslaveholders. Moreover, only two later enlists criticized the war for being a "slave owner's conflict," and Noe's work suggests that about one-third to one-half of late enlisters were motivated by the issue of slavery—primarily those from the Lower South.[6]

Though most Confederate soldiers were not slave owners, most supported the institution of slavery. Many had encountered African Americans and some even had personal relationships with them. One could easily imagine a spectrum of emotions developing between white southerners and enslaved or free peoples that ranged on one end from sheer hatred to, on the other end and in rare cases, mutual affection. The central problem for historians today attempting to understand the relationship between Blacks and white southerners is that few primary source materials were left behind by African Americans. In many southern states, it was illegal to teach free or enslaved Blacks to read or write. Those who attempt to do so could face prison. African Americans who learned to read or write could face beatings, being sold, or even worse. Moreover, most relationships between enslaved Blacks were isolated to the plantation on which they worked, or to surrounding plantations if their labor was sold to others. Thus, they had little reason to write, even if they could. On the other hand, it must be noted that in a society marked by racist paternalism, there are a number of primary source materials that indicate a range of emotions among southern whites toward African Americans, spanning from hatred to affection. The lack of primary source materials from African Americans means that it is difficult to know if these feelings were ever reciprocated by African Americans. Logically, it can be surmised that very few of them felt any tenderness toward whites. No human being wants to be enslaved, controlled, and demeaned. But it is impossible for historians to gain a crystal-clear picture of the emotional relationship between southern whites and African Americans. Nonetheless, the extant primary source materials do offer some insight into the feelings of Confederate soldiers *toward* African Americans even if there are comparatively few explaining how African Americans felt about white southerners.

Apart from cultural and social expectations, Confederate soldiers felt a range of emotions toward African Americans which are believed to have been generally dependent upon their level of exposure to Blacks, their level of personal involvement with slavery, and their political views. From birth, white southerners were raised in a society that was wholly engineered to justify slavery and white supremacy. In his speech to the U.S. Senate on March 4, 1858, Senator James Henry Hammond reflected this, stating, "In all social systems there must be a class to do the menial duties, to perform the drudgery of life . . . requiring but a low order of intellect and but little skill. . . . It constitutes the very mud-sill of society and of political government; and you might as well attempt to build a house in the air, as to build either the one or the other, except on this mud-sill. Fortunately for the South, she found a race adapted to that purpose to her hand. . . . We use them for our purpose, and call them slaves."[7]

Though Hammond's words do not fully encapsulate the broader range of white emotions toward African Americans, they nonetheless represent a central truss upon which southern society was built. If, as we have previously noted, social norms shaped the contours of expressed feelings between white southerners, they also shaped the expression of white feelings toward Black individuals. Writ large, white southerners did not view African Americans with great esteem. As a society, the South's agricultural economy was built on the continued subjugation of their race. Slavery was what enabled the South to become economically competitive in both domestic and international markets and thus its survival depended on slavery's defense in every arena, including politics, economics, religion, and culture. Southerners lived within a world that required them to perform vast feats of mental gymnastics to protect their economic interests and soothe their consciences.

Historian Michael W. Woods argues that the emotional norms encapsulating the institution of slavery in the South can be described as "ambivalent." This ambivalence was rooted in the sentimentalism of the antebellum period, which emphasized the cultivation of "love, gratitude, and affection within the home, and to eliminate anger from domestic relationships." This desire for domestic tranquility meshed well with the impulse toward self-mastery, and thus it was believed that men were responsible for maintaining familial harmony by cultivating love and affection for those in their care while stifling their own personal anger. In effect, though they could not fully control their families or circumstances, they could control themselves. This impulse was also expected to carry over into their relationships with their slaves, whose care, they believed, God had entrusted them with.[8] Yet, with slaves it was different. In this case, unlike their families, white southerners were expected to control African Americans in almost every regard. They would have to if they wanted to protect their own financial interests. But "owning" and controlling others represents a moral pitfall that would be difficult both to navigate and to justify. Much rested on white southerners' ability to deftly do so.

In the almost nine decades between the American Revolution and the outbreak of the American Civil War, the United States witnessed an explosion in the expansion of the institution of slavery. The federal census of 1790 counted 697,897 slaves in the country. By 1860, that number had increased over five times to 3,953,760 slaves and the number kept increasing as slavery continued to spread across the North American continent. By the outbreak of the American Civil War, slavery in the South still flourished even as it had largely died out in the North due to industrialization and immigration. Increasingly, cultural and political institutions shaped social expectations, class structures, laws, and politics around the institution of slavery. It was important to project slavery as a benevolent institution to justify its existence in a Judeo-Christian society. As such, slaveowners were expected to promote the well-being of their slaves—largely by creating the illusion of Black docility and material dependence. For example, slaves did not often have their own money and their survival depended upon those who purchased them. By making African Americans dependent upon their white "masters," southerners used their material wealth to reinforce cultural conceptions of Black inferiority and dependence. In some ways, they believe that this mirrored the parent-child relationship in which the dependent child relies upon the material largesse of his or her parents to survive. Gracious masters, southerners would argue, would always do so for those who were considered obedient and "good" slaves (or children). White southerners appropriated the framework of familial love and dependence to delineate their way of life from that of the industrial North, which had little room for interpersonal connection in the ongoing drive to decrease costs and increase profits.[9]

This is not to say that white southerners may not have believed in the humaneness of the institution of slavery. Many in fact did. They had to. For those who did believe, this belief was rooted in the culture of sentimentality of the prewar period. Some even went so far as to promote "Christian slavery."[10] Presbyterian minister Charles C. Jones reflected this in his book *The Religious Instruction of the Negroes* (1842), writing that "being brought here [from Africa] they were brought as *slaves;* in the providence of God we were constituted *masters;* superiors; and constituted their *guardians.* And all the laws in relation to them, civilly, socially, and religiously considered, were framed by ourselves. They thus were placed under our control, and not exclusively for our benefit but for theirs also."[11] This intertwining of Christian morality and sentimentality with the institution of chattel slavery represented a study in contradictions that could only be overcome by a complex system of cognitive dissonance and moral denial. This system provided emotional resolution to the anxiety-producing moral inconsistences of slavery. Moreover, it made certain conceptions of slavery intellectually and morally normative. Regardless of how one may have felt, surely ministers, politicians, parents, schoolteachers, and other prominent members of society could not be wrong about the religious, moral, and intellectual basis for the protection and propagation of slavery. Thus, many white southerners deferred to those who they saw as their social and intellectual "betters."

Southerners were inculcated with decades of culturally produced psychological defensive mechanisms to help assuage any feelings of regret or remorse. The institution of slavery was undergirded by a sort of fantasy land in which everyone was forced to play roles that, over a lifetime, must have been exhausting. Whites had to paint African Americans as bestial individuals driven by both a lack of moral certitude and intellect, even though their interactions with them would prove this to be false. Meanwhile, Blacks had to play along with this fantasy or face physical punishment for either themselves or their family members. Psychologist H. D. Kirkpatrick argued that "enslaved people had a powerful, emotionally eroding effect on their masters, an effect that was not much noticed or admitted by the slaveholder." The slaveholder's repeated attempts at intellectual and moral anesthetization were driven by the lust for wealth or the desire to elevate oneself over another, both of which are rooted in feelings of insecurity. These acts, in the words of Kirkpatrick, "murdered [slaveholders'] conscience. Slaveholding, in effect, was to be the cause of [a slaveholder's] psychic death."[12] Yet the willful denial of Black humanity in the face of evidence to the contrary was problematic. The only way for individuals not suffering from psychopathy to sidestep feelings of remorse for their involvement in chattel slavery was to recast the enslavement of others as an act born out of their empathy and benevolence toward those whom they saw as their natural inferiors. Only white southerners, as they saw it, were courageous enough to do the difficult but necessary work to elevate another race from their savagery while also building a wealthier and more prosperous civilization that benefited all whites.

This belief is demonstrated by a letter written by Corporal F. E. Duggar of the Gid Nelson Alabama Light Artillery to his mother. Like many others, Corporal Duggar used the motif of benign paternalism to assuage his guilt over owning slaves in pursuit of wealth and power. In an effort to purchase more land and provide for his mother and slaves, Corporal Duggar asks her to sell some of their slaves. To purchase the land, he writes that "I am willing to advance you five thousand, taking that much interest in it, if you will buy it as I expect to sell Jim for that, if I can find him a master that he likes. I don't wish to sell him at public Auction for fear he might fall in the hands of some one who would abuse him. Tell him for me, that I think I will be obliged to sell him, mainly because I have no home for him and have no regular place of hiring him." Facing the ingrained moral hazards of chattel slavery, Corporal Duggar agonized over what to do with the rest of his slaves, writing that "I am at a loss to know what to do with Louisa Agnes and Alex. If you want Agnes take her—but I am afraid as she never did do much at home that she will not suit you. I would like for Mrs Cobbs to take Julia and Thomas another year as she is doubtless a good mistress and will make them good servants. Alex I think I will have to sell or hire out as he is so troublesome to you at home. If you wish to keep him you can do so—though he doesn't suit you or Bro Rueben."[13]

What is clear from Corporal Duggar's letter is that he felt some affection or concern for his slaves. Seeing himself as their caretaker, as well as that of his mother and family, he agonizes over what is best for all involved. The fact that he is wholly unconcerned with buying and selling human beings, much less splitting them up from their families, is telling. Duggar's psychological dissonance is representative of that of thousands of southern slaveowners. On the one hand, he is willing to debase other human beings (though he does not probably see them that way) to meet his family's financial needs. On the other hand, he agonizes about what to do with them and wants to place them with individuals who he believes would better care for them. He is, in effect, taking on the role of their paternal caretaker. In this regard, Duggar is elevating himself above those who neglected or abused enslaved individuals, while also consoling himself with the belief that he is agonizing more over the care of his slaves than any northern factory would for its workers. Slavery's inherent inhumaneness was often ignored in favor of cultural constructs of black uplift and paternalistic care—a dichotomy that created immense moral and intellectual ambiguity among white southerners. By building their entire culture around the protection and promulgation of slavery, southerners could drown out the negative feelings wrought by the moral impropriety of slavery while also strengthening the collective belief in slavery's goodness and rightness through repeated exposure to racist and paternalistic narratives of white duty to Black uplift.

The emotional confusion wrought by this ambiguity allowed individuals like Duggar to pick and choose their reality. Devoid of absolute truth, slaveowners made their own truths which were designed to meet the emotional needs of the moment. If they could persuade themselves that enslaving individuals or splitting them up and selling them off was ultimately for their own good, they could rest easier knowing that they were doing what was best in a thorny situation. That they created this thorny situation out of their own greed and selfishness could be ignored as they could instead focus on the fact that, regardless of whether slaveowners like Duggar created the problem, they were providing the solution. If Blacks needed "civilizing," they were providing it. If they needed to be converted to Christianity, they would do so. The problem for slaveowners was not so much slavery but that they wanted to believe that Africans needed to be "improved." Slavery was just the means by which this would be accomplished and by seeing it this way, men like Duggar could feel good and righteous about their actions.

In Duggar's letter, he curiously refers to his slaves as "servants" rather than "slaves"—as if they had the option to be anything else. The use of this term found widespread use among southern slaveowners who used it to obfuscate the reality of slavery. "Servants" was ambiguous enough a term that it could denote those who willingly served or those who were forced to serve. Though this may denote a denial of reality on the part of Duggar, it is also possible that he really saw those whom he enslaved as something more than just property. The ambiguity of his choice in words allows him to navigate between the stark reality of those who were enslaved and those who willingly wanted to serve his family. By being ambiguous, he could choose whatever he needed for the moment. If he felt happy or content, they were "servants." If he was angry, he could call them "slaves." Either way, they were his to do with as he wished.

Though many cynics (including myself) could easily describe Duggar's letter as one in which an individual engaged in a moral wrong is simply trying to delude himself and others into thinking that he cares for those whom he is harming, the uncomfortable truth is that he actually may have cared. In fact, to placate their potential gnawing sense of guilt and shame, many slaveowners like Duggar would have had to recast what they were doing as acts borne out of concern for others rather than selfish gain. In some ways, this may not have been all smoke and mirrors. Slaveowners may have really believed that they not only cared for their slaves, but that they had a real paternal duty to care for them. The relationship between slave masters and slaves was often one of forced reciprocity in which masters sought to justify their enslavement of others. Meanwhile, those enslaved often used this paternalistic ambiguity to protect themselves and their families while also obtaining what they needed to survive. Within this ambiguous matrix of white sentimentality and Black practicality, the play acting and moral denial of southern chattel slavery could stretch on without, it was hoped, the possibility of it spilling over into violence.[14] Though Duggar may have been sincere in his belief that he cared for his slaves, it is doubtful that they generally felt the same way toward him. But they could not tell him so, lest they be punished or sold. Instead, they would have to play along and by doing so, placate Duggar's emotions and help soothe his conscience. As historian Eugene Genovese noted, "cruel, unjust, exploitative, oppressive, slavery bound two peoples together in bitter antagonism while creating an organic relationship so complex and ambivalent that neither could express the simplest human feelings without reference to the other."[15]

As early as 1979, historian Paul D. Escott argued "that masters and slaves lived in different worlds" and that "the strength of cultural differences set these two groups apart from each other and gave the slaves a fundamental sense of themselves as an oppressed racial group. For most individuals, physical proximity only heightened the sense of mental separation that existed under slavery." However, Escott also recognizes that there could have been cases of genuine feelings between slaves and masters and that "in such cases the individuals involved made an exception of each other without forgetting the enmity that existed between their groups." These relationships, as uncomfortable as they are to recognize, probably developed because of the close physical proximity wrought by plantation life. However, there was no guarantee that this would occur, and it is doubtful that most of the warm feelings felt by self-deluded slave masters were ever truly ever reciprocated by their slaves.[16]

Yet some white southerners truly believed that they were "lifting up" those whom they saw as their inferiors. Many slaveholders interacted with their slaves on a daily basis and were personally involved in many of the major events of their lives. Some even went so far as to hold celebrations for milestones such as weddings and births.[17] Apart from the delusion that they were God's appointed paternalistic caretakers, slave masters sought to soothe their consciences while also practically protecting their investment. Slaves found themselves trapped within the delusions of those who held power. As former slave Henry Box Brown noted, "the religion of the slave-holder is everywhere a system of mere delusion, got up expressly for the purpose of deceiving the poor slaves, for everywhere the leading doctrine in the slave-holder's religion is, that it is the duty of the slave to obey his master in all things."[18]

This relational dynamic began early in both masters' and slaves' childhoods. On many plantations, white and Black children played together and grew up together and this relationship often carried over into adulthood. In his tours of the South in 1853, writer Frederick Law Olmsted noted that he was "struck with the close co-habitation and association of black and white—negro women are carrying black and white babies together in their arms; black and white children are playing together." While seated on a train, he noticed a white woman and her daughter sit down with one of her slaves, whom Olmsted described as a "very pretty mulatto girl." The writer was astonished as he saw that "they all talked and laughed together, and the girls munched confectionary out of the same paper, with a familiarity and closeness of intimacy that would have been noticed with astonishment, if not with manifest displeasure, in almost any chance company at the North." Yet this would always be a relationship built on feelings of white superiority and Black inferiority. As Olmsted noted, "When the negro is definitely a slave, it would seem that the alleged natural antipathy of the white race to associate with him is lost."[19] Unlike the relationships between white southern men and their wives and children, there was no room for emotional equality between white slaveowners and Black slaves. Whereas white southern men cared about the emotional status of their loved ones and took part in their emotional development, the emotional status and development of Black slaves were not considered to be a white man's concern. To make it their concern would have been to allow themselves to see the humanity of their property and the inherent contradictions of chattel slavery and Christian morality.

Yet, as noted before, this does not mean that white southern men did not care at all about their slaves. Peculiarly, the letters read for this project indicate that white slaveowners were sometimes very interested in interacting with their slaves, even from a distance. For example, Sergeant John Crittenden of the 34th Alabama Infantry Regiment asked his wife to say hello to his family's slaves in 59 of 123 (47.97 percent) of his letters. Strangely, these entreaties were generally found in his closing comments after bidding his family adieu and reminding them how much he loved them. Writing to his mother, he asked her to "Kiss Bettie and the babies for [me]. Tell all the negroes howdy. Give my respects to all enquiring friends. I remain as ever your son John Crittenden."[20] More strikingly, he signs off one of his letters by exhorting his wife to "give my love to all Pa Ma & your Pa and all of the negroes."[21] Even his brother William exhorted his mother to give "my love to the Negroes."[22] In a striking representation of his own cognitive dissonance, Sergeant Crittenden often wrote letters to his wife in which he exhorted her to say hello to his slaves on ledgers used to catalog the slave inhabitants of a given area.[23]

By refusing to see the implications of their actions and beliefs, white slaveowners could protect themselves from feeling the negative emotions attached to the moral compromise of slavery. Likewise, they lived in a society that normalized slavery and encouraged slaveowners to treat their slaves with kindness and to eschew anger as a source of control. Family members and slaves, in the eyes of many southerners, were to be bound by mutual love and the ideal of domestic tranquility and reciprocity.[24] White enslavers could feel good about what they saw as their contributions to an inferior race and by taking on the role of their paternal care-takers, they were fulfilling the cultural mandate in which men were expected to serve their families and communities. In this sense, they could tell themselves that slavery served their family's financial needs while also serving the needs of Blacks who they saw as intellectually, morally, and psychologically deficient. In reality, white slaveowners were trying to avoid the shame and guilt of their true motivation: serving only themselves.

It is clear from the examples above, however, that some white southerners did feel positive emotions toward their slaves. Many young men started out their lives by interacting and playing with young slaves. As they got older, these relationships became much more formal, and whites and Blacks were expected to find their place in the racial hierarchy. Thus, some of these positive feelings on the part of whites may have developed organically. More often, however, they were rooted in paternal-istic ideology and masters and slaves lived in a bizarre emotional symbiosis in which a master's level of affection for their slaves was often in direct proportion to the latter's perceived "good conduct." This fact is important as popular advice literature of the period exhorted masters to treat their slaves with kindness and to maintain emotional restraint in dealing with them. This proved immensely difficult when slaves' conduct was perceived as "bad" and their actions drew out feelings of anger and resentment—emotions which are far more difficult to control. The result was that slaves could use their behavior to manipulate the feelings of enslavers and in this way, the power structure of the master-slave relationship was sometimes turned upside down. Those enslaved could either play into their enslavers' expectations for Black docility and obedience and leave them with positive feelings of them or they could act in ways which ran contrary to these expectations and evoke a loss of emotional control. Either way, at least in regards to emotions, slaves actually exerted immense power over their enslavers—to a degree that many slaveholders did not understand or want to admit.[25] According to historian Erin Austin Dwyer, "Slave narratives reveal that enslaved people were acutely aware of the effect they could have on slaveholders' emotions, whether they were intentionally trying to evoke certain feelings or not. . . . Some enslaved people deliberately tried to influence their owners' feelings."[26] Like their children, white slaveowners looked to slaves as sources of happiness, comfort, and self-confidence. The more obsequious slaves were to their masters, the more this belief was reinforced. Yet slaves could also use this to their advantage. In effect, many became adept at manipulating their "masters'" emotions for their own purposes.

Likewise, Dwyer notes that the emotional exchange between slaveowners and their slaves represented a "currency of power" in which proslavery advocates "wielded feelings like love, terror, and jealousy to maintain and justify the institution."[27] This could take a variety of forms, including using anger on a broad scale to stoke widespread discontent with northern policies or on a small scale by using love or terror to attempt to control their slaves. On the other hand, slaves could wield emotional power by upsetting the equanimity of the plantation and drawing out feelings of anger on the part of their masters.[28] In this way, slaves could impel white southerners to violate the masculine norms of self-mastery and emotional stoicism. It is no wonder then that many enslavers reacted with such anger when slaves shattered the illusion of patriarchy, white hegemony, and emotional self-control.

Members of the planter class often viewed slaves as lacking emotional capacity.[29] After watching his family divided up by slaveowners and himself being removed from the plantation, former slave Henry Box Brown noted that "the tyrant slaveholder regards not the social, or domestic feelings of the slave, and makes his division according to the moneyed value they possess, without giving the slightest consideration to the domestic or social ties by which the individuals are bound to each other; indeed their common expression is that 'n——rs have no feelings.'"[30] This exaltation of self and denial of others' emotions is representative of the abuse and the self-aggrandizement of white planter culture in the nineteenth century. To deny that Blacks felt emotion was another justification for the protection of slavery and, most importantly, slaveowners' own pecuniary gain.

***

Historian Michael E. Woods sees the development of affective norms surrounding slavery as due to four distinct factors, namely "the end of the international slave trade, the rise of sentimentalism, the growth of organized abolitionist and proslavery movements, and the western expansion of slavery." With the U.S. Constitution's abolishment of American involvement in the international slave trade in 1808, slaveowners sought to protect their "investment" by encouraging slaves to reproduce. Much as they had with cattle, sheep, and goats, white slaveowners believed that the purchase of Black women would provide an almost limitless return on their investment. Moreover, the children of these women could be sold off to make extra money, if necessary. To justify these actions, white southerners denied Black affective norms, going so far as to argue that Black mothers lacked the maternal affection so celebrated among white mothers.[31] In the minds of many, the absence or presence of emotion was the delineating line between human and animal.

Meanwhile, abolitionists railed against the embrace of Black slavery as a logical fallacy, the degradation of Christian nobility, white morality, and democratic justice. Abolitionists appealed to the sentimentalism of their age by providing vivid pictures of slavery's horrors. In some ways, they juxtaposed the failure of white slaveowners to maintain emotional self-control with the emotional maturity of Black slaves who learned to control their emotions for fear of facing brutal consequences. Thus, it was not African Americans who were animal-like. Rather, it was those who enslaved them—individuals who denied their own humanity for selfish gain and who acted out of the basest of emotions—who were acting brutish. One example of this juxtaposition is Harriet Beecher Stowe's book *Uncle Tom's Cabin,* published in 1852. The novel's central character was a slave named Tom who represented Christian nobility and moral virtue and who stood in sharp contrast to his white "owner" Simon Legree—a man marked by savagery and moral depravity. Stowe thus exposed slavery as a system in which whites debased themselves by becoming the very things that they accused Blacks of being—emotionally infantile creatures who lived only out of their animal instincts. Many private letters and diaries of slaveholders demonstrate that, on the eve of the war, they "strove to cultivate love and repress anger within their plantation households. But it was a losing battle. Bedeviled by their inability to meet the lofty emotional standards of domestic sentimentalism," Woods notes, "masters increasingly blamed meddling outsiders for corroding the social bonds of the plantation South. By 1861, many slaveholders turned to separate nationhood as a solution to their persistent and disturbing emotional dilemma."[32] The issue of slavery represented a clash of emotional appeals as proslavery factions justified slavery as a morally good, paternalistic institution that uplifted those who were emotionally and intellectually inferior. Meanwhile, antislavery forces sought to counter this approach by presenting African Americans as human beings who not only felt emotions but were in many ways the moral betters of slaveowners. Both sides used emotional appeals to push their points to a broader non-slaveholding public.

Strikingly, displays of emotion surrounding the issue of slavery are not prominent in the letters read for this project. While some letters acknowledged or defended the institution of slavery, most who addressed the subject of African Americans made racist statements that were not in direct reference to slavery. This is not to argue that soldiers did not believe in slavery. Their racist beliefs were in large part born out of the cultural zeitgeist of a system purpose-built to preserve and promulgate slavery. But it does indicate that the issue of slavery was not top of mind for many Confederate soldiers during the war—at least when writing to their families. Historian James McPherson's study of Civil War soldiers notes that "only 20 percent of the sample of 429 Southern soldiers explicitly voiced proslavery convictions in their letters or diaries," and that slaveholding families expressed these views at a much larger rate (33 percent to 12 percent for nonslaveholding families). McPherson also notes that no Confederate soldier dissented from a proslavery view—though in this case, the adage that "the absence of evidence is not the evidence of absence" applies. Rather than explicitly referencing slavery, soldiers in his sample more often chose to pontificate on "liberty, rights, and the horrors of subjugation."[33] The ideals of liberty and rights (that is, to own slaves) were a hallmark of Confederate ideology. So too was the belief that Confederate soldiers must either fight or themselves become slaves of the industrial North.[34] In this way, they could cast themselves as victims of injustice rather than as perpetrators.

Psychologist H. D. Kirkpatrick noted in his study of elite slaveholders that they utilized four specific techniques to cope with their participation in chattel slavery. These included denial, projection, delusional projection, and rationalization. The denial of Black humanity was used to justify the physical brutality and sexual exploitation of slaves while also holding onto white moral certitude. "Projection" involved the attribution of feelings to others that one denies having oneself and the act of projection is often intertwined with denial. Slaveowners and slave supporters often fell into both projection and denial. Though slaveowners were expected to be models of Christian virtue, paternalistic care, and emotional control, many violently punished their slaves for even the smallest of perceived slights or infractions. In punishing the "sinful acts" of others, they were themselves committing sinful acts. In punishing others for living out of their passions, whites were living out of their own. In some ways, the worst punishments may have been enacted upon those slaves in whom a master saw more of himself. To justify these actions, slaveowners couched their punishment as discipline for their wayward "children." In doing so, they were merely inflicting pain for the betterment of their victims' personal growth and character development. Punishment was not about asserting his dominance and control, the slaveowner could contend. Rather, it was a tool for maturing those whom God had burdened him to care for.

Slaveowners resorted to "delusional projection" by projecting false beliefs upon others out of incorrect inferences about external reality. For example, Europeans saw African Americans as inferior and animal-like as they compared the latter's dark skins to those of apes. Likewise, African American males were stereotyped as having a predilection for raping white women due to their lack of moral development and uncontrolled lust. This cognitive dissonance becomes more prominent when one realizes that the stereotypes served primarily as a tool for white slaveowners to deny the reality and prevalence of their own sexual violence. Finally, slaveowners justified slavery through a process of rationalization, in which they framed slavery as a business which, in the words of John C. Calhoun, "united the interests of capital and labor." With so many reaping the financial rewards of slavery, it was important to everyone involved to cloak the reality of slavery in terms of dollars and cents. Focusing on the ends helped take many eyes off the means.[35] Slave labor and the economic and social benefits that it conferred on whites (even on those who did not own slaves) left white society in a sort of tenuous equilibrium in which social order depended upon the degradation of an entire race. The threat of slave insurrections (such as John Brown's Raid in 1859) evinced mass anxiety among whites of all social and economic castes. So entrenched was the institution of slavery in the South that it seemed as if the entirety of the South's emotional state depended upon the preservation of slavery and the suppression of slave rebellions.[36] If white southerners could control their external worlds through maintaining a rigid racial

hierarchy, securing vast sums of wealth, and creating a world in which the degradation of others would lead to the exaltation of themselves, then maybe they could
feel some internal peace. This attempt to control the externalities of one's life to
bring about positive feelings of security and peace represents an impulse that is
very strong in the Western world into the present day. It was no different in the
nineteenth century.

The anxiety surrounding slavery was largely due to the fact that it was the glue
that held elite white society together. By stoking fears of black insurrection or the
violation of white purity, white southerners used anxiety as an important tool for
motivating southerners to defend the institution of slavery. Slave powers hyped up
their rhetoric around abolitionism and Republicanism to paint them as groups bent
on dissolving the very bonds that held southern society together. The South's entire
worldview was predicated on white hegemony and anything that threatened the
rewards reaped from this hegemony needed to be eliminated. Moreover, as has been
noted, Confederate soldiers were anxious to protect their families', and particularly
their children's, futures, many of which were dependent upon the financial rewards
of enslaving others.

The irony of the Confederate army is that it was filled with men who fought to
subjugate others and who, in the process, found themselves subjugated. If sentimentalism and self-mastery represented the paragon of nineteenth-century masculinity,
the military had little room for either. Over time, many Confederates felt that they
too had become slaves. As enlisted men, they no longer had control over their lives.
Officers dictated almost every aspect of their lives, and their decisions could cost
a man his life or the lives of his friends. They now served at the whim of distant
politicians and nearby officers. Sergeant R. E. Corry of the 11th Alabama Cavalry
felt this acutely, writing to his wife that "I can hardly bear the thought of going off
without seeing or hearing from you in some way but the 'powers that be' care not
for this and I suppose it is my duty to go on where ever bid without murmuring.
O, how I wish to be a free man again without masters or mistress save your own
dear indulgent self. I could serve willingly and happily for you would smile upon
and love me."[37] Corry's sentiments are a familiar refrain for anyone who has read
letters of Confederate soldiers. Though certainly a statement born of Victorian
sentimentality, Corry's assertion that he would be willing to subjugate himself to

his wife is reflective of the feelings of many Confederate soldiers. Their wives and children were their whole worlds and men like him reshaped what it meant to be a man. Men like Corry simply wanted to go home, not prove their manhood. In the latter two years of the war, much of the masculine bravado had been quashed. Yet, much of the anxiety over the dissolution of slavery remained. Slave ownership was a well-worn path to economic and social advancement and its pecuniary rewards were potentially so great that few wanted to let it go. Likewise, if slavery was eliminated, what would prevent white southern men themselves from becoming slaves? They would be tied to working the land in perpetuity to survive. Their children could hope for little better. Southerners captivated by the Jeffersonian vision of agrarian self-sufficiency and economic independence saw the abolishment of slavery as the path down which they would become cogs in the industrial machinery of the North.[38]

Yet with the outbreak of war, white southerners bound themselves to an army in which they were now beholden to the whims of their government, country, and officers. Little did many realize that enlistment involved the fervent circumscription of their freedom and ambition. For the average Confederate soldier, wartime service provided little hope of seeing the fulfillment of their grand pre-war visions. There would be no self-sufficiency now. Though they feared becoming cogs in the industrial machines of the North, white southerners instead submitted themselves to becoming cogs in the machinery of the Confederate army. No longer did the individual matter. Now, only the totality was important.[39]

The frustration that soldiers felt about their own perceived enslavement was exacerbated by what many saw as superior treatment toward African Americans in camp. Many soldiers of means brought bondservants with them and these individuals became integral to the machinations of unit officers and, in some cases, messes of enlisted men. These slaves were sent to forage for food, and in the process they often foraged for themselves; others were forced to bury the Union dead and sometimes they helped themselves to their equipment; and almost all of them avoided the horror of participating in battle. Meanwhile, many hungry Confederate soldiers found Richmond's promises of bounteous provisions as hollow as their stomachs, looking upon these bondservants with jealous malice. Likewise, the fact that those who they saw as their racial inferiors did not have to participate in battle or face being shot for refusing to fight caused immense widespread anger among Confederate soldiers.[40] One Virginia artillerist wrote in his diary "I wish I were an *army* n——r until 'this cruel war is over.' They are the happiest dogs I ever saw."[41] Likewise, Sergeant John Crittenden of the 34th Alabama Infantry Regiment complained to his wife that "we drew to day two crackers to the man for one days rations. I made a calculation to day and find that it takes not quite eight bushels of meal to bread 1 Soldier a year That is cheap living. Not as much as is allowed a negro and he where he can get other things besides. Some alteration will have to take place or else serious results will take place."[42]

This frustration was generally rooted in perception rather than reality. Confederate soldiers steeped in the beliefs of their own racial superiority fed their resentment of Black bondservants. Moreover, the growing sense that they themselves had become enslaved and had every part of their lives dictated, much like those of the bondservants who worked beside them, stirred feelings of humiliation and resentment. Soldiers could not leave their unit as they wished, were told what to do, were made to perform menial and backbreaking tasks, and had their entire lives circumscribed by the whims of their officers and the needs of the Confederacy. Whereas before the war, they may have felt some power over African Americans, now all they could do was stand by and watch as those who they considered inferior now *seemingly* had more freedom than themselves. Southern men, who were often sensitive to any perceived slight to their own power, burned with white hot rage.[43]

Some of this anger was stoked by the Emancipation Proclamation. Issued by U.S. president Abraham Lincoln in January 1863, the Emancipation Proclamation was a direct attempt to undercut the Confederacy's ability to carry out the war by taking away their primary labor force. Already facing a manpower shortage, without Black slaves, the Confederacy would have no hope of winning the war, as enslaved laborers were integral both to the operations along the home front and in many cases along the battle front as well. In his first inaugural address, Lincoln promised that "I have no purpose, directly or indirectly, to interfere with the institution of slavery in the States where it exists. I believe I have no lawful right to do so, and I have no inclination to do so."[44] After secession, he used his background as a lawyer to bend the war's aims to include emancipation. Though Lincoln argued that secession was constitutionally unsound, he also stated that since these states were no longer under the U.S. Constitution (which protected the institution of slavery), he now had the right to abolish slavery in the seceded states by fiat, and he did so only a few months after the battle of Antietam. This act confirmed southerners' suspicions that Lincoln and his ilk were radical abolitionists who wanted to pull apart the entire social structure of the South, and as it collapsed, drag their families, fortunes, and futures down with it.[45] Seeing the growing movement towards abolitionism as the war progressed, the anxiety produced by this shift led to a future in which white anger would spill over into decades of rage. Finding themselves losing control in the face of abolition, southern whites would spend the next century attempting to reclaim that control.

Even more infuriating than abolitionism was President Lincoln's plan to turn former slaves and free African Americans into Union soldiers. Armed Blacks were the clearest representation of white powerlessness. Much angst and violence had been enacted before the war out of the fear of slave insurrections. Southerners could not believe that those for whom they expended so much treasure and turmoil to guide and uplift would ever rebel, apart from some malevolent external force— usually northerners. Now tens of thousands of them were flocking to Union lines and donning blue uniforms on their own volition. Even still, cognitive dissonance reared its head, as southerners sought out simplified explanations for this behavior. Moreover, their anxieties at armed Black soldiers accelerated as they believed that giving them weapons would allow them to rape white women and destroy white communities at will.[46] By freeing Black slaves, southerners believed that northerners were extricating Black men from the only institution (and from the only people) who could keep their worst impulses in check. By arming them, southerners believed that northerners were allowing men of rapacious urges almost unchecked power to enact their desires on others.

The very presence of Black soldiers marching through the streets of southern towns pushed many Confederate soldiers to the point of unbridled rage. White hegemony required the physical and social oppression of those considered "less than" to continue propagating the ideology that undergird the South's racial and social structure.[47] Because of this, some Confederate soldiers promised to kill every Black soldier that they came across.[48] Many more itched to reassert their hegemony. John Crittenden again wrote that "the enemy is reported to be perfectly quiet at this time. I am told that they have a Brigade of Negroes at Ringgold If such is a fact our boys may get what they have been wishing for sometime and that is to have a fight with a negro Regt."[49] Crittenden and others would have plenty of opportunities, as it is estimated that more than 186,000 Black and white soldiers eventually served under the umbrella of the Bureau of Colored Troops—a number that represents "a force larger than the field armies that either Lt. Gen. Ulysses S. Grant or Maj. Gen. William T. Sherman directly oversaw at the height of their campaigns in 1864 and 1865."[50]

White southerners felt betrayed. So inculcated from birth had they been with the idea of Black docility that many could not fathom why African Americans rebelled against their caretakers. Why were their "children" now wanting to kill their "parents?" This insouciance enraged them and this often led to the murder of hundreds of Black soldiers in the wake of battle.[51] Atrocities committed against United States Colored Troops increased exponentially as the war progressed and the country drew closer to complete abolition. In 1864 alone, reacting emotionally to what they saw as Black mutiny, Confederate soldiers massacred United States Colored Troops at the Battle of Poison Spring, the Battle of the Crater, the Battle of Saltville, and the Battle of Fort Pillow.[52] Their white officers would fare little better. Less than a year before, in May 1863, the Confederate Congress authorized the execution of captured white officers of Black regiments and implied that captured Black soldiers should either be resold into slavery, placed in the service of the Confederate Army, or summarily executed.[53] Many Confederate soldiers heartily obliged.

On one end of the spectrum, Confederate soldiers were motivated to fight due to their emotional connections to family, friends, and comrades. Their love for these individuals and the support which they received from them was instrumental to the continuance of the Confederate war effort and the ability of southern men to stay in the army. On the other end of the spectrum, their anger at the arming of Black soldiers and the undermining of their racist preconceptions also motivated them to keep fighting. Black soldiers threatened to undermine the entire economic and social order of the South. Thus, they were a threat that needed to be subjugated or, if control could not again be reasserted, eliminated. Likewise, Black soldiers knew that if they were captured, they would most likely meet a terrible end. It is no wonder therefore that when white Confederate and Black Union soldiers met on the field of battle, as one historian noted, "no fraternization or tacit truces took place along the lines where they confronted each other."[54]

In August 1864, outside of Petersburg, Virginia, North Carolinian Henry Biggs openly admitted to picking off what he and his regiment believed were Black Union soldiers stationed across from them. One morning, his regiment attacked the enemy's skirmish line and, to their disappointment, found that the troops before them were white.[55] Likewise, Lieutenant Edmund Dewitt Patterson of the 9th Alabama Infantry Regiment was captured at Gettysburg and imprisoned at Johnson's Island in Ohio. After learning that Union officials halted prisoner exchanges due to Confederate officials' unwillingness to treat Black soldiers as protected prisoners of war, Patterson wrote in his diary that "I hope there may never be another exchange. If the Yankee government will persist in arming the negroes of the South and sending them against us, I believe it will amount to the 'Black Flag.' One thing I think is very certain and that is that the army in Virginia will not take negro prisoners. . . . If we lose everything else, let us preserve our honor."[56] Civilians were not immune to these intense feelings as well. Black soldiers who survived being captured at the Battle of the Crater were paraded through the streets of Danville, Virginia, where citizens demanded their execution. Some citizens even went so far as to attempt to hang two white officers of Black soldiers.[57]

By 1864, as the tide of war turned in the Union's favor, Confederate soldiers believed that the looming racial apocalypse was imminent. Not only were Confederate armies losing on the battlefield, but former slaves and free Blacks enlisted in the Union army en masse, slaves abandoned their plantations, and Union soldiers marched throughout the South virtually unhindered. Before their eyes, the social equilibrium that had held white southern society together was collapsing. In response, many soldiers doubled down.[58] Fear and anxiety encouraged members of all white southern social strata to coalesce around their mutual hatred for Yankees and Black troops.[59] White men were losing control. No longer could they control their own emotions, nor could they control those over whom they had once dangled the prospect of slavery or freedom, life or death.

During the war, arguably the greatest collective outpouring of emotion among Confederate soldiers on the issue of race came when the Confederate Congress passed the "Negro Soldier Bill" on March 13, 1865, allowing the enlistment of Black soldiers in the Confederate army. This was an act of utter desperation and a sign of how much things had changed from the beginning of the war. Regarding the sample for his book *For Cause and Comrades,* historian James McPherson noted that half of his sample who commented on the arming of Black soldiers supported it while the other half angrily opposed it. Some were so enraged at what they saw as the humiliating prospect of arming former slaves and free Blacks that they willingly deserted.[60] In this vein, Sergeant Joseph F. Maides of the 27th North Carolina Infantry Regiment wrote to his mother that "I did not volunteer my services to fight for a free negroes country but to fight for a free white mans country & I do not think I love my country well enough to fight with black soldiers."[61] Many men in Maides's company had already deserted by the time that he wrote this letter. Relatively few supported the arming of Black soldiers and it was only when the Confederacy was drawing its final breaths that many relented on the matter.[62] The irony was not lost on everyone. "Now it is proposed that *we* should do the same thing—should 'lay aside our scruples,' and commit this great sin against our slaves, against ourselves, against humanity, and against God," William W. Holden wrote in the *North Carolina Standard.* "Is our government going to do it? If it does, it will proclaim by such an act that the white men of the Confederate States are not able to achieve their own liberties, and will thus in reality give up a contest which it will seek to prolong by the cowardly sacrifice of an unwarlike and comparatively innocent race."[63]

Though the idea of white unity did not fade even in the final year of the war, many Confederate soldiers were amenable to the idea of arming Black men and giving them their freedom if it meant the survival of the Confederacy.[64] This was again an act of cognitive dissonance rooted in the overwhelming desire to assuage their anxiety through control. While Confederate soldiers felt immense anxiety at the prospect of freeing some slaves and turning them into Confederate soldiers, they felt even more anxiety at the prospect of losing the political and social system which made slavery possible. The war shattered the illusion of white control. As it progressed, and Union forces marched to and fro throughout the South, slaves ran away or enlisted in the Union army. Instead of admitting their own self-deception, white southerners argued that slaves ran away or enlisted in the Union army only because they were deceived or unduly influenced by Union soldiers. Most slaveowners could not stomach the idea that their slaves never really cared for or needed them. This realization was too painful for many white southerners whose own emotional equanimity lay in the lie of paternalism and racial hegemony. This cognitive dissonance was a powerful force that shaped attempts on the part of white southerners to reimpose this hegemony during Reconstruction.

In the waning months of the war, as Confederate soldiers increasingly faced the prospect of a nation without slavery, their emotions pooled into a cauldron of fear, anger, anxiety, and insecurity. They feared for their families' livelihoods, the collapse of a racial order that seemed to hold society together, and, more importantly, the possibility of becoming enslaved themselves. White southerners (particularly elites), who once held so much power, now found themselves overpowered by those whom they considered their inferiors—Yankees and African Americans. White southerners could only see the economic and social degradation that awaited them if they surrendered and as a result, many fought on even when it was pointless.[65] No doubt, some found death preferable to a world in which whites would have to face the social, moral, and emotional reality of the web of lies and self-deception that they had constructed.

The collapse of the war effort in 1865 marked an emotional turning point for many dyed-in-the-wool Confederates. Their continued fighting in the face of clear evidence of its futility was further evidence of their need for control. They were again trying to control external circumstances in order to quell the overwhelming anxieties that would come with the collapse of their fabricated world. When the end did come, the overwhelming feelings of gloom on the part of Confederates would be exacerbated by the decision to station Black Union soldiers throughout the South during Reconstruction.[66] At the same time, Radical Republicans in Congress pushed vociferously for Black political equality, thus fulfilling many of the worst prophecies expressed by white southerners before the war. As is often the case, feelings of sadness intermingled with hopelessness eventually yielded to rage. This collective and self-righteous anger gave white southerners a feeling of control, even when they had none. Once again, during Reconstruction, they would try to control their external world (and its actors) to bring about what they felt was internal peace. In effect, control felt like safety.

However, this is not to say that all white southerners were incensed at the loss of white social and economic power. According to historian Reid Mitchell, many Confederate soldiers *knew* that they were defeated and were thus "more willing to accept changes in the South than they would ever be again . . . they believed that the North had the power and the will to create a revolution in Southern society." Many Union soldiers, who also had deep feelings of racial superiority to Blacks, were frustrated that in the postwar period they were now tasked with protecting the rights of African Americans when they had originally only enlisted to preserve the Union.[67] The seeds of white unity were thus sown and this fact would later lead to the betrayal of African Americans at the tail end of Reconstruction.

Yet some southerners came through the war having their perceptions of slavery altered by their horrific experiences in combat. At the end of the war, Captain Samuel T. Foster wondered in his diary, "Who is to blame for all this waste of human life?" and "What does it amount to? Has there been anything gained by all this sacrifice? What were we fighting for, the principles of slavery?" His opinion of the war shifted as he came to the inevitable conclusion that all that he fought for was for naught. "Men's minds can change so sudden from opinions, of life long, to new ones a week old," he wrote; "men who have not only been taught from their infancy that the institution of slavery was right; but men who actually owned and held slaves up to this time have now changed in their opinions regarding slavery, so as to be able to see the other side of the question—to see that for many to have property in man was wrong, and that the Declaration of Independence meant more than they had ever been able to see before." "These ideas come not from the Yanks or northern people," Foster surmised, "but come from reflection and reasoning among ourselves."[68] For many southerners, the very worst that could have happened *did happen* and while some were wracked with anxiety over the tectonic changes, others came to accept this new world. The Old South was gone. It would be up to them to build a new one.

CONCLUSION

REUNION
AND
REALITY

HOW THE WAR SHAPED SOUTHERN MEN'S
POSTWAR LIVES, RELATIONSHIPS, AND MOTIVATIONS

On the morning of April 9, 1865, Private William Abernathy and his comrades of the 17th Mississippi Infantry Regiment stood around the regimental colors for the last time. Enlisting in the Confederate army in April 1861 at the tender age of seventeen, Abernathy transitioned to adulthood beneath these colors. Though young, he fought in some of the bloodiest battles in the war including the Battle of Seven Pines, Antietam, Fredericksburg, Chancellorsville, Gettysburg, Chickamauga, and Cold Harbor. Though wounded six times over the course of the war, Abernathy served to the bitter end. In the end, he and his comrades' masculine courage and sacrifice were not enough and they all knew that they were defeated. In one last show of defiance, each member of the regiment stepped forward and tore a piece of their beloved flag until there was nothing left. Soon, Abernathy recounts, "we gave way to womanish tears . . . and shall I say it, cried bitterly." Writing thirty-seven years after Robert E. Lee's surrender at Appomattox Courthouse, Virginia, Abernathy grew wistful as he remembered the men of his company and all that they had endured together. "We had entered the Confederate Army one hundred and thirty strong," he wrote, "the faces of whom gathered around the old flag that night and parted; among them of the old company comes vividly before me. . . . All of them bore scars of the siege in battle. And now, when the Heavens were black, they parted the old flag, and wending their way homeward, took up life again."[1]

Men who faced four years of unrelenting suffering and self-sacrifice now found themselves with no country to speak of. For all their toil—only made possible by the emotional support of their families, friends, and comrades—Confederate soldiers were now left without a sense of place in the world. The Confederacy and all that it embodied—white supremacy, black slavery, agricultural dominance, classical morality, and the Jeffersonian vision for America—were in ashes. Along with them were the hopes and dreams of men who before the war believed that along with their own courage and character, the rightness of their cause meant that God had predestined them to eventual victory. Now, many were left in confusion and some even went so far as to end their own lives rather than face this new world.[2]

Yet many also felt a rush of joy at the prospect of seeing their families again. The war had changed them. Four years of struggle and loss had eroded much of the exuberance they felt about the war's political and social causes. Moreover, it had stripped many of them of their youthful innocence. Now what lay before them was the hope of joyful reunion. Life would no longer be a constant struggle to survive. When soldiers from the Army of Northern Virginia streamed through the streets of Atlanta on their way home, one newspaper noted that they walked with "buoyant steps and exulting smiles at the thought of soon again meeting with 'loved ones at home,' from whom they had been separated for years." Others, however, openly expressed their "anxiety and despondency."[3]

"Many a weak, puny boy was returned to his parents a robust, healthy, *manly man,*" Carlton McCarthy waxed poetically. "Many a timid helpless boy went home a brave, independent man. Many a wild, reckless boy went home sobered, serious, and trustworthy. And many whose career at home was wicked and blasphemous went home changed in heart, with principles fixed, to comfort and sustain the old age of those who gave them to their country, not expecting to receive them again."[4] Yet as these soldiers crossed the thresholds of their homes, they unknowingly entered a world that was as much changed by the war as they were. Little children were now big, wives were more independent, and everyone wanted to put the awful experience of the war behind them. In many cases, the soldier couldn't. Even now, the common soldier felt the loss of control. The horrors of the war often plagued him and now instead of being surrounded by those who understood his experience, he was surrounded by those who never tasted the spartan lifestyle of the soldier, much less the trauma of combat. Some soldiers felt as if they entered a sort of purgatory in which, McCarthy notes, they "felt that they were not yet returned to civil life, but 'foraging' on the neutral ground between war and peace, neither soldiers nor citizens" and were now tasked with, on their own, "the responsibility of 'finding themselves.'"[5]

Shedding their uniforms, former Confederate soldiers could not shed the effects that the war had upon them. During the war, they sought emotional stasis and reunion with the very people who now surrounded them. But how could a man leave behind all that he experienced in war and still be expected to take on domestic duties? Moreover, why did he often feel as if he never escaped the war? The sights, sounds, smells, and emotions often haunted him.[6] In many cases, he had lost good friends, and this loss made putting the war behind him feel like a betrayal of those who could not return. This was the experience of thousands of returning soldiers. Many refused to forget.

Out of a total population of 5.5 million, 450,000 white southerners were casualties of the war, representing 8.2 percent of the total population. In comparison, 1.8 percent of the total northern population were casualties of the war.[7] The dead were friends and comrades of those who now found themselves trying to reintegrate into the alien world of domesticity. Indeed, the very family members upon whom these former soldiers had depended for years themselves seemed to be alien. What had they known of the terror of battle? What had they known of losing a comrade upon whom one's life depends? The dissolution of the Confederacy and their growing fear of abolitionism's dominance meant that many former Confederate soldiers felt detached from their world, their country, and, in some cases, their families. Unwilling to accept these changes, many hoped that the Confederacy would rise once again. Others simply fled. Between 1865 and 1867, roughly eight to ten thousand former Confederates fled for Mexico, the Caribbean, Canada, and Central and South America.[8]

Those who remained often turned their despondency into action. "The idea that Confederate veterans came home catatonic with despair is a gross exaggeration of the mental state of Southern men," historian Peter Carmichael argues. "Internally, to be sure, returning veterans were in turmoil, but in public they had little choice but to show a brave face, now that power was up for grabs." As such, former Confederate soldiers used the emotional strength and self-confidence gained from surviving the war to launch a collective insurrection aimed at overturning racial equality and establishing the hierarchy of the Old South.[9] Doing so, they believed, would lead to social harmony and a society enveloped by an illusion of peace, much as it had been before the war. This harmony and peace felt like security. By controlling their outward circumstances, thousands of Confederate soldiers hoped to control their inward feelings. Meanwhile, others simply sought to leave the war behind them and did their best to return to a life of domestic bliss. Most eventually did so.

Men who made up this latter group continued to rely upon the families who had sustained them during the war. But their families were not always enough. Soldiers found that they still needed each other. The war had bound them together. Men who had once depended solely upon themselves before the war now desperately craved the connection that they had with their comrades during the war. The incommunicable experience of suffering which soldiers shared bound them with one another in ways that their own families could not always understand.[10] Because of this, many families urged former soldiers to embrace their old comrades for emotional support. These relationships are fondly remembered in dozens of postwar memoirs. Sergeant-Major David Johnston of the former 7th Virginia Infantry Regiment wrote his memoir, at the behest of old comrades, friends, and family, as a remembrance of the "patriotic, self-sacrificing, brave company of men with whose fortunes and destiny my own were linked for four long years of blood and carnage, and to whom during that period I was bound by ties stronger than hooks of steel; whose confidence and friendship I fully shared, and as fully reciprocated."[11] The competitive drive and "standoffishness" which marked prewar masculinity were replaced with a recognition of mutual interdependence and a need for emotional support. Many still found emotional succor in the men from their hometown with whom they had enlisted. For others, veterans' groups would soon emerge and draw men together from various cities and states. After its founding in 1889, a national group known as the United Confederate Veterans grew to include over eighty thousand former Confederate soldiers.[12]

One way that former soldiers supported one another was by encouraging each other to record their remembrances of the war. Though dripping with syrupy reminiscences, these accounts represent a medium through which men processed feelings of the war. In many ways, they represented a widespread and prolific outpouring of emotions that would have been unheard of before the war. Many grizzled veterans found comfort in reconnecting with the myriad of characters that they had met along the way, many of whom did not survive the war. For these latter individuals, remembrances were the only connection that could be had. Writing them down and sharing them with others was a way of keeping those connections alive, even as one's memory faded. "I suffered more at Home on the subject of the war than I have since I have been in the army," wrote Private Horace McLean of the 59th Alabama Infantry Regiment during the war, "for the reason that I was studying about my friends in the service and thinking that I was no better to be by their side with a gun in hand."[13] Many others felt this way after the war.

After the war, Mississippian William Abernathy wondered "if when this toil-some life is over for all of us, shall we meet again, and if so, will the imprint of our life here have any trace left upon us." After recalling the war's toll on his messmates, he declared that when one of them [Scott Lynch] "starts to Heaven, he will have to go by Gettysburg to get part of his bones, and then, he shall have to go down to North Carolina to get the balance. And so with Bill Phillips. . . . He will have to visit Knoxville, Tennessee to make himself a full proportioned man. And so, with you, Cal Cummings, if you do not want to appear maimed before St. Peter, you will have to go to Gettysburg."[14]

The war had taught men that they needed each other. Until they all passed and were hopefully once again reunited, soldiers' societies and reminiscences would have to do. The insular nature of soldiers' groups fostered intimacy between those who experienced the war as combatants and their bonhomie provided an emotional buffering effect well into their old age. In their study of Union veterans, researchers Dora L. Costa and Matthew E. Kahn found that the war affected soldiers long after the guns fell silent. Their research indicates "that Union Army veterans of the American Civil War who faced greater wartime stress (as measured by higher battlefield mortality rates) experienced higher mortality rates at older ages, but that men who were from more cohesive companies were statistically significantly less likely to be affected by wartime stress." Social networks often mitigated the negative effects of stress by providing oppositional beneficial effects on a soldier's psychological and physical well-being.[15]

Still, many men struggled with their emotions as they began to process what they had endured. Some who were single or courting were now physically disfigured, and they became exceedingly preoccupied with what they saw as their diminished prospects for marriage.[16] "I constantly hear the unmarried ones," one nurse recounted of her amputee patients, "wondering if the girls will marry them now."[17] Whether psychologically or physically disfigured by the war, many soldiers awoke to a deep-seated insecurity that no one could understand them or love them. For many, it was only in each other—those who had shared in the experience of war—that they would find the sense of belonging that they were searching for.

The war cut through an entire generation of young white males like a scythe. Hundreds of thousands were dead, millions in property destroyed, and the physical and psychological trauma lingered well into the twentieth century. Men who were promised a short and relatively bloodless war encountered devastation unlike anything the Western hemisphere had previously seen. Though exhibiting greater restraint and far less grandiose visions at the end of the war, many of these men once again took up prewar cultural norms of service to their families and their communities and found their purpose in this service.

The American Civil War represented an important emotional epoch in which white southern males were far more emotionally effusive than their prewar cultural standards would have allowed. This expressed emotionalism was the result of internal responses on the part of Confederate soldiers to external stimuli that led to a collective restructuring of emotional and masculine norms. Men discovered that they could not survive on their own. Interpersonal intimacy was no longer a sign of weakness but rather a recognition of their primal needs. Many entered the war knowing that survival required the willingness to fight. Through indomitable courage and limitless self-confidence, they believed that they could overcome a foe who was better armed, better trained, and far more numerous. The war's suffering taught them that a vast gulf existed between the abstract ideals of stoic masculinity and the painful reality of their own fragility. This realization required a new kind of courage—the courage to eschew cultural norms, and the courage to express their feelings—even the ones that made them feel weak or needy.

The war forced southern men to reshape masculine norms. The depth of their sacrifice and suffering gave them enough social cachet to do so. These men were different. They had changed because, unlike those at home, theirs was a war that was both *fought and felt*. Returning home, Carlton McCarthy noted, these men had "learned that life was passable and enjoyable without a roof or even a tent to shelter from the storm," and "that cheerfulness was compatible with cold and hunger; and that a man without money, food, or shelter need not feel utterly hopeless."[18] Though they had lost much, they still had hope. They were alive. And no matter how they felt, they still had *each other.*

NOTES

INTRODUCTION

1. L. White Duggar to Mother, Atlanta, August 7, 1864, Duggar Family Papers, AU Archives.

2. For an excellent exploration of southern males' belief in themselves, see Berry, *All That Makes a Man*. For a monograph on the subject, see Phillips, *Diehard Rebels*.

3. Glover, "Let Us Manufacture Men." *Southern Manhood: Perspectives on Masculinity in the Old South,* 29. See also Glover, *Southern Sons,* 86–87.

4. Glover, *Southern Sons,* 104, 145. See also Broomall, *Private Confederacies,* 62. See also Berry, *All That Makes a Man,* 11.

5. For an excellent analysis of southerners' fears over the loss of autonomy and slavery (two interlinked concepts for many white southerners), see Charles B. Dew, *Apostles of Disunion: Southern Secession Commissioners and the Causes of the Civil War* (Charlottesville, VA: University of Virginia Press, 2001). For another excellent analysis of manhood and fear, see Kimmel, *Manhood in America,* 1–4. For the relationship between southern fears and secession, see Woods, *Emotional and Sectional Conflict.* See also Glover, *Southern Sons.*

6. Adolphs, "The Biology of Fear," 79–80.

7. This is not to argue that hegemony, patriarchy, white supremacy, and insecurity were not important facets of the collective experiences of nineteenth-century southern white males. However, these four concepts have become four boundaries within which historians have sought to conceptualize and understand the masculine experience. The four concepts are just a handful of many pillars upon which white southern masculinity must be reconstructed if we are to understand the totality of the historical actors' experience. Rather than refuting these concepts, I have sought to build off them and to add one more dimension to our understanding of the male experience of the American Civil War. For excellent books on the role of hegemony, patriarchy, and white supremacy, see Wyatt-Brown, *Southern Honor;* McCurry, *Masters of Small Worlds;* and Rable, *Civil Wars.* For excellent books on white southern male insecurities and their role in shaping the conflict, see Berry, *All That Makes a Man* and Broomall, *Private Confederacies.*

8. Woodworth, ed., *The Loyal, True, and Brave,* xi. While this is true of all eras of historical study, it is important for historians to recognize their own biases and to make their best attempt at understanding the past with as much clarity as they can muster. At the same time, new cultural milieus in which historians research and write allow them to see and shine light upon previously obscured areas or perspectives of historical events. For example, the emergence of second- and third-wave feminism in the twentieth century led historians to look at masculinity through lenses of patriarchy and hegemony. These new approaches provided valuable new perspectives in our understanding of masculinity in the Old South.

9. Kimmel, *Manhood in America,* 1–4.

10. Attridge et al., eds., *Post-Structuralism,* 1.

11. Eustace et al., "AHR Conversations: The Historical Study of Emotions," 1491–92.

12. Ibid., 1504.

13. For a further exploration of white hegemony, see McCurry, *Masters of Small Worlds;* Wyatt-Brown, *Southern Honor;* Ira Berlin, *Many Thousands Gone: The First Two Centuries of Slavery in North America* (Cambridge, MA: Harvard University Press, 1998); Drew Gilpin Faust, *James Henry Hammond and the Old South: A Design for Mastery* (Baton Rouge: Louisiana State University Press, 1982).

14. James R. McCutchan to Rachel Ann McCutchan, Camp Near Fairfax C.H., September 22, 1861, James B. McCutchan Papers, Leyburn Library, WLUSC.

15. For Wiley's interpretation of Union soldiers' motivations, see Wiley, *The Life of Billy Yank: The Common Soldier of the Union* (Baton Rouge: Louisiana State University Press, 1952).

16. Wiley, *The Life of Johnny Reb,* 15–18.

17. The lack of emphasis on the motivational power of emotions is particularly noteworthy among military historians. The field of military psychology grew exponentially in the years after World War II and yet it is largely a field which has witnessed little embrace from historians. Though historians must be careful in "psychologizing" history since the actors involved are deceased and it is far more difficult to understand the psyche of an individual who can no longer speak for him or herself, this overwrought hesitancy can hinder our understanding of why human beings acted or reacted the way that they did. While historians have long been comfortable embracing external motivators for understanding human behaviors, it is important to now embrace internal motivators as well. Without this approach, we are left without some of the most important premises that could fundamentally alter our conclusions.

18. Woodworth, ed., *The Loyal, True, and Brave,* xi. One of the first books to seek to understand the soldier's individual experience of war is John Keegan's *The Face of Battle* (New York: Viking Press, 1976).

19. For greater insight on the sociocultural explanations of soldier motivations during the American Civil War, see Linderman, *Embattled Courage;* Michael Fellman, *Inside War: Guerilla Conflict in Missouri during the American Civil War* (New York: Oxford University Press, 1989); Sheehan-Dean, ed., *The View from the Ground;* Sheehan-Dean, *Why Confederates Fought;* Phillips, *Diehard Rebels;* Glatthaar, *General Lee's Army;* and Noe, *Reluctant Rebels.* For greater insight on the ideological explanations of soldier motivations during the American Civil War, see Drew Gilpin Faust, *The Creation of Confederate Nationalism: Ideology and Identity in the Civil War South* (Baton Rouge: Louisiana State University Press, 1988); Mitchell, *Civil War Soldiers;* McPherson, *For Cause and Comrades;* Peter S. Carmichael, *The Last Generation: Young Virginians in Peace, War, and Reunion* (Chapel Hill: University of North Carolina Press, 2005); Manning, *What This Cruel War Was Over.* For greater insight on historians who incorporate both sociocultural and ideological explanations for soldier motivations, see Randall Jimerson, *The Private Civil War: Popular Thought during the Sectional Conflict* (Baton Rouge: Louisiana State University Press, 1988). One of the most important works from this period include James McPherson's book *For Cause and Comrades,* which became the most influential book in the field of Civil War soldier studies. Not only did McPherson provide more complex analysis by borrowing historian John A. Lynn's three-pronged framework for analyzing soldiers' motivations, including *initial motivation*—that is, why men enlisted, *sustaining motivation*—what kept them in military service, and *combat motivation*—what sustained them in combat, but he also placed ideology as the centerpiece of both initial and sustaining motivators while also placing sociocultural factors in symbiosis with these ideological explanations. Thus, he provided a far more nuanced understanding of the individual experience of the Civil War soldier than those who came before him. At the same time, McPherson's book (much like many of those published in the 1980s and 1990s) not only privileged analysis over description, but also reflected the leveraging of quantitative and social history, which has been useful in broadening the scope of soldier studies beyond traditional boundaries of military history. McPherson's approach would become the norm for historians of soldier studies until the fourth epoch of soldier's studies, which focused on the emotions of soldiers.

20. Rosenwein, "Worrying about Emotions in History," 821.

21. Eustace et al., "AHR Conversations: The Historical Study of Emotions," 1522.

22. Dwyer, *Mastering Emotions,* 14.

23. Eustace et al., "AHR Conversations: The Historical Study of Emotions," 1506.

24. Barbara H. Rosenwein, in Eustace et al., "AHR Conversations: The Historical Study of Emotions," 1497.

25. Harry S. Laver, "Refuge of Manhood: Masculinity and the Militia Experience in Kentucky," in Friend and Glover, eds., *Southern Manhood,* 1–3. For an excellent monograph on this subject, see Glover, *Southern Sons.*

26. Sommerville, *Aberration of Mind,* 12–14.

1. MASTERS OF MANHOOD

1. Kann, *Republic of Men,* 5–8.

2. Volo, *Family Life in 17th- and 18th-Century America,* 41–42.

3. James Iredell, quoted in Watson, *Colonial North Carolina,* 22.

4. Watson, *Colonial North Carolina,* 22–24.

5. Miranda, *The New Democracy in America,* 6.

6. Kant, *"What Is Enlightenment?"* 1.

7. David Williams, "Introduction: The Enlightenment," 7.

8. Mintz, *Huck's Raft,* 57–58.

9. Hutcheson, *A System of Moral Philosophy,* 2:192.

10. Fliegelman, *Prodigals and Pilgrims,* 1; Kann, *Republic of Men,* 8.

11. Lockridge, *On the Sources of Patriarchal Rage,* 88.

12. Volo, *The Boston Tea Party,* 61.

13. Arthur Iredell to James Iredell, January 31, 1775, Charles E. Johnston Collection, North Carolina Department of Archives and History, Raleigh, NC.

14. Volo, *Boston Tea Party,* 61.

15. Lockridge, *Patriarchal Rage,* 109.

16. Wood, *Empire of Liberty,* 495–96.

17. Quoted in Norton, *Liberty's Daughters,* 235.

18. Murray, *The Gleaner: A Miscellaneous Production,* 133.

19. Mintz, *Huck's Raft,* 54.

20. Ibid., 71.

21. Kagan et al., *Infancy,* 135–36.

22. Webster, "On the Education of Youth in America," 173

23. Kagan et al., *Infancy,* 135–36.

24. Wood, *Empire of Liberty,* 502–3. For more information on republican motherhood, see Linda K. Kerber, *Women of the Republic: Intellect and Ideology in Revolutionary America* (Chapel Hill: University of North Carolina Press, 1980), Norton, *Liberty's Daughters,* Jeanne Boydston, *Home and Work: Housework, Wages, and the Ideology of Labor in the Early Republic* (New York: Oxford University Press, 1994), and Rosemarie Zagari, "Morals, Manners, and the Republican Mother," *American Quarterly* 44 (June 1992): 192–215.

25. Smith, "Remarks on Education," 207.

26. Paine Wingate, quoted in Mintz, *Huck's Raft,* 74.

27. Lewis, *The Pursuit of Happiness,* 214.

28. Blanning, *Romantic Revolution,* xv–xvii.

29. *Merriam-Webster's Encyclopedia of Literature,* 964.

30. McClymond, "Jonathan Edwards," 407. For a greater understanding of Jonathan Edwards and his emotional and religious influence upon American history, see George M. Marsden, *Jonathan Edwards: A Life* (New Haven, CT: Yale University Press, 2003).

31. Kidd, *The Great Awakening,* xiv.

32. Ibid., xiv–xv.

33. Galatians 3:26–28 (New International Version).

34. Kidd, *The Great Awakening,* 265–66.

35. Hankins, *The Second Great Awakening,* 1–5.

36. Charles G. Finney to the Female Missionary Society of the Western District, September 30, 1824, in *The Eighth Annual Report of the Trustees,* 17–19.

37. Stokes, *The Altar at Home,* 41–43.

38. Wyatt-Brown, *Southern Honor,* xv.

39. Ibid., 15.

40. Memminger, "Lecture Delivered," 14–15.

41. McCurry, *Masters of Small Worlds,* 304.

42. Johnson, "Planters and Patriarchy," 46–47. He also noted what may be a problem with McCurry's choice of geographic study as he noted that "it is doubtful if any planters were more self-consciously patriarchal than the rice planters of the South Carolina low country. . . . It is difficult to think of other Americans of the era who came closer to being ideal-typical patriarchs." For more information on patriarchal families in England, see Lawrence Stone, *The Family, Sex and Marriage in England, 1500–1800* (New York: Harper and Row, 1977).

43. Broomall, "Personal Confederacies," 28.

44. Lewis, *Pursuit of Happiness,* 214.

45. Broomall, "Personal Confederacies," 39, 42.

46. Wyatt-Brown, *Hearts of Darkness,* xiii–xiv.

47. Berry, *All That Makes a Man,* 39.

48. Kimmel, *Manhood in America,* 5–8.

49. Berry, *All That Makes a Man,* 46.

50. Ibid., 85–86.

51. Tocqueville, *Democracy in America,* 2:183.

52. Ott, *Confederate Daughters,* 26, 100–101.

53. Berry, *All That Makes a Man,* 89.

54. Stevens Jr., "The Anatomy of Mass Literacy," 101.

55. Berry, *All That Makes a Man,* 90–97, 107.

56. Tocqueville, *Democracy in America,* 2:202.

57. Ibid., 2:195.

58. Mercer, *Understanding Attachment,* 2–3.

59. Hanania and Davidow, "Attachment," 192.

60. Ibid., 198–99.

61. Ott, *Confederate Daughters,* 22–24.

62. Scherer, "What Are Emotions?," 697–701.

2. EROS AND IMPETUS

1. James Barnett Painter to Father and Mother, Camp Near Frederick City, September 8, 1862, James Barney Painter Letters, UVA.

2. W. R. Stilwell to Molly, September 18, 1862, in *The Stillwell Letters,* 49–50.

3. J. R. Redmond to His Wife, Children, and Mother, November 2, 1864, NCDAH.

4. Perry, *Civil War Courts-Martial,* 284–85.

5. Carmichael, *War for the Common Soldier,* 45.

6. Sommerville, *Aberration of Mind,* 34.

7. Berry, *All That Makes a Man,* 12.

8. Hammond, *Secret and Sacred,* 150.

9. Sommerville, *Aberration of Mind,* 3.

10. Friend and Glover, "Rethinking Southern Masculinity," *Southern Manhood,* ix.

11. S. Hubert Dent to wife, Chattanooga, TN, July 11, 1863, S. H. Dent Papers, AU.

12. Smith, *Historian and History,* 202–16.

13. Stinson, "Leopold von Ranke: History of the Popes (1834–1836)," 155.

14. Smith, *Historian and History,* 142.

15. McPherson, *For Cause and Comrades,* 131.

16. Phillips, *Diehard Rebels,* 88.

17. Karageorgos, *Australian Soldiers in South Africa and Vietnam,* 149.

18. Ibid., 155.

19. Feldman et al., "The Use of Writing," 368.

20. McPherson, *Battle Cry of Freedom,* 35–36.

21. Selcer, *Civil War America,* 301. This statistic includes slave and free, male and female, making no distinctions by the Census Bureau. See also Stephens, "Literacy in England, Scotland, and Wales," 555.

22. McPherson, *For Cause and Comrades,* 11.

23. Hager, *I Remain Yours,* 3–5.

24. William Addison Tesh to Father and Mother, Camp Gregg, May 17, 1863, William A. Tesh Papers, Duke.

25. Ann L. Bowen to Henry Bowen, Plymouth Washington County, November 11, 1864, Henry H. Bowen Papers, NCDAH.

26. Rotundo, *American Manhood,* 2; Rose, *Victorian America and the Civil War,* 147.

27. Rotundo, *American Manhood,* 3–4.

28. Ott, *Confederate Daughters,* 27–29.

29. Berry, *All That Makes a Man,* 18, 41–44, 80.

30. Robertson Jr., *Soldiers Blue and Gray,* 112.

31. Harvey Black to Mary Black, Brandy Station, November 1, 1863; Black, Kent, and Apperson Family, VT.

32. Sheehan-Dean, *Why Confederates Fought,* 4.

33. Berry, *All That Makes a Man,* 11.

34. Kimmel, *Manhood in America,* 6, 9.

35. Cornelius Morris to Sarah Morris, Camp Davis Near Wilmington, June 9, 1862, Cornelius Morris Letters, SHC-UNC.

36. J. T. Scott to Miss Philo, Camp Near Yorktown, April 16, 1862, John T. Scott Letters, AU.

37. Carroll, *Invisible Wounds,* 19.

38. Joseph Kinsey to Sister, Wilmington, North Carolina, August 12, 1862, Joseph Kinsey Papers, ECU.

39. J. David Hacker et al., "Southern Marriage Patterns," 44. Some historians dispute these claims. See Drew Gilpin Faust, *Mothers of Invention: Women of the Slaveholding South in the American Civil War* (Chapel Hill: University of North Carolina Press, 1996), 149–51; E. Susan Barber, "'The White Wings of Eros': Courtship and Marriage in Confederate Richmond," in *Southern Families at War: Loyalty and Conflict in the Civil War South,* ed. Catherine Clinton (New York: Oxford University Press, 2000), 120.

40. Hacker et al., "Southern Marriage Patterns," 45.

41. McGuire, *Diary of a Southern Refugee,* 243–44.

42. Hacker et al., "Southern Marriage Patterns," 46.

43. Robertson, *Soldiers Blue and Gray,* 112.

44. Elodie Breck Todd to Nathaniel Henry Rhodes Dawson, Selma, May 9, 1861, Nathaniel Henry Rhodes Dawson Papers, SHC-UNC.

45. Cimbala, *Soldiers North and South,* 77.

46. J. T. Scott to Miss Philo, Camp Pickens, Dec. 9, 1861, John T. Scott Letters, AU.

47. Broomall, *Private Confederacies,* 67.

48. John W. Cotton to Wife, August 3, 1862, in *Yours til Death: Civil War Letters of John W. Cotton,* 14.

49. Harrison Hanes to Nancy Williams, Manassas, VA, September 30, 1861, Harrison Hanes Papers, Duke.

50. Leon, *Diary of a Tar Heel Confederate Soldier,* 35–37.

51. Kellett, *Combat Motivation,* 277.

52. S. Hubert Dent to Wife, Chattanooga, TN, July 11, 1863, S. H. Dent Letters, AU.

53. John Futch Jr. to Martha Ramsey Futch, Camp Near the United States Ford, May 9, 1863, Futch Letters, NCDAH.

54. Dean Jr., *Shook over Hell,* 51–66. Some historians have taken the perspective that Civil War soldiers got "used to combat" and experienced a "hardening" of their attitudes toward death and destruction including McPherson, *For Cause and Comrades,* 74; Linderman, *Embattled Courage,* 240–41; and Earl Hess, *The Union Soldier in Battle: Enduring the Ordeal of Combat* (Lawrence: University Press of Kansas, 1997), 146–49.

55. Dean Jr., *Shook over Hell,* 74–75. Other historians follow Dean's lead, arguing that soldiers' reactions varied and often they remained feeling throughout the war including Broomall, *Private Confederacies,* 84; Carmichael, *War for the Common Soldier,* 111.

56. Gimbel and Booth, "Why Does Military Combat Experience Adversely Affect Marital Relations?," 691, 701–2.

57. Nadelson, *Trained to Kill*, 100.

58. Jesse Hill to Dear Companion, New Market, VA, October 21, 1864, Jesse Hill Letters, NCDAH.

59. Silas Stepp to Eleanor Stepp, June 12, 1864, Silas Stepp Letters, UNCA.

60. Horace McLean to Mary, Camp Mary, May 4, 1862, Horace McLean Letters, AU.

61. S. Hubert Dent to wife, Barracanas, Florida, November 7, 1861, S. H. Dent Papers, AU.

62. John Marcus Hefner to Keziah Hefner, Richmond, VA, March 7, 1864, Marcus Hefner Papers, NCDAH.

63. James W. Watkins to Francis Maxwell Watkins, Atlanta, GA, October 18, 1863, James W. Watkins Papers, EU.

64. Silas Stepp to Eleanor, April 8, 1864, Silas Stepp Letters, UNCA.

65. Ellis, *North Carolina English*, xl.

66. Cotton to Wife, Tennessee, December 9, 1862, in *Yours Til Death*, 36.

67. Robertson, *Soldiers Blue and Gray*, 105–8.

68. John Samuel Shropshire to Carrie, September 5, 1861, John S. Shropshire Papers, NML.

69. William F. Testerman to Jane Davis, July 25, 1863, William F. Testerman Letters, VT.

70. Cimbala, *Soldiers North and South*, 117.

71. Hager, *I Remain Yours*, 9.

72. Susann Cloer to William Cloer, October 17, 1862, "Civil War Voices: Soldier Studies," http://www.soldierstudies.org/index.php?action=view_letter&Letter=492 (accessed April 2, 2015).

73. Mary Bell to Husband, July 8, 1864, Alfred W. Bell Papers, Duke.

74. Robertson, *Soldiers Blue and Gray*, 114.

75. Hiram Talbert Holt to Carrie, Fort Pillow, TN, April 25, 1862, Hiram Talbert Holt Letters, UM.

76. McPherson, *For Cause and Comrades*, 135–40.

77. Carmichael, *War for the Common Soldier*, 176.

78. S. Hubert Dent to wife, Barracanas, Florida, November 7, 1861, S. H. Dent Papers, AU.

79. Ted Ownby, quoted in Clinton, *Southern Families at War*, 229–34.

80. Noe, *Reluctant Rebels*, 74–76.

81. Marten, *The Children's Civil War*, 69.

82. Noe, *Reluctant Rebels*, 74.

83. Rable, *Civil Wars*, 59–60.

84. Armistead L. Galloway to Eliza, June 22, 1862, Armistead L. Galloway Letters, AU.

85. Feldman et al., "The Use of Writing," 366–67.

86. Ibid., "The Use of Writing," 368.

87. John A. Smith to Sister, January 24, 1864, in Watford, *The Civil War in North Carolina: The Piedmont*, 145–46.

88. Robertson, *Soldiers Blue and Gray*, 111.

89. Madden, *Beyond the Battlefield*, 223–27.

90. McPherson, *For Cause and Comrades*, 132.

91. Ann L. Bowen to Henry H. Bowen, January 14, 1865, Civil War Collection, Henry H. Bowen Papers, NCDAH.

92. Rable, *Civil Wars*, 64–67.

93. Spencer Welch to Wife, June 29, 1862, in Welch, *A Confederate Surgeon's Letters to his Wife*, 17.

94. Little, "Buddy Relations and Combat Performance," 219.

95. Patterson, *Yankee Rebel*, 83.

96. Samuel King Vann to Nancy Elizabeth Neel Vann, Atlanta in the Ditches, August 17, 1864, in Vann, *Most Lovely Lizzie*, 41.

97. William Irby Box to Margaret and Rachel Box, Camp Near Winchester, October 6, 1862, Box Family Papers, USC.

98. Nancy King to Jasper King, March 14, 1863, Barkley Family Letters, Southern Historical Collection, SHC-UNC.

99. White, "In Their Heads," 28.

100. McPherson, *For Cause and Comrades*, 134.

101. See Berry, *All That Makes a Man*, 179; Dean Jr., *Shook over Hell*, 92; McPherson, *For Cause and Comrades*, 140–41; Linderman, *Embattled Courage*, 216–18; Phillips, *Diehard Rebels*, 88–90.

102. Hiram Talbert Holt to Wife, Fort Pillow, TN, April 25, 1862, Hiram Talbert Holt Letters, UM.

103. Thomas Inglet to Martha Inglet, Fredericksburg, VA, February 20, 1862, Thomas W. G. Inglet Letters, UGA.

104. Derrick Ho, "Homesickness Isn't Really About 'Home.'" CNN, https://www.cnn.com/2010/HEALTH/08/16/homesickness.not.about.home/index.html (accessed March 17, 2025).

105. E. Tom Broughton to Wife, January 29, 1862, "Civil War Voices: Soldier Studies," http://www.soldierstudies.org/index.php?action=view_letter&Letter=691 (accessed April 2, 2015).

106. Unknown to "My very dear Sister," June 6, 1861, James Eldridge Papers, Henry Huntington Library, quoted in Sheehan-Dean, *Why Confederates Fought*, 60.

107. Carmichael, *War for the Common Soldier*, 36.

108. Rable, *Civil Wars*, 50; Weitz, *A Higher Duty*, 144.

109. John Wesley Williams to Mother, Brothers, and Sisters, Petersburg, VA, July 12, 1862, John Wesley Williams Papers, Duke.

110. John A. Everett to Patience Everett, Brigade Hospital Near Chancellorsville, VA, May 10, 1864, John A. Everett Papers, EU.

111. Nadelson, *Trained to Kill*, 37.

112. Grossman, *On Killing*, 54.

113. The debate over whether soldiers in the American Civil War experienced PTSD on a large scale is a hotly contested one with very little concrete statistical answers. Certainly, some Civil War soldiers experienced PTSD but the exact number is unknown. For more information on Civil War soldiers and PTSD, see Michael Adams, *Living Hell*; Dean Jr., *Shook over Hell*; Dennis W. Brandt, *Pathway to Hell: A Tragedy of the American Civil War* (Bethlehem, PA: Lehigh University Press, 2008); Brian Matthew Jordan, *Marching Home: Union Veterans and Their Unending War* (New York: Liveright Publishing, 2015); James Marten, *Sing Not War: The Lives of Union and Confederate Veterans in Gilded Age America* (Chapel Hill: University of North Carolina Press, 2011); David T. Courtwright, "Opiate Addiction as a Consequence of the Civil War," *Civil War History* 24 (June 1978): 101–11; and Sommerville, *Aberration of Mind*.

114. Van der Kolk, *The Body Keeps the Score*, 30.

115. Grossman, *On Killing,* 75.

116. Lewis Sylvester Branscomb to Bennett Hill Branscomb, Camp Near Richmond, June 7, 1862, Branscomb Family Letters, ADAH.

117. Kennedy-Moore and Watson, *Expressing Emotion,* 77–78.

118. Van der Kolk, *The Body Keeps the Score,* 212–18.

119. Harvey Black to Mollie, November 1, 1863, Black, Kent, and Apperson Family Papers, VT.

3. PHILIA AND FRIENDSHIP

1. Soldier Profile: James Robert Montgomery, "Civil War Voices: Soldier Studies," http://www.soldierstudies.org/index.php?action=soldier_profile&Soldier=489 (accessed September 11, 2018).

2. J. R. Montgomery to A. R. Montgomery, May 10, 1864, CSA Collection, ACWM.

3. Ethelbert Fairfax to Mother, May 15, 1864, Fairfax Letters, ACWM.

4. Ethelbert Fairfax to Parents of J. R. Montgomery, quoted in Faust, *Republic of Suffering,* 17.

5. Weitz, *More Damning Than Slaughter,* 303.

6. Adams, *Living Hell,* 5–6.

7. Sommerville, *Aberration of Mind,* 13.

8. Staub and Vollhardt, "Altruism Born of Suffering," 267.

9. Berry, *All That Makes a Man,* 39.

10. W. L. Jones to R. B. Paschall, August 14, 1863, Civil War Collection, Military Collection, NCDAH.

11. Linderman, *Embattled Courage,* 65.

12. Mitchell, *The Vacant Chair,* 7.

13. Van der Kolk, *The Body Keeps the Score,* 85.

14. Ibid., 100–102.

15. Paul Schilder quoted in Van der Kolk, *The Body Keeps the Score,* 102.

16. Van der Kolk, *The Body Keeps the Score,* 102–3.

17. Feldman et al., "The Use of Writing," 384.

18. Smith, *The American Civil War,* 130.

19. Gray, *The Warriors,* 90.

20. Verweij, "Comrades or Friends?," 289–90.

21. Dunaway, *Reminiscences of a Rebel,* 41.

22. Booth, Personal *Reminiscences of a Maryland Soldier,* 117–18.

23. Sommerville, *Aberration of Mind,* 40.

24. McPherson, *For Cause and Comrade,* 13.

25. McCarthy, *Detailed Minutiae of Soldier Life,* 3.

26. Sheehan, "Treating Intimacy Issues," 95.

27. Scurfield, "War-Related Trauma," 181.

28. Alfred Wilson to James Watson, March 8, 1862, James Watson Papers, WCU.

29. H. C. Ward to John E. Morgan, May 17, 1863, Daniel W. Revis Letters, Private Collections, NCDAH.

30. Dickert, *History of Kershaw's Brigade,* 131–32.

31. McPherson, *Battle Cry of Freedom,* 317.

32. Guelzo, *Fateful Lightning,* 239–41.

33. McKim, *A Soldier's Recollections,* 23.

34. McPherson, *For Cause and Comrades,* 80.

35. Berry, *All That Makes a Man,* 179.

36. Noe, *Reluctant Rebels,* 157–58.

37. William F. Broaddus, "In Camp," Duke.

38. Eggleston, *A Rebel's Recollections,* 169.

39. Nathaniel Henry Rhodes Dawson to Elodie Breck Todd, May 10, 1861, Nathaniel Henry Rhodes Dawson Papers, SHC-UNC.

40. Matthew Clanton to Miss Sallie, Camp Davis Ford VA, February 2, 1862, James T. Jones Collection, JWL-UM.

41. Weitz, "Drill, Training, and the Combat Performance of the Civil War Soldier," 271–72, 276–78.

42. Glatthaar, *Lee's Army,* 51.

43. McCarthy, *Detailed Minutiae,* 37.

44. John Hartman to Partha Hartman, Culpepper Courthouse, June 8, 1863, John H. Hartman Papers, Duke.

45. Hamilton and Cameron, eds., *The Papers of Randolph Abbott Shotwell,* 1:95.

46. James R. McCutchan to Rachel Ann McCutchan, Camp Near Fairfax C.H., September 22, 1861, WLU.

47. Watkins, *Co. Aytch,* 70.

48. Abernathy, "The Confederate Memoir of William M. Abernathy," 12.

49. Liberty Independence Nixon Diary, Liberty Independence Nixon Papers, AU.

50. Eggleston, *Rebel's Recollections,* 33–34.

51. S. H. Dent to Anna Dent, August 14, 1861, S. H. Dent Papers, AU.

52. J. J. Young to Henry King Burgwyn, Raleigh, North Carolina, July 31, 1863, William Hyslop Sumner Burgwyn Papers, NCDAH.

53. McCarthy, *Detailed Minutiae,* 37.

54. Broomall, "Band of Brothers," 298.

55. Henry C. Semple to Emily Virginia James Semple, 1861–62, Mobile, Alabama. Henry C. Semple Papers, ADAH.

56. William Batts to Father, Camp Allegany Virginia, November 30, 1861, William M. Batts Letters, EU.

57. Kolditz et al., *Why They Fought,* 12–13.

58. Broomall, "Band of Brothers," 298.

59. McCarthy, *Detailed Minutiae,* 204.

60. James T. Jones to Sister, Near Manassas Virginia, December 10, 1861, James T. Jones Collection, JWL-UM.

61. Kolditz et al., *Why They Fought,* 13–14.

62. Mitchell, *The Vacant Chair,* 158.

63. John J. Jefcoat to Rachel E. Jefcoat, Sullivans Island, May 20, 1862, John J. Jefcoat Papers, Duke.

64. Elisha Kindred Flournoy to Martha Flournoy, Vicksburg, MS, April 10, 1863, E. K. Flournoy Letters, ADAH.

65. Watkins, *Co. Aytch,* 52.

66. Dobbs, "Trying it On," 59.

67. Daniel H. Whitener to Eliza Whitener, Camp Mangum Near Raleigh, December 14, 1861, Eliza Whitener Papers, Duke.

68. Benjamin L. Mobley to Susan Mobley, December 26, 1861, Benjamin L. Mobley Papers, EU.

69. Tarr et al., "Music and Social Bonding," 6.

70. George K. Evans to Burnell Shephard, Hanover Hospital, September 2, 1862, George K. Evans Letters, Duke.

71. Dickert, *History of Kershaw's Brigade,* 205.

72. Pinkser, *Lincoln's Sanctuary,* 84. For a discussion of nineteenth-century sleeping habits that developed into intimate sexual relationships between men, see Jonathan Ned Katz, *Love Stories: Sex between Men before Homosexuality* (Chicago: University of Chicago Press, 2003).

73. Glatthaar, *Lee's Army,* 221–23.

74. Robert Pressly Boyd to Fenton and Mary Jane Hall, Viana, Virginia, August 4, 1861, Robert Boyd Papers, Duke.

75. RWS to Carolina Virginia Taliaferro Miller, Aug. 17, 1861, in Simpson and Simpson, *Far, Far from Home,* 61.

76. Henry Bowen to Ann L. Bowen, C.S. Flag Ship, Charleston, SC, December 15, 1864, Henry H. Bowen Papers, NCDAH.

77. Kimmel, *Manhood in America,* 8.

78. Broomall, "Band of Brothers," 293, 273.

79. McCarthy, *Detailed Minutiae,* 88.

80. Rable, *God's Almost Chosen Peoples,* 8–9.

81. Alfred N. Profitt to Rachel Profitt, Camp Gregg, VA, March 11, 1863, Profitt Family Letters, SHC-UNC.

82. James C. Zimmerman to Adaline Zimmerman, Fredericksburg, VA, December 14, 1862, James C. Zimmerman Papers, Duke.

83. Jesse M. Frank to Alexander Frank, Orange C.H., VA, April 26, 1864, Alexander Frank Papers, Duke.

84. Freeman, *R. E. Lee,* 241.

85. Carroll, "The God Who Shielded Me Before," 270.

86. Partin, "The Sustaining Faith of an Alabama Soldier," 434–35.

87. Simeon Skinner to Elizabeth Mobley, Camp Iverson, January 30, 1862, Benjamin L. Mobley Papers, EU.

88. Rable, *God's Almost Chosen Peoples,* 107–8, 125; Brinsfield Jr., ed., *The Spirit Divided,* 38.

89. Wilcox, "Weeping Tears of Blood," 178.

90. Edwards, *The Wounded Soldier,* 5.

91. Eggleston, *Rebel's Recollections,* 180–82.

92. McKim, *Soldier's Recollections,* 220.

93. Dickert, *Kershaw's Brigade,* 247.

94. C. M. Avery to Father of John Caldwell, July 18, 1863, Tod Robinson Caldwell Papers, SHC-UNC.

95. Watkins, *Co. Aytch,* 139–40.

96. Dupre, *Fagots from the Camp Fire,* 53.

97. Faust, *Republic of Suffering,* 9–14.

98. G. B. Samuels to Kathleen Boone Samuels, July 26, 1861, in Samuels et al., comps., *A Civil War Marriage in Virginia,* 99–101.

99. T. J. Hodnett to William F. Hodnett, Camp Near Darksville, VA, July 18, 1863, John W. Hodnett Letters, Duke.

100. Abernathy, "Memoir of William M. Abernathy," 29–30.

101. Nathaniel Henry Rhodes Dawson to Elodie Breck Todd, Manassas Junction, August 4, 1861, Nathaniel Henry Rhodes Dawson Papers, SHC-UNC.

102. Ahronson and Cameron, "The Nature and Consequences of Group Cohesion," 13.

103. S. E. Hobfolland and S. Walfisch, "Coping with a Threat to Life: A Longitudinal Study of Self-Concept, Social Support, and Psychological Distress," cited in Costa and Kahn, "Health, War-time Stress, and Unit Cohesion," 47.

104. Dunaway, *Reminiscences of a Rebel,* 40–41.

105. Holmes Jr. "The Soldier's Faith." Holmes gave an earlier version of this speech in Keene, New Hampshire, on Memorial Day in 1884.

106. Staub and Vollhardt, "Altruism Born of Suffering," 53–54.

107. Ibid., 272.

108. Kolditz et al., *Why They Fought,* 10–11.

109. Dickert, *History of Kershaw's Brigade,* 47–48.

110. Abernathy, "Memoir of William M. Abernathy," 15; Dickert, *History of Kershaw's Brigade,* 132–33.

111. Grossman, *On Killing,* 150–53.

112. Charles A. Derby to Sister, Falling Creek, Chesterfield, July 15, 1862, Charles A. Derby Papers, VMI.

113. Speer, *Portals to Hell,* 57.

114. Heartsill, *Fourteen Hundred and 91 Days,* 113.

115. William Tilmon Bishop to Sarah Adeline Bishop, Johnson's Island, October 20, 1863, William Tilmon Bishop Letters, ADAH.

116. Owen and Owen, *History of Alabama,* 1493.

117. *Berry Benson's Civil War Book,* 127.

118. Heartsill, *Fourteen Hundred and 91 Days,* 106.

119. Dunaway, *Reminiscences of a Rebel,* 115–16.

120. Speer, *Portals to Hell,* 60–61.

121. Costa and Kahn, "Surviving Andersonville," 1467–68, 1482.

122. Williamson, *Prison Life in the Old Capital,* 29.

123. Speer, *Portals to Hell,* 63.

4. STORGE AND STEADFASTNESS

1. Asa T. Martin to Mary E. Martin, Manassas, Virginia, August 10, 1861, Asa T. Martin Papers, AU.

2. Isaac Lefevers to Catherine Lefevers, Camp Near Richmond, VA, August 24, 1862, Isaac Lefevers Papers, NCDAH.

3. B. F. McGruder to Mary E. Martin, Richmond, Virginia, August 23, 1862, Asa T. Martin Papers, AU.

4. Charles Carroll Morey, quoted in Edward Alexander, "And Then We Kill."

5. Frank, "Rendering Aid and Comfort," 6.

6. Glatthaar, *Soldiering in the Army of Northern Virginia,* 127.

7. Ebenezer B. Coggin to Ann E. Coggin, Petersburg, VA, June 20, 1862, E. B. Coggin Papers, ADAH.

8. Wilburn Thompson to Charlotte Thompson, Jackson County, AL, July 17, 1862, Wilburn Thompson Papers, Duke.

9. James E. Wesson to Rachel Jane Wesson, Camp Stonewall, Talladega, AL, January 11, 1863, Joseph E. Wesson Letters, ADAH.

10. Seidman, "The Power of Desire," 47.

11. Rotundo, "American Fatherhood: A Historical Perspective," 12.

12. Marten, "Fatherhood in the Confederacy," 269–70.

13. Rotundo, "American Fatherhood," 8.

14. Marten, "Fatherhood in the Confederacy," 270.

15. Keister and Southgate, *Inequality,* 21–22.

16. Marten, "Fatherhood in the Confederacy," 270.

17. Marten, *The Children's Civil War,* 21.

18. Gordon and Nair, "Domestic Fathers," 554.ee

19. Boettger, "Eastman Johnson's 'Blodgett Family,'" 51–52.

20. *State Journal,* February 20, 1861.

21. McWhiney and Jamieson, *Attack and Die,* 170.

22. Carroll, *Invisible Wounds,* 12.

23. T. B. Deaver to Thomas Hendricks, October 8, 1861, in McLaughlin, ed., *Cherished Letters,* 86.

24. Marten, *Children's Civil War,* 10–11, 81–82.

25. Cotton to wife, Montgomery County Alabama, May 5, 1862 in *Yours Till Death,* 4.

26. R. E. Corry to Eliza, Camp Near Okalona, November 25, 1863, Robert Emmett Corry Letters, AU Archives.

27. Marten, *Children's Civil War,* 99.

28. Daniel W. Murphy to Wife and Children, Fort French Near Wilmington, NC, August 8, 1863, Daniel W. Murphy Papers, Duke.

29. George A. Williams to his children, Line of Battle Near Malrins, June 17, 1864, Williams-Womble Papers, NCDAH.

30. Franklin Setzer to Wife and Children, Camp Vance, Burke County, NC, March 2, 1864, Franklin A. Setzer Correspondence, UVA.

31. R. E. Corry to wife, Camp Near Okalona, November 25, 1863, Robert Emmett Corry Letters, AU.

32. Marten, *Children's Civil War,* 77.

33. Asa T. Martin to Mary, Manassas Junction, Virginia, January 13, 1862, Asa T. Martin Papers, AU.

34. Benjamin Mason to "Dear Wife," Bristol, TN, February 10, 1863, Benjamin Mason Letters, AU.

35. William V. Fleming to Mary Susan Fleming, Camp Near Blakely, September 14, 1864, W. V. Fleming Correspondence, ADAH.

36. Charles A. Derby to Mary E. Stancell, Camp Near Falling Creek, July 15, 1862, Charles A. Derby Papers, VMI.

37. Little, "Buddy Relations and Combat Performance," 219.

38. A. L. Galloway to Eliza, July 1, 1862, Armistead L. Galloway Letters, AU.

39. Liberty Independence Nixon Diary, April 3, 1862, entry, Liberty Independence Nixon Papers, AU.

40. Marten, *Children's Civil War,* 70.

41. Francis M. Parker to Wife, Near James River, July 3, 1862, Francis M. Parker Papers, NCDAH.

42. Dunkelman, *Brothers One and All,* 110–11.

43. Isaac Lefevers to Catherine Lefevers, Spotsylvania Courthouse, VA, May 20, 1864, Isaac Lefevers Papers, NCDAH.

44. Frank, "Rendering Aid and Comfort," 24, 8.

45. Francis Marion Poteet to Martha Hendley Poteet, Petersburg, VA, December 31, 1864, Poteet-Dickson Letters, NCDAH.

46. Marten, *Children's Civil War,* 111–12.

47. Kezia Stradley Osborne to Roland C. Osborne, Asheville, NC, March 16, 1862, Roland C. Osborne and Kezia Stradley Osborne Civil War Letters, WCU.

48. Sarkadi et al., "Fathers' Involvement," 153.

49. Silas Stepp to Eleanor Stepp, May 29, 1864. Silas H. Stepp Letters, UNCA.

50. Marten, *Children's Civil War,* 50–52.

51. Werner, *Reluctant Witnesses,* 53–54.

52. Moore, *The Geographical Reader,* 13–14.

53. Marten, *Children's Civil War,* 147–49.

54. Marten, *Children's Civil War,* 69–70.

55. John T. Scott to Miss Philo, Camp Near Tunnel Hill, January 4, 1863, John T. Scott Letters, AU.

56. Isham Simms Upchurch to Brother, Camp Gregg, June 1, 1863, Isham Upchurch Papers, Duke.

57. White, "In Their Heads," 28.

58. Marten, *Children's Civil War,* 69.

59. Haines, "The White Population of the United States," 308.

60. Brosco, "The Early History of the Infant Mortality Rate in America." *Gale General OneFile* (accessed February 14, 2020) <https://link-gale-com.spot.lib.auburn.edu/apps/doc/A53877078/ITOF?u=avl_auburnu&sid=ITOF&xid=84283be3>.

61. Friend, "Little Eva's Last Breath," 62–64.

62. Ibid., 74–75.

63. J. H. Everett to Patience Everett, Manassas Junction, VA, October 26, 1861, John A. Everett Papers, EU.

64. Marten, *Children's Civil War,* 71.

65. George A. Williams to children, Line of Battle Near Malrins, June 11, 1854, Williams-Womble Papers, Private Collections, NCDAH.

66. William T. Presley to Henrie, Gate City Hospital, Atlanta, October 22, 1862, William T. Presley Papers, AU.

67. Benjamin Mason to "Darling Daughter," January 28, 1863, Benjamin Mason Letters, AU.

68. Marten, *Children's Civil War,* 87–89.

69. Rafuse, *Stonewall Jackson,* 152.

70. Bean, *Stonewall's Man,* 108–9.

71. Marten, *Children's Civil War,* 74–75.

72. Loughborough, *My Cave Life in Vicksburg,* 128–31.

73. Werner, *Reluctant Witnesses,* 151–54.

74. Weitz, *More Damning Than Slaughter,* 287–88.

75. King-Owen, "Conditional Confederates," 351.

76. Ibid., 359.

77. Weitz, "A Higher Duty," 24.

78. Eluctius W. Treadwell to Mattie Treadwell, Shelbyville, TN, April 5, 1863, E.W. Treadwell Letters, ADAH.

79. Daniel Webster Revis to Sarepta Revis, Knoxville, TN, December 7, 1862, Daniel W. Revis Letters, NCDAH.

5. ETHNOS AND AUTHORITY

1. Adams, *Our Masters the Rebels,* 4.

2. Kirkpatrick, *Marse,* 69.

3. Glatthaar, *General Lee's Army,* 19–20.

4. Ibid., 203–4.

5. Ibid., 28.

6. Noe, *Reluctant Rebels,* 59.

7. Hammond, "Speech of Hon. James H. Hammond."

8. Woods, *Emotional and Sectional Conflict,* 82.

9. Kolchin, *American Slavery,* 93–94.

10. Genovese and Genovese, *Fatal Self-Deception,* 1.

11. Jones, *The Religious Instruction of the Negroes,* 159.

12. Kirkpatrick, *Marse,* 23–24.

13. F. E. Duggar to Mother, Camp Beulah, Mobile, Alabama, December 4, 1863, Duggar Family Papers, AU.

14. Genovese, *Roll Jordan Roll,* 146

15. Ibid, 3.

16. Escott, *Slavery Remembered,* 20–21.

17. Kolchin, *American Slavery,* 115.

18. Brown, *Narrative of the Life of Henry Box Brown,* 29.

19. Olmsted, *A Journey in the Seaboard Slave States,* 17–18.

20. John Crittenden to Mother, Camp Lomax, June 15, 1862. John Crittenden Papers 1862–1865. AU.

21. John Crittenden to Bettie Browning Crittenden, Tynersville, TN, August 10, 1862. John Crittenden Papers 1862–1865, AU.

22. WD Crittenden to Mother, Camp Brown, MS, July 27, 1862. John Crittenden Papers 1862–1865, AU.

23. For examples, see John Crittenden to WD and BB Crittenden, Near Dalton, GA, April 9, 1864; John Crittenden to Father, Marietta, GA, July 1, 1864; and John Crittenden to BB Crittenden, St. Clair County Near Gadsden, October 22, 1864, in John Crittenden Papers 1862–1865, AU.

24. Woods, *Emotional and Sectional Conflict,* 87–88.

25. Woods, *Emotional and Sectional Conflict,* 92.

26. Dwyer, *Mastering Emotions,* 15.

27. Ibid., 3.

28. Woods, *Emotional and Sectional Conflict,* 89.

29. Dwyer, *Mastering Emotions,* 5.

30. Brown, *Narrative of the Life of Henry Box Brown,* 17.

31. Dwyer, *Mastering Emotions,* 6.

32. Woods, *Emotional and Sectional Conflict,* 17.

33. McPherson, *For Cause and Comrades,* 109–10.

34. Ibid., 20.

35. Kirkpatrick, *Marse,* 70–75.

36. Sheehan-Dean, *Why Confederates Fought,* 34.

37. R. E. Corry to Eliza, February 25, 1865, Robert Emmett Corry Letters, AU.

38. Phillips, *Diehard Rebels,* 54.

39. Berry, *All That Makes a Man,* 176–78.

40. Carmichael, *War for the Common Soldier,* 42.

41. John Waldrop Diary, August 29, 1863, Richard Woolfolk Waldrop Papers, UNC.

42. John Crittenden to Bettie Browning Crittenden, November 1, 1864, in John Crittenden Papers 1862-1865, AU.

43. Broomall, *Private Confederacies,* 47–48.

44. Abraham Lincoln, *First Inaugural Address,* March 4, 1861.

45. Sheehan-Dean, *Why Confederates Fought,* 99.

46. Cimbala, *Soldiers North and South,* 160.

47. Sheehan-Dean, *Why Confederates Fought,* 33–34.

48. Noe, *Reluctant Rebels,* 53.

49. John Crittenden to Bettie Browning Crittenden, March 29, 1864, in John Crittenden Papers 1862-1865, AU.

50. Glatthaar, *Forged in Battle,* 10.

51. Cimbala, *Soldiers North and South,* 160.

52. Glatthaar, *Forged in Battle,* 156.

53. Foote and Hess, eds., *The Oxford Handbook of the American Civil War,* 145. See also Cimbala, *Soldiers North and South,* 185.

54. McPherson, *For Cause and Comrades,* 152.

55. Henry Biggs to Sister, August 28, 1864, Biggs Family Papers, Duke University, quoted in Carmichael, *War for the Common Soldier,* 71.

56. Patterson, *Yankee Rebel,* 128.

57. Cimbala, *Soldiers North and South,* 185.

58. Manning, *What This Cruel War Was Over,* 172.

59. Ibid., 66.

60. McPherson, *For Cause and Comrades,* 171.

61. Joseph F. Maides to mother, February 18, 1865, quoted in McPherson, *For Cause and Comrades,* 172.

62. McPherson, *For Cause and Comrades,* 171–72.

63. William W. Holden, *North Carolina Standard,* October 18, 1864, quoted in Durden, *The Gray and the Black,* 95.

64. Levine, *Confederate Emancipation,* 115.

65. Cimbala, *Soldiers North and South,* 188–90.

66. Mitchell, *Civil War Soldiers,* 197–98.

67. Ibid., 204.

68. Captain Samuel T. Foster, quoted in Mitchell, *Civil War Soldiers,* 204–5.

CONCLUSION

1. Abernathy, "The Confederate Memoir of William M. Abernathy," 17.

2. Sommerville, *Aberration of Mind,* 4.

3. "War-Worn Veterans," *Intelligencer* (Atlanta, GA), May 10, 1865.

4. McCarthy, *Detailed Minutiae,* 215–16.

5. Ibid., 193.

6. Mitchell, *Civil War Soldiers,* 208.

7. Carmichael, *War for the Common Soldier,* 269.

8. Broomall, *Private Confederacies,* 93.

9. Carmichael, *War for the Common Soldier,* 293–94.

10. Sommerville, *Aberration of Mind,* 3.

11. Johnston, *The Story of a Confederate Boy,* iii.

12. Hattaway, "Clio's Southern Soldiers," 214.

13. Horace McLean to Wife, Beans Station, May 4, 1863, Horace McLean Letters, AU.

14. Abernathy, "The Confederate Memoir of William M. Abernathy," 17.

15. Costa and Kahn, "Health, Wartime Stress, and Unit Cohesion," 45–46.

16. Hacker, "Southern Marriage Patterns," 49.

17. Cumming, *A Journal of Hospital Life,* 117.

18. McCarthy, *Detailed Minutiae,* 215.

BIBLIOGRAPHY

PRIMARY SOURCES

Manuscript Collections

Alabama Department of Archives and History, Montgomery
    William Tilmon Bishop Letters
    Branscomb Family Letters
    E. B. Coggin Papers
    W. V. Fleming Correspondence
    E. K. Flournoy Letters
    E. W. Treadwell Letters
    Henry C. Semple Papers
    Joseph E. Wesson Letters
Auburn University, Special Collections and Archives, Auburn, AL
    Robert Emmett Corry Letters
    John Crittenden Papers
    S. H. Dent Papers
    Duggar Family Papers
    Armistead L. Galloway Letters
    Asa T. Martin Papers
    Benjamin Mason Letters
    Horace McLean Letters
    Liberty Independence Nixon Papers
    William T. Presley Papers
    John T. Scott Letters
Duke University, David M. Rubenstein Rare Book and Manuscript Library, Durham, NC
    Tilmon F. Baggarly Papers
    Alfred W. Bell Papers

Robert Boyd Papers
William F. Broaddus Papers
George K. Evans Letters
Alexander Frank Papers
Harrison Hanes Papers
John H. Hartman Papers
John W. Hodnett Letters
John J. Jefcoat Papers
Daniel W. Murphy Papers
John W. Reese Papers
William A. Tesh Papers
Wilburn Thompson Papers
Isham Upchurch Papers
Eliza Whitener Papers
John Wesley Williams Papers
James C. Zimmerman Papers
East Carolina University, Joyner Library Special Collections, Greenville, NC
Joseph Kinsey Papers
Ellen Brockenbrough Library, American Civil War Museum, Richmond, VA
Barksdale Letters
CSA Collection
Fairfax Letters
Emory University, Manuscripts, Archives, and Rare Book Library, Atlanta, GA
William M. Batts Letters
John A. Everett Papers
Jesse Fuller Letters
William Harmon Harden Papers
Benjamin L. Mobley Papers
Henry W. Robinson Letters
James W. Watkins Papers
Nesbitt Memorial Library, Columbus, TX (NML)
John S. Shropshire Papers
North Carolina Department of Archives and History, Raleigh
Henry H. Bowen Papers
William Hyslop Sumner Burgwyn Papers
Civil War Collection
Faison Family Papers
Futch Letters
Marcus Hefner Papers
Jesse Hill Letters

Charles E. Johnston Collection
Isaac Lefevers Papers
Francis M. Parker Papers
Poteet-Dickson Letters
Daniel W. Revis Letters
Stephen Whitaker Papers
Williams-Womble Papers
University of Georgia, Hargrett Rare Boko and Manuscript Library, Athens
Thomas W. G. Inglett Letters
Thomas A. Woodham Papers
University of Michigan, William L. Clements Library, Ann Arbor
Hiram Talbert Holt Letters
University of Mississippi, J. D. Williams Library, Oxford
James T. Jones Collection
University of North Carolina Asheville, D. H. Ramsey Library Special Collections
and University Archives
Silas Stepp Letters
University of North Carolina, Southern Historical Collection, Chapel Hill
Barkley Family Letters
Tod Robinson Caldwell Papers
Nathaniel Henry Rhodes Dawson Papers
Cornelius Morris Letters
North Carolina Collection
Profitt Family Letters
Richard Woolfolk Waldrop Papers
University of North Carolina Wilmington, William Madison Randall Library
Special Collections
Wilmington, North Carolina and the Lower Cape Fear Area Manuscript Collection
University of South Carolina, Caroliniana Library, Columbia
Box Family Papers
University of Virginia, Albert and Shirly Small Special Collections Library, Charlottesville
James Barney Painter Letters
Franklin A. Setzer Correspondence
Virginia Military Institute, VMI Archives, Lexington.
Charles A. Derby Papers
Virginia Tech, Special Collections and University Archives, Blacksburg
Black, Kent, and Apperson Family Papers
William F. Testerman Letters
Washington and Lee University, Special Collections, Lexington, VA
James B. McCutchan Papers

Western Carolina University, Special Collections, Cullowhee, NC
    Edmonston-Kelly Family Papers
    Roland C. Osborne and Kezia Stradley Osborne Civil War Letters
    C. W. Slagle Collection
    James Watson Papers

BOOKS AND ARTICLES

Abernathy, William M. "The Confederate Memoir of William M. Abernathy." *Confederate Veteran* 3 (2003): 11–19.

Benson, Berry. *Berry Benson's Civil War Book: Memoirs of a Confederate Scout and Sharpshooter.* Edited by Susan Williams Benson. Athens: University of Georgia Press, 1962.

Booth, George Wilson. *Personal Reminiscences of a Maryland Soldier in the War Between the States, 1861–1865.* Baltimore: Privately published, 1898.

The Boston Weekly Messenger: Politics, Agriculture, Literature, and Miscellaneous Intelligence 7. Boston: Boston Daily Advertiser, 1818.

Brown, Henry Box. *Narrative of the Life of Henry Box Brown, Written by Himself.* Manchester, UK: Lee & Glynn, 1851.

Burton, John. *Lectures on Female Education and Manners.* Dublin: J. Milliken, 1794.

Clausewitz, Carl von. *On War.* Translated by J. J. Graham. New York: Barnes & Noble Books, 2004.

Cotton, John W. *Yours til Death: Civil War Letters of John W. Cotton.* Edited by Lucille Griffith. Tuscaloosa: University of Alabama Press, 1951.

Cumming, Kate. *A Journal of Hospital Life in the Confederate Army of Tennessee: From the Battle of Shiloh to the End of the War.* Louisville, KY: John P. Morton., 1866.

Dickert, David Augusts. *History of Kershaw's Brigade with Complete Roll of Companies, Biographical Sketches, Incidents, Anecdotes, Etc.* Newberry, SC: Elbert H. Aull, 1899.

Dobbs, Charles Holt. "Trying it On." In *The Spirit Divided: Memoirs of Civil War Chaplains: The Confederacy,* edited by John Wesley Jr. Macon, GA: Mercer University Press, 2006.

Dunaway, Wayland F. *Reminiscences of a Rebel.* New York: Neale, 1913.

Dupre, Louis J. *Fagots from the Camp Fire.* Washington, D.C.: E. T. Charles, 1881.

Edwards, John E. *The Wounded Soldier.* N.P., 1860. In Documenting the American South, UNC Chapel Hill. https://docsouth.unc.edu/imls/soldier/soldier.html.

Eggleston, George Cary. *A Rebel's Recollections.* New York: G. P. Putnam's Sons, 1905.

The Eighth Annual Report of the Trustees of the Female Missionary Society of the Western District. Utica, NY: William Williams, 1824.

Fulmer, John Kent, ed. *From That Terrible Field: Civil War Letters of James M. Williams, Twenty-First Alabama Infantry Soldiers.* Tuscaloosa: University of Alabama Press, 1981.

Gierke, Otto. *Natural Law and the Theory of Society, 1500 to 1800; with a Lecture on the Ideas of Natural Law and Humanity by Ernst Troeltsch.* Translated by Ernest Barker. Cambridge: Cambridge University Press, 1934.

Hamilton, J. G. de Roulhac, and Rebecca Cameron, eds. *The Papers of Randolph Abbott Shotwell.* 3 vols. Raleigh: North Carolina Historical Commission, 1929–36.

Hammond, James H. "Speech of Hon. James H. Hammond, of South Carolina, On the Admission of Kansas, Under the Lecompton Constitution: Delivered in the Senate of the United States, March 4, 1858." Washington, DC: 1858.

———. *Secret and Sacred: The Diaries of James Henry Hammond, a Southern Slaveholder.* Edited by Carol Bleser. New York: Oxford University Press, 1988.

Heartsill, W. W. *Fourteen Hundred and 91 Days in the Confederate Army: A Journal Kept by W. W. Heartsill, For Four Years, One Month, and One Day, or Camp Life: or, Camp-Life: Day-by-Day, of the W. P. Lane Rangers, from April 19th 1861 to May 20th 1865.* Edited by Bell Irvin Wiley. 1876. Reprint, Jackson, TN: McCowat-Mercer Press, 1954.

Hendricks, Thomas W. *Cherished Letters of Thomas Wayman Hendricks.* Edited by Josie Armstrong McLaughlin. Birmingham, AL: Birmingham Publishing, 1947.

Holmes Jr., Oliver Wendell. "The Soldier's Faith: An Address Delivered on Memorial Day, May 30, 1895 at a Meeting Called by the Graduating Class of Harvard University." Boston: Little, Brown, 1895.

Hutcheson, Frances. *A System of Moral Philosophy.* Vol. 2. London: R. and A. Poulis, 1755.

Johnston, David E. *The Story of a Confederate Boy in the Civil War.* Portland, OR: Glass & Prudhomme, 1914.

Jones, Charles C. *The Religious Instruction of the Negroes.* Savannah, GA: Thomas Purse, 1842.

Kant, Immanuel. *An Answer to the Question: "What is Enlightenment?"* Translated by H. B. Nisbet. New York: Penguin Books, 2009.

Leon, Louis. *Diary of a Tar Heel Confederate Soldier.* Charlotte, NC: Stone, 1913.

McCarthy, Carlton. *Detailed Minutiae of Soldier Life in the Army of Northern Virginia, 1861–1865.* Richmond: Carlton McCarthy, 1882.

McGuire, Judith W. *Diary of a Southern Refugee, During the War.* New York: E. J. Hale, 1867.

McKim, Randolph H. *A Soldier's Recollections: Leaves from the Diary of a Young Confederate with an Oration on the Motives and Aim of the Soldiers of the South.* New York: Longmans, Green, 1910.

Memminger, C. G. "Lecture Delivered Before the Young Men's Library Association of Augusta, April 10, 1851." Augusta, GA: W. S. Jones, 1851.

Miranda, Francisco de. *The New Democracy in America: Travels of Francisco de Miranda in the United States, 1783–84.* Translated by Judson P. Wood and edited by John S. Ezell. Norman: University of Oklahoma Press, 1963.

Moore, Marinda Branson. *The Geographical Reader for the Dixie Children.* Raleigh, NC: Branson, Farrar, 1863.

Morey, Charles Carroll. Quoted in Edward Alexander, "And Then We Kill." *Hallowed Ground* 14 (Winter 2013), https://www.battlefields.org/learn/articles/life-civil-war-soldier-battle (accessed February 11, 2020).

Murray, Judith Sargent. *The Gleaner: A Miscellaneous Production.* Boston: I. Thomas and E. T. Andrews, 1798.

Norton, Oliver W. *Army Letters 1861–1865.* Chicago: O. L. Deming, 1903.

Olmsted, Frederick Law. *A Journey in the Seaboard Slave States; With Remarks on Their Economy.* New York: Dix & Edwards, 1856.

Patterson, Edmund D. *Yankee Rebel: The Civil War Journal of Edmund DeWitt Patterson.* Edited by John G. Barrett. Chapel Hill: University of North Carolina Press, 1966.

Rush, Benjamin. "The Amusements and Punishments Which are Proper for Schools." In *The Selected Writings of Benjamin Rush,* edited by Dagobert D. Runes, 106–16. New York: Philosophical Library, 1947.

Samuels, G. B., and Katie Samuels. *A Civil War Marriage in Virginia: Reminiscences and Letters.* Compiled by Bernard Samuels, Walter Berry Samuels, and Carrie Esther-Spencer. Boyce, VA: Carr Publishing, 1956.

Simpson, Dick, and Tally Simpson. *"Far, Far from Home": The Wartime Letters of Dick and Tally Simpson, Third South Carolina Volunteers.* Edited by Guy R. Everson and Edward H. Simpson Jr. (New York: Oxford University Press, 1994.

Smith, Samuel Harrison. "Remarks on Education: Illustrating the Close Connection Between Virtue and Wisdom: To which is Annexed, a System of Liberal Education." In *The Founding Fathers, Education, and "The Great Contest,"* edited by Benjamin Justice, 205–17. New York: Palgrave Macmillan, 2013.

Stillwell, William R. *The Stillwell Letters: A Georgian in Longstreet's Corps, Army of Northern Virginia.* Edited by Ronald Mosely. Macon, GA: Mercer University Press, 2002.

Tocqueville, Alexis de. *Democracy in America.* Translated by Henry Reeve. Vol. 2. London: Longmans, Green, 1875.

Vann, Samuel K. *Most Lovely Lizzie: Love Letters of a Young Confederate Soldier.* Edited by William Young Elliot. Birmingham, AL: Privately published, 1958.

Walker, Francis A. *A Life of Francis Amasa Walker.* Edited by James P. Munroe. New York: H. Holt, 1923.

Watford, Christopher M., ed. *The Civil War in North Carolina: Soldiers' and Civilians' Letters and Diaries, 1861–1865: The Piedmont.* Jefferson, NC: McFarland, 2003.

Watkins, Samuel R. *Co. Aytch, Maury Grays, First Tennessee Regiment; or, A Side Show of the Big Show.* Chattanooga, TN: Times Printing, 1900.

Webster, Noah. "On the Education of Youth in America." In *The American Museum or University Magazine, Part II: July to December,* 173–75. Philadelphia: M. Carey, 1792.

Welch, Spencer G. *A Confederate Surgeon's Letter to His Wife.* New York: Neale Publishing Company, 1911.

Williamson, James J. *Prison Life in the Old Capital and Reminiscences of the Civil War.* West Orange, NJ: J. J. Williamson, 1911.

SECONDARY SOURCES

Adolphs, Ralph. "The Biology of Fear." *Current Biology* 23 (January 2013): 79–93.

Adams, Michael. *Living Hell: The Dark Side of the Civil War.* Baltimore: Johns Hopkins University Press, 2014.

———. *Our Masters the Rebels: A Speculation on Union Military Failure in the East, 1861–1865.* Cambridge, MA: Harvard University Press, 1978.

Ahronson, Arni, and James E. Cameron. "The Nature and Consequences of Group Cohesion in a Military Sample." *Military Psychology* 19 (2007): 9–25.

Attridge, Derek, George Bennington, and Robert Young, eds. *Post-Structuralism and the Question of History.* New York: Cambridge University Press, 1987.

Barber, E. Susan. "'The White Wings of Eros': Courtship and Marriage in Confederate Richmond." In *Southern Families at War: Loyalty and Conflict in the Civil War South,* edited by Catherine Clinton, 119–32. New York: Oxford University Press, 2000.

Barloon, Mark C. "Combat Reconsidered: A Statistical Analysis of Small-Unit Actions during the American Civil War." PhD diss., University of North Texas, 2001.

Bean, W. G. *Stonewall's Man: Sandie Pendleton.* Chapel Hill: University of North Carolina Press, 1959.

Benjamin Jr., Ludy T. "A History of Clinical Psychology as a Profession in America (and a Glimpse at Its Future)." *Annual Review of Clinical Psychology* 1 (April 2005): 1–30.

Berry, Stephen W. *All That Makes a Man: Love and Ambition in the Civil War South.* New York: Oxford University Press, 2003.

Blanning, Tim. *The Romantic Revolution: A History.* New York: Modern Library, 2010.

Boettger, Suzaan. "Eastman Johnson's 'Blodgett Family' and Domestic Values during the Civil War Era." *American Art* 6 (Autumn 1992): 50–67.

Brinsfield Jr., John Wesley, ed. *The Spirit Divided: Memoirs of Civil War Chaplains: The Confederacy.* Macon, GA: Mercer University Press, 2006.

Broomall, James J. "Personal Confederacies: War and Peace in the American South, 1840–1890." PhD diss., University of Florida, 2011.

———. *Private Confederacies: The Emotional Worlds of Southern Men as Citizens and Soldiers.* Chapel Hill: University of North Carolina Press, 2019.

———. "'We Are a Band of Brothers': Manhood and Community in Confederate Camps and Beyond." *Civil War History* 60 (September 2014): 270–309,

Brosco, Jeffrey P. "The Early History of the Infant Mortality Rate in America: 'A Reflection upon the Past and a Prophecy of the Future.'" *Pediatrics* 103 (February 1999): 478–85.

Carmichael, Peter S. *The War for the Common Soldier: How Men Thought, Fought, and Survived in Civil War Armies.* Chapel Hill: University of North Carolina Press, 2018.

Carroll, Dillon J. *Invisible Wounds: Mental Illness and Civil War Soldiers.* Baton Rouge: Louisiana State University Press, 2021.

———. "'The God Who Shielded Me Before, Yet Watches Over Us All': Confederate Soldiers, Mental Illness, and Religion." *Civil War History* 61, no. 3 (September 2015): 252–80.

Cimbala, Paul A. *Soldiers North and South: The Everyday Experiences of the Men Who Fought America's Civil War.* New York: Fordham University Press, 2010.

Costa, Dora L., and Matthew E. Kahn. "Health, Wartime Stress, and Unit Cohesion: Evidence from Union Army Veterans." *Demography* 47 (February 2010): 45–66.

———. "Surviving Andersonville: The Benefits of Social Networks in POW Camps." *American Economic Review* 97 (September 2007): 1467–1487.

Cott, Nancy F. "On Men's History and Women's History." In *Meanings for Manhood: Constructions of Masculinity in Victorian America,* edited by Mark C. Carnes and Clyde Griffin, 205–12. Chicago: University of Chicago Press, 1990.

Collingwood, R. G. *The Idea of History.* New York: Oxford University Press, 1946.

Dean Jr., Eric T. *Shook over Hell: Post-Traumatic Stress, Vietnam, and the Civil War.* Cambridge, MA: Harvard University Press, 1999.

DuBose, John W. *The Life and Times of William Lowndes Yancey.* Birmingham, AL: Roberts & Son, 1892.

Dunkelman, Mark H. *Brothers One and All: Esprit de Corps in a Civil War Regiment.* Baton Rouge: Louisiana State University Press, 2004.

Durden, Robert F. *The Gray and the Black: The Confederate Debate on Emancipation.* Baton Rouge: Louisiana State University Press, 1972.

Dwyer, Erin A. *Mastering Emotions: Feeling, Power, and Slavery in the United States.* Philadelphia: University of Pennsylvania Press, 2021.

Ellis, Michael. *North Carolina English, 1861–1865: A Guide and Glossary.* Knoxville: University of Tennessee Press, 2013.

Escott, Paul D. *Slavery Remembered: A Record of Twentieth-Century Slave Narratives.* Chapel Hill: University of North Carolina Press, 1979.

Eustace, Nicole. Eugenia Lean, Julie Livingston, Jan Plamper, William M. Reddy, and Barbara H. Rosenwein. "AHR Conversations: The Historical Study of Emotions." *American Historical Review* 117, no. 5 (December 2012): 1487–1531.

Fahs, Alice. "The Sentimental Soldier in Popular Civil War Literature, 1861–65." *Civil War History* 46 (June 2000): 107–31.

Faust, Drew Gilpin. "Christian Soldiers: The Meaning of Revivalism in the Confederate Army." *Journal of Southern History* 53, no. 1 (February 1987): 63–90.

———. *Mothers of Invention: Women of the Slaveholding South in the American Civil War.* Chapel Hill: University of North Carolina Press, 1996.

———. *This Republic of Suffering: Death and the American Civil War.* New York: Alfred A. Knopf, 2008.

Feldman, Susan C., David Read Johnson, and Marilyn Ollayos. "The Use of Writing in the Treatment of Post-Traumatic Stress Disorders." In *Handbook of Post-Traumatic Therapy,* edited by Mary Beth Williams and John F. Sommer Jr, 366-85. Westport, CT: Greenwood Press, 1994.

Fisher, David Hackett. *Albion's Seed: Four British Folkways in America.* New York: Oxford University Press, 1989.

Fliegelman, Jay. *Prodigals and Pilgrims: The American Revolution against Patriarchal Authority, 1750–1800.* New York: Cambridge University Press, 1982.

Foote, Lorien, and Earl J. Hess, eds. *The Oxford Handbook of the American Civil War.* New York: Oxford University Press, 2021.

Frank, Stephen M. "'Rendering Aid and Comfort': Images of Fatherhood in the Letters of Civil War Soldiers from Massachusetts and Michigan." *Journal of Social History* 26, no. 1 (Autumn 1992): 5–31.

Freeman, Douglass Southall. *R. E. Lee: A Biography.* New York: Charles Scribner's Sons, 1934.

Friend, Craig T. "'The Crushing of Southern Manhood': War, Masculinity, and the Confederate Nation-State, 1861–1865." In *Masculinities and the Nation in the Modern World: Between Hegemony and Marginalization,* edited by Pablo Dominguez Andersen and Simon Wendt, 19–38. New York: Palgrave Macmillan, 2015.

———. "Little Eva's Last Breath: Childhood Death and Parental Mourning in 'Our Family, White and Black.'" In *Family Values in the Old South,* edited by Craig Thompson Friend and Anya Jabour, 62-85. Gainesville: University Press of Florida, 2010.

Friend, Craig T., and Lorri Glover, eds. *Southern Manhood: Perspectives on Masculinity in the Old South.* Athens: University of Georgia Press, 2004.

Gallagher, Gary W. *The Confederate War.* Cambridge, MA: Harvard University Press, 1997.

Genovese, Eugene. *In Red and Black: Marxian Explorations in Southern and Afro-American History.* Knoxville: University of Tennessee Press, 1971.

———. *Roll Jordan Roll: The World the Slaves Made.* New York: Pantheon Books, 1974.

Genovese, Eugene, and Elizabeth Fox Genovese. *Fatal Self-Deception: Slaveholding Paternalism in the Old South.* New York: Cambridge University Press, 2011.

Gimbel, Cynthia, and Alan Booth. "Why Does Military Combat Experience Adversely Affect Marital Relations?" *Journal of Marriage and the Family* 56 (August 1994): 691–703.

Glatthaar, Joseph T. *Forged in Battle: The Civil War Alliance of Black Soldiers and White Officers.* New York: Free Press, 1990.

———. *General Lee's Army: From Victory to Collapse.* New York: Free Press, 2008.

———. *Soldiering in the Army of Northern Virginia: A Statistical Portrait of the Troops Who Served under Robert E. Lee.* Chapel Hill: University of North Carolina Press, 2011.

Glover, Lorri. *Southern Sons: Becoming Men in the New Nation.* Baltimore: Johns Hopkins University Press, 2007.

Gordon, Eleanor, and Gwyneth Nair. "Domestic Fathers and the Victorian Parental Role." *Women's History Review* 15, no. 4 (September 2006): 551–59.

Gray, Jesse Glenn. *The Warriors: Reflections on Men in Battle.* New York: Harcourt, Brace, 1959.

Grossman, David A. *On Killing: The Psychological Cost of Learning to Kill in War and Society.* New York: Back Bay Books, 1996.

Guelzo, Allen C. *Fateful Lightning: A New History of the Civil War and Reconstruction.* Oxford University Press, 2012.

Hacker, J. David, Libra Hilde, and James Holland Jones. "The Effect of the Civil War on Southern Marriage Patterns." *Journal of Southern History* 76 (February 2010): 39–70.

Haines, Michael R. "The White Population of the United States, 1790–1920." In *A Population History of North America,* edited by Michael R. Haines and Richard H. Steckel, 305–70. New York: Cambridge University Press, 2000.

Hager, Christopher. *I Remain Yours: Common Lives in Civil War Letters.* Cambridge, MA: Harvard University Press, 2018.

Hanania, Ronit Roth, and Maayan Davidow. "Attachment." In *Encyclopedia of Applied Psychology,* edited by Charles Spielberger, 191–202. San Diego, CA: Elsevier Academic Press, 2004.

Hankins, Barry. *The Second Great Awakening and the Transcendentalists.* Westport, CT: Greenwood Press, 2004.

Hattaway, Herman. "Clio's Southern Soldiers: The United Confederate Veterans and History." *Louisiana History* 3 (Summer 1971): 213–42.

Ho, Derrick. "Homesickness Isn't Really about 'Home.'" CNN Health. http://www.cnn.com/2010/HEALTH/08/16/homesickness.not.about.home/index.html (accessed June 19, 2019).

Johnson, Michael P. "Planters and Patriarchy: Charleston, 1800–1860." *Journal of Southern History* 46 (February 1980): 45–72.

Kagan, Jerome, Richard B. Kearsley, and Philip R. Zelazo. *Infancy: Its Place in Human Development.* Cambridge, MA: Harvard University Press, 1980.

Kann, Mark E. *A Republic of Men: The American Founders, Gendered Language, and Patriarchal Politics.* New York: New York University Press, 1998.

Karageorgos, Effie. *Australian Soldiers in South Africa and Vietnam: Words from the Battlefield.* New York: Bloomsbury Academic, 2016.

Karson, Albert, and Martha Karson. "The Influence of American Parenting Styles of Puritanism, Rationalism, and Romanticism." Institute of Education Sciences, 1976.

Keister, Lisa A., and Darby E. Southgate. *Inequality: A Contemporary Approach to Race, Class, and Gender.* New York: Cambridge University Press, 2012.

Kellett, Anthony. *Combat Motivation: The Behavior of Soldiers in Battle.* Boston: Kluwer Nijhoff, 1982.

Kennedy-Moore, Eileen, and Jeanne C. Watson. *Expressing Emotion: Myths, Realities, and Therapeutic Strategies.* New York: Guilford Press, 1999.

Kidd, Thomas S. *The Great Awakening: The Roots of Evangelical Christianity in Colonial America.* New Haven, CT: Yale University Press, 2007.

Kimmel, Michael. *Manhood in America: A Cultural History.* New York: Free Press, 1996.

King-Owen, Scott. "Conditional Confederates: Absenteeism among Western North Carolina Soldiers, 1861–1865." *Civil War History* 57 (December 2011): 349–79.

Kirkpatrick, H. D. *Marse: A Psychological Portrait of the Southern Slave Master and His Legacy.* Lanham, MD: Prometheus Books, 2022.

Kolchin, Peter. *American Slavery, 1619–1877.* New York: Hill & Wang, 1993.

Kolditz, Thomas A., Raymond Millen, Terrence M. Potter, and Leonard Wong. *Why They Fought: Combat Motivation in the Iraq War.* Washington, DC: Strategic Studies Institute, 2003.

Levine, Bruce. *Confederate Emancipation: Southern Plans to Free and Arm Slaves during the Civil War.* New York: Oxford University Press, 2006.

Lewis, Jan. *The Pursuit of Happiness: Family and Values in Jefferson's Virginia.* New York: Cambridge University Press, 1983.

Linderman, Gerald. *Embattled Courage: The Experience of Combat in the American Civil War.* New York: Free Press, 1987.

Little, Roger W. "Buddy Relations and Combat Performance." In *The New Military: Changing Patterns of Organization,* edited by Morris Janowitz, 195–223. New York: Russell Sage Foundation, 1964.

Lockridge, Kenneth A. *On the Sources of Patriarchal Rage: The Commonplace Books of William Byrd and Thomas Jefferson and the Gendering of Power in the Eighteenth Century.* New York: New York University Press, 1992.

Loughborough, Mary Ann. *My Cave Life in Vicksburg: With Letters of Trial and Travel.* New York: D. Appleton, 1864.

Madden, David. *Beyond the Battlefield: The Ordinary Life and Extraordinary Times of the Civil War Soldier.* New York: Touchstone, 2000.

Manning, Chandra. *What This Cruel War Was Over: Soldiers, Slavery, and the Civil War.* New York: Alfred A. Knopf, 2007.

Marshall, S. L. A. *Men against Fire: The Problem of Battle Command.* 1947. Reprint, Norman: University of Oklahoma Press, 2000.

Marten, James. "Fatherhood in the Confederacy: Southern Soldiers and Their Children." *Journal of Southern History* 63 (May 1997): 269–92.

———. *The Children's Civil War.* Chapel Hill: University of North Carolina Press, 1998.

McClymond, Michael, "Jonathan Edwards." In *Oxford Handbook of Religion and Emotion,* edited by John Corrigan, 404–17. New York: Oxford University Press, 2008.

McCurry, Stephanie. *Masters of Small Worlds: Yeoman Households, Gender Relations, and the Political Culture of the Antebellum South Carolina Low Country.* New York: Oxford University Press, 1995.

McPherson, James M. *Battle Cry of Freedom: The Civil War Era.* New York: Oxford University Press, 1988.

———. *For Cause and Comrades: Why Men Fought in the Civil War.* New York: Oxford University Press, 1997.

McWhiney, Grady, and Perry D. Jamieson. *Attack and Die: Civil War Military Tactics and the Southern Heritage.* Tuscaloosa: University of Alabama Press, 1982.

Mercer, Jean. *Understanding Attachment: Parenting, Child Care, and Emotional Development.* Westport, CT: Praeger, 2006.

Merriam-Webster's Encyclopedia of Literature. Springfield, MA: Merriam-Webster, 1995.

Miller, Brian Craig. *John Bell Hood and the Fight for Civil War Memory.* Knoxville: University of Tennessee Press, 2010.

Mintz, Steven. *Huck's Raft: A History of American Childhood.* Cambridge, MA: Belknap Press, 2004.

Mitchell, Reid. *Civil War Soldiers: Their Expectations and Their Experiences.* New York: Touchstone Books, 1988.

———. *The Vacant Chair: The Northern Soldier Leaves Home.* New York: Oxford University Press, 1993.

Morillo, Stephen, and Michael F. Pavkovic. *What Is Military History?* Malden, MA: Polity Press, 2006.

Nadelson, Theodore. *Trained to Kill: Soldiers at War.* Baltimore: Johns Hopkins University Press, 2005.

Nelson, Megan Kate. *Ruin Nation: Destruction and the American Civil War.* Athens: University of Georgia Press, 2012.

Noe, Kenneth. *Reluctant Rebels: The Confederates Who Joined the Army after 1861.* Chapel Hill: University of North Carolina Press, 2010.

Norton, Mary Beth. *Liberty's Daughters: The Revolutionary Experience of American Women, 1750–1800.* Ithaca, NY: Cornell University Press, 1980.

Ott, Victoria E. *Confederate Daughters: Coming of Age during the Civil War.* Carbondale: Southern Illinois University Press, 2008.

Owen, Thomas McAdory, and Marie Bankhead Owen. *History of Alabama and Dictionary of Alabama Biography, Volume 4.* Chicago: S. J. Clarke, 1921.

Ownby, Ted. "Patriarchy in the World Where There Is No Parting: Power Relations in the Confederate Heaven." In *Southern Families at War: Loyalty and Conflict in the Civil War South,* edited by Catherine Clinton, 229–41. New York: Oxford University Press, 2000.

Partin, Robert. "The Sustaining Faith of an Alabama Soldier." *Civil War History* 6 (December 1960): 425–38.

Perry, Aldo S. *Civil War Courts-Martial of North Carolina Troops.* Jefferson, NC: McFarland, 2012.

Phillips, Jason. *Diehard Rebels: The Confederate Culture of Invincibility.* Athens: University of Georgia Press, 2007.

Pinkser, Matthew. *Lincoln's Sanctuary: Abraham Lincoln and the Soldiers' Home.* New York: Oxford University Press, 2003.

Plamper, Jan. *The History of Emotions: An Introduction.* New York: Oxford University Press, 2012.

Rable, George C. *Civil Wars: Women and the Crisis of Southern Nationalism.* Urbana: University of Illinois Press, 1989.

———. *God's Almost Chosen Peoples: A Religious History of the American Civil War.* Chapel Hill: University of North Carolina Press, 2010.

Rafuse, Ethan S. *Stonewall Jackson: A Biography.* Santa Barbara, CA: Greenwood Publishing, 2011.

Robertson Jr., James I. *Soldiers Blue and Gray*. New York: Warner Books, 1991.

Rose, Anne C. *Victorian America and the Civil War*. Cambridge: Cambridge University Press, 1994.

Rosenwein, Barbara H. "Worrying about Emotions in History." *American Historical Review* 107 (June 2002): 821–45.

Rotundo, Anthony E. "American Fatherhood: A Historical Perspective." *American Behavioral Scientist* 29 (September/October 1985): 7–23.

———. *American Manhood: Transformations in Masculinity from the Revolution to the Modern Era*. New York: Basic Books, 1993.

Sarkadi, Anna, Robert Kristiansson, Frank Oberklaid, and Sven Bremberg. "Fathers' Involvement and Children's Developmental Outcomes: A Systematic Review of Longitudinal Studies." *Acta Pediatrica* 97 (February 2008): 153–58.

Scherer, Klaus R. "What Are Emotions? And How Can They Be Measured?" *Social Science Information* 4 (December 2005): 695–729.

Schivelbush, Wolfgang. *The Culture of Defeat: On National Trauma, Mourning, and Recovery*. Translated by Jefferson Chase. New York: Picador, 2004.

Scurfield, Raymond M. "War-Related Trauma: An Integrative, Experiential, Cognitive, and Spiritual Approach." In *Handbook of Post-Traumatic Therapy,* edited by Mary Beth Williams and John F. Sommer Jr, 204–18. Westport, CT: Greenwood Press, 1994.

Seidman, Steven. "The Power of Desire and the Danger of Pleasure: Victorian Sexuality Reconsidered." *Journal of Social History* 24 (Autumn 1990): 47–67.

Selcer, Richard F. *Civil War America: 1850 to 1875*. New York: Infobase Publishing, 2006.

Sheehan, Patricia L. "Treating Intimacy Issues of Traumatized People." In *Handbook of Post-Traumatic Therapy,* edited by Mary Beth Williams and John F. Sommer Jr, 94–105. Westport, CT: Greenwood Press, 1994.

Sheehan-Dean, Aaron, ed. *The View from the Ground: Experiences of Civil War Soldiers*. Lexington: University Press of Kentucky, 2007.

———. *Why Confederates Fought: Family and Nation in Civil War Virginia*. Chapel Hill: University of North Carolina Press, 2009.

Smith, Adam I. P. *The American Civil War*. New York: Palgrave Macmillan, 2007.

Smith, Page. *The Historian and History*. New York: Alfred A. Knopf, 1964.

Sommerville, Diane. *Aberration of Mind: Suicide and Suffering in the Civil War–Era South*. Chapel Hill: University of North Carolina Press, 2018.

Speer, Lonnie R. *Portals to Hell: Military Prisons of the Civil War*. Mechanicsburg, PA: Stackpole Books, 1997.

Staub, Ervin, and Johanna Vollhardt. "Altruism Born of Suffering: The Roots of Caring and Helping after Victimization and Other Trauma." *American Journal of Orthopsychiatry* 78 (July 2008): 267–80.

Stephens, W. B. "Literacy in England, Scotland, and Wales, 1500–1900." *History of Education Quarterly* 30 (Winter 1990): 545–71.

Stevens Jr., Edward. "The Anatomy of Mass Literacy in Nineteenth-Century United States."

In *National Literacy Campaigns: Historical and Comparative Perspectives,* edited by R.F. Arnove and H. J. Graff, 99–122. New York: Plenum Press, 1987.

Stinson, Robert. "Leopold von Ranke: History of the Popes (1834–1836)." In *The Faces of Clio: An Anthology of Classics in Historical Writing from Ancient Times to the Present,* edited by Robert Stinson, 155–72. Chicago: Nelson-Hall, 1987.

Stokes, Claudia. *The Altar at Home: Sentimental Literature and Nineteenth-Century American Religion.* Philadelphia: University of Pennsylvania Press, 2014.

Tarr, Bronwyn, Jacques Launay, and Robin I. M. Dunbar. "Music and Social Bonding: 'Self-Other' Merging and Neurohormonal Mechanisms." *Frontiers in Psychology* 5 (September 2014): 1–10.

Taylor, Amy Murrell. *The Divided Family in Civil War America.* Chapel Hill: University of North Carolina Press, 2005.

Thurber, Christopher A., Edward Walton, and the Council on School Health. "Preventing and Treating Homesickness." *Pediatrics: The Journal of the American Academy of Pediatrics* 119 (January 2007): 192–201.

Van der Kolk, Bessel. *The Body Keeps the Score: Brain, Mind, and Body in the Healing of Trauma.* New York: Penguin Books, 2014.

Verweij, Desiree. "Comrades or Friends? On Friendship in the Armed Forces." *Journal of Military Ethics* 6 (2007): 280–91.

Volhardt, Johanna Ray. "Altruism Born of Suffering and Prosocial Behavior Following Adverse Life Events: A Review and Conceptualization." *Social Justice Research* 22 (March 2009): 53–97.

Volo, James M. *The Boston Tea Party: The Foundations of Revolution.* Santa Barbara, CA: Praeger, 2012.

Volo, James M., and Dorothy Denneen Volo. *Family Life in Seventeenth- and Eighteenth-Century America.* Westport, CT: Greenwood Press, 2006.

Watson, Alan D. *Society in Colonial North Carolina.* Raleigh: Office of Archives and History North Carolina Department of Cultural Resources, 1996.

Weitz, Mark A. *A Higher Duty: Desertion among Georgia Troops during the Civil War.* Lincoln: University of Nebraska Press, 2000.

———. "Drill, Training, and the Combat Performance of the Civil War Soldier: Dispelling the Myth of the Poor Soldier, Great Fighter." *Journal of Military History* 62 (April 1998): 263–89.

———. *More Damning Than Slaughter: Desertion in the Confederate Army.* Lincoln: University of Nebraska Press, 2005.

Werner, Emmy E. *Reluctant Witnesses: Children's Voices from the Civil War.* Boulder, CO: Westview Press, 1998.

White, Jonathan W. "In Their Heads: Soldiers Dreamed of Battle, Loved Ones and Infidelity, and Cheese." *Civil War Times* 54 (December 2015): 26–31.

Wilcox, Vanda. "'Weeping Tears of Blood': Exploring Italian Soldiers' Emotions in the First World War." *Modern Italy* 17, no. 2 (May 2012): 171–84.

Wiley, Bell I. *The Life of Johnny Reb: The Common Soldier of the Confederacy.* Baton Rouge: Louisiana State University Press, 1943.

Williams, David. "Introduction: The Enlightenment." In *Cambridge Readings in the History of Political Thought: The Enlightenment,* edited by David Williams, 7–70. New York: Cambridge University Press, 1999.

Wood, Gordon. *Empire of Liberty: A History of the Early Republic, 1789–1815.* New York: Oxford University Press, 2009.

Woods, Michael E. *Emotional and Sectional Conflict in the Antebellum United States.* New York: Cambridge University Press, 2014.

Woodworth, Stephen, ed. *The Loyal, True, and Brave: America's Civil War Soldiers.* Wilmington, DE: Scholarly Resources Inc., 2002.

Wyatt-Brown, Bertram. *Hearts of Darkness: Wellsprings of a Southern Literary Tradition.* Baton Rouge: Louisiana State University Press, 2003.

———. *Southern Honor: Ethics & Behavior in the Old South.* New York: Oxford University Press, 1982.

INDEX

Abernathy, William, 96, 108, 171, 175
altruism: born of suffering, 84, 107–10
Asbury, Francis, 29–30
attachment: and children, 38–39, 54; definition of, 38; and emotions, 38; insecure attachment, 38; and internal working models, 38–39; and killing, 104, 110–11; and parents, 38; secure attachment, 38; and soldiers, 61, 64, 80, 104, 108, 116; theory, 38; thoughts, 38
Aubury, Luke, 144
Avery, C. M., 105–6

Baird, Alfred H., 43
Batts, William, 97
Benson, Berry, 112–13
Biggs, Henry, 167
Bishop, William T., 112
Black, Harvey, 56, 81

Booth, George, 90
Bowen, Ann, 54, 74
Bowen, Henry, 54, 74, 100
Box, William I., 75
Boyd, Robert P., 100
Branscomb, Lewis S., 80
Broaddus, William, 94
Brooks, Preston, 26–27
Broughton, Edward T., 77

Brown, Henry B., 155, 158
Burgwyn, Henry, 97
Butler, Andrew, 26–27

Calhoun, John C., 161
Campbell, Sam, 98
Carter, Charlie, 112
children: and anxiety, 127, 138; and attachment, 38–39, 54, 142; in the colonial period, 38, 121; and death, 138, 145; and desertion, 128, 143; and education, 135–36; as emotional sanctuaries, 54, 123; and the Enlightenment, 22; and fatherly affection, 38, 123–26, 129–32, 134, 137, 139; and fatherly guidance, 125–26, 139–40; "hands off" parenting, 54; influence on parents, 32–33, 39; and letter writing, 72, 117, 127–31; and loss of innocence, 141–42; and morale, 135; and mothers, 24–25, 36, 122, 13; as a motivation for fighting, 16, 70, 114, 117–18, 120, 124; and new roles, 136–37; and parental affection, 22, 24, 117, 119–21; participation in war effort, 135–37; and patriarchy, 19, 22–24, 32, 121; and race, 155; and rights, 22; and Romanticism, 54; and sacrifice, 136; and self-confidence, 54–55; and self-cultivation, 24; and sentimentality, 54–55; and slavery, 158–61; and trauma, 141–42

.

www.ingramcontent.com/pod-product-compliance
Lightning Source LLC
Chambersburg PA
CBHW031546260326
41914CB00002B/300